MOBILE
RENAISSANCE

Celebrating Mobile's Tricentennial

Produced in Cooperation with the Mobile Area Chamber of Commerce

In its early years, Mobile would never have come to national prominence without the cotton trade. An essential part of the trade took place in the New Cotton Exchange housed on the northwest corner of Commerce and St. Michael Streets, built in 1886. Here, cotton merchants set prices and bought and sold the commodity. The building shared quarters with two other concerns central to the business life of the city, the Chamber of Commerce and the offices of the Mobile and Ohio Railroad. *Photo courtesy of Mobile in Photo Gravure/University of South Alabama Archives*

ON THE COVER Admiral Raphael Semmes, sporting a wreath of Mardi Gras beads, serenely stands watch over Mobile River. Though a native of Maryland, the Confederate naval hero was so impressed with Mobile that he settled in the city and considered himself a citizen of the state of Alabama. *Cover photos by Steve Goraum/Studio G!*

MOBILE

RENAISSANCE

Celebrating Mobile's Tricentennial

Editorial Content by Barbara N. Spafford • Featuring the Photography of Steven L. Goraum
Historical Research and Captions Written by George H. Ewert, Jr. • Corporate Profiles by Barbara N. Spafford

*The Mobile Area Chamber of Commerce and Community Communications, Inc.
would like to express our gratitude to the following companies for their leadership in the development of this book.*

Atlantic

degussa.

EnergySouth, Inc.

maa
mobile airport authority

MINOLTA
QMS

Mobile Register

USA
University of South Alabama ™

Library of Congress Cataloging-in-Publication Data

Spafford, Barbara N., 1951-
Mobile renaissance : celebrating Mobile's tricentennial / editorial content and corporate profiles written by Barbara N. Spafford ; featuring the photography of Steve Goraum ; historical research and captions written by George H. Ewert, Jr.
p. cm.
Includes index.
ISBN 1-58192-039-3
1. Mobile (Ala.)—Civilization. 2. Mobile (Ala.)—Pictorial works. 3. Mobile (Ala.)—Economic conditions. 4. Business enterprises—Alabama—Mobile. I. Goraum, Steve, 1958- . II. Ewert, George H., 1950- . III. Title.
F334.M6 S73 2001
976.1'22—dc21

2001004179

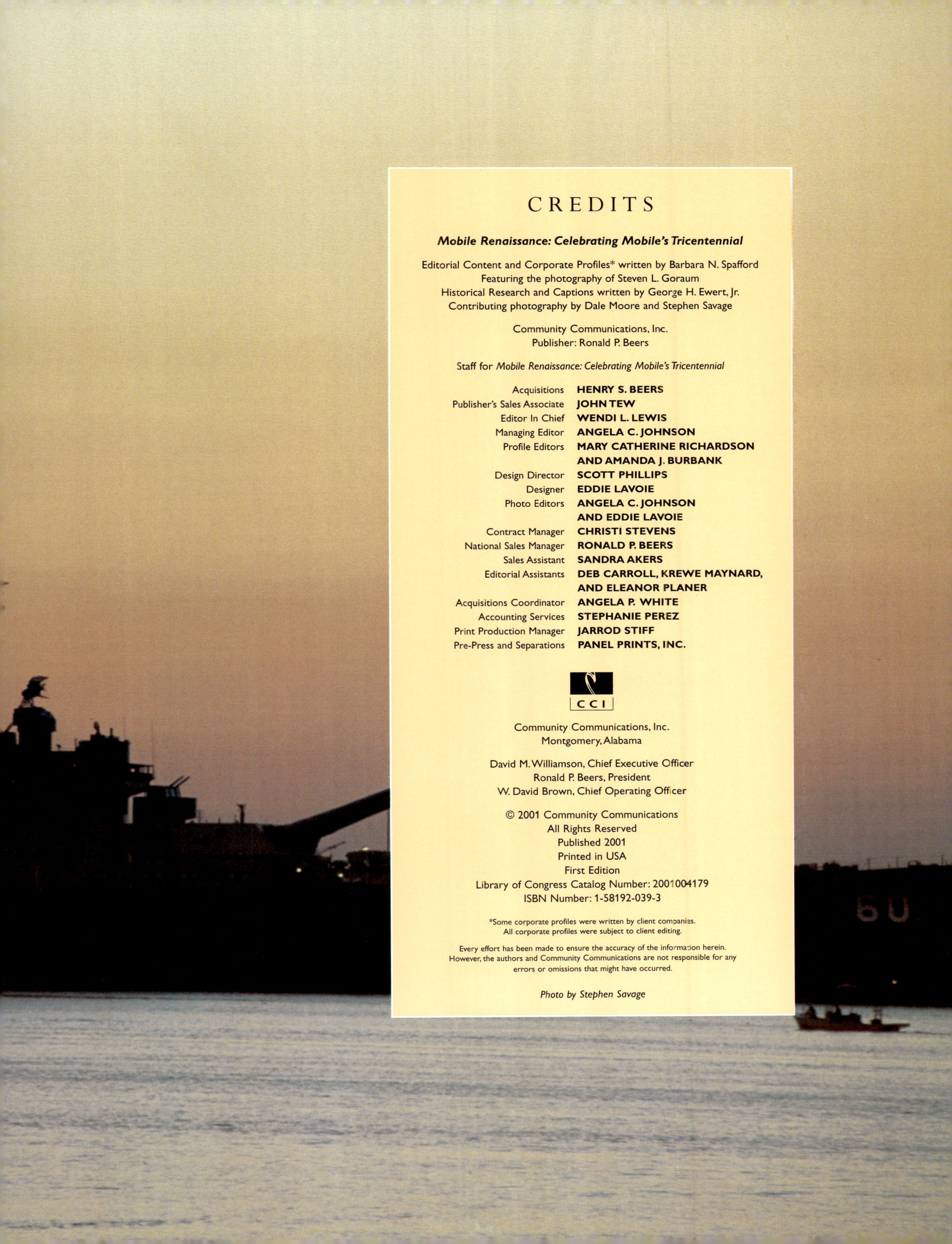

CREDITS

Mobile Renaissance: Celebrating Mobile's Tricentennial

Editorial Content and Corporate Profiles* written by Barbara N. Spafford
Featuring the photography of Steven L. Goraum
Historical Research and Captions written by George H. Ewert, Jr.
Contributing photography by Dale Moore and Stephen Savage

Community Communications, Inc.
Publisher: Ronald P. Beers

Staff for *Mobile Renaissance: Celebrating Mobile's Tricentennial*

Acquisitions	**HENRY S. BEERS**
Publisher's Sales Associate	**JOHN TEW**
Editor In Chief	**WENDI L. LEWIS**
Managing Editor	**ANGELA C. JOHNSON**
Profile Editors	**MARY CATHERINE RICHARDSON AND AMANDA J. BURBANK**
Design Director	**SCOTT PHILLIPS**
Designer	**EDDIE LAVOIE**
Photo Editors	**ANGELA C. JOHNSON AND EDDIE LAVOIE**
Contract Manager	**CHRISTI STEVENS**
National Sales Manager	**RONALD P. BEERS**
Sales Assistant	**SANDRA AKERS**
Editorial Assistants	**DEB CARROLL, KREWE MAYNARD, AND ELEANOR PLANER**
Acquisitions Coordinator	**ANGELA P. WHITE**
Accounting Services	**STEPHANIE PEREZ**
Print Production Manager	**JARROD STIFF**
Pre-Press and Separations	**PANEL PRINTS, INC.**

CCI

Community Communications, Inc.
Montgomery, Alabama

David M. Williamson, Chief Executive Officer
Ronald P. Beers, President
W. David Brown, Chief Operating Officer

Published 2001
Printed in USA
First Edition
Library of Congress Catalog Number: 2001004179
ISBN Number: 1-58192-039-3

*Some corporate profiles were written by client companies.
All corporate profiles were subject to client editing.

Photo by Stephen Savage

table of contents

FOREWORD

Mobile, Alabama—one of the oldest and most beautiful cities in America—has been captured in this rich, beautiful book that leads you through a tour of its neighborhoods, parks, and historic sites; gives you a glimpse of its many sporting events and festivals; introduces you to its friendly people, and provides a sample of its Southern culture that beckons you to visit in person.

This book is special. It is our tricentennial edition and is one of the many ways we are celebrating 300 years of Mobile, Alabama, and America's history. We've named it *Renaissance* because it symbolizes a revival in our community that continues today. Our strong economy, downtown projects, convention and tourism programs, growing neighborhoods, improved infrastructure, diverse business community, entertaining arts programs, and enticing quality of life here on the Gulf of Mexico all reflect a community with vision and spirit.

Let this book be just the beginning of your introduction to Mobile. Plan to experience its rich history by visiting its many historic homes and sites. World War II enthusiasts can climb aboard the Battleship USS *Alabama* or view the aircraft and equipment at Battleship Memorial Park. Lovers of water sports will find a haven here where fishing, swimming, and boating are daily activities. And, of course, our annual Mardi Gras celebration—the first in the U.S.—attracts tens of thousands to its colorful parades and parties.

There's so much more to say about this wonderful community. But, they say a picture is worth a thousand words, so relax, and enjoy this glimpse of our Port City—Mobile, Alabama.

Ann Bedsole
President
Mobile Tricentennial, Inc.

Photo by Steve Goraum/Studio G!

PREFACE

It's true.

The metamorphosis is real.

Mobile is experiencing an amazing renaissance.

While celebrating 300 years of our history and heritage, we in the city of "perpetual potential" have grabbed hold of the reins and are charging full speed ahead into a bright, exciting future.

We took the first steps by implementing a mayor-council form of city government—opening the door to new ideas and attitudes.

Then, to welcome the world to our doorstep, we built a new waterfront convention center—a beautifully concrete symbol of the city's rebirth, and a reconnection with the maritime legacy that shaped our history.

Since then, revitalization efforts have flourished. The once-sleepy downtown area is now a lively city center—with the Dauphin Street entertainment district, the refurbished Saenger Theatre, Cooper Riverside Park, the Gulf Coast Exploreum Museum of Science, and the new Museum of Mobile, which is a regional history center. In the thriving western section of the city, the redesigned and expanded Mobile Art Museum and the new, state-of-the-art West Regional Library are serving a growing population.

Mobile also is making its mark as a sports town—with the BayBears AA professional baseball team, the Mysticks hockey team, and the Revelers of the NBA's Developmental League.

Looming on the horizon—literally—is the proposed Retirement Systems of Alabama Office Tower in downtown Mobile, soon to be the tallest building in the state.

As a native Mobilian, it's extremely gratifying for me to see the changes taking place here. And it's a pleasure to escort you on a visit to our city.

Welcome to the renaissance.

—Barbara Spafford

Photo by Steve Goraum/Studio G!

PART ONE

The Bragg-Mitchell Mansion is the city's finest surviving example of the splendid two-story country homes that graced the area during the mid-1850s. Built in 1855 by Judge John Bragg, brother of Confederate General Braxton Bragg, the house is listed on the National Register of Historic Places and is said to be the most-photographed home in the city. The 14-room structure, which gracefully combines Classical and Italianate design elements, features spacious double parlors with 15-foot ceilings. *Photo by Steve Goraum/Studio G!*

RAMONA DOYLE
MOBILE FIRE-RESCUE
DEPARTMENT

CHAPTER ONE

1

The Eclectic Flavor of Life in Mobile

NEIGHBORHOODS, PARKS & ARCHITECTURE

Mobile, where dynamic growth caused the population center to shift inland, is returning to its roots, thanks to a waterfront renaissance spurred on by development along the Mobile River—including Cooper Riverside Park and the Arthur R. Outlaw Convention Center. *Photo by Steve Goraum/Studio G!*

A city presents many faces to the world—faces crafted by visitor's bureaus, economic developers, and historic preservationists. Perhaps the most authentic image of a city is the one that shows her citizens carrying on the business of daily life—the neighborhoods where they live, the buildings in which they work, the parks and public spaces where they play.

Like any city with a 300-year history, Mobile displays a complex and often contradictory face to the world. Downtown on Dauphin Street, an edgy jazz riff drifts from a music club housed in a nineteenth-century Victorian townhouse. In Bienville Square, a pensive business woman checks for e-mail on a laptop while sitting on a wrought iron bench in the shade of a one-hundred-year-old oak tree. Everywhere you look, Mobile is a heady blend of old and new.

Take a walk through Mobile's neighborhoods—east from the river, west to the city limits—and you'll walk through three centuries of history. The downtown area is dominated by seven historic districts that architecturally document Mobile's past, ranging from the stately DeTonti Square Historic District, Mobile's oldest existing neighborhood that once housed river pilots and cotton brokers, to the Leinkauf Historic District, home to Mobilians who commuted the long three miles to town in the new sensation, the automobile. In the western part of the city, vibrant new neighborhoods of spacious custom-built homes and garden townhouses are mushrooming as the city's population shifts and expands.

Throughout the city, greenspaces large and small dot the landscape. Mobile is home to more than eighty parks ranging from the grassy triangular third-of-an-acre sliver of Ryan Park to the rambling 720-acre Langan Park—complete with golf course, tennis center, and performing arts pavilion. The addition of "pocket parks" in the business district offer shady retreats for downtown workers, while large, multi-use play areas, like Medal of Honor Park cater to growing families in the western part of the city.

Mobile has a rich legacy of fine architecture that chronicles its evolution from an eighteenth-century colonial outpost to a major port city of the twenty-first century. Each year, visitors stream through lovingly restored buildings ranging from elegant federal townhomes to raised Creole cottages designed for steamy gulf coast summers.

Pictured on the opposite page is one popular "face" of Mobile. It is an image, however, that must take its place within the context of the city's new spirit of renaissance. Scratch the surface of Mobile and you'll find a vibrant city that is an eclectic mix of the old and the new—with respect for the past and a passion for the future.

Turn the page and see for yourself.

(above) Cannons roar a friendly greeting to visitors at Fort Condé, Mobile's official Welcome Center. *Photo by Steve Goraum/Studio G!*

(opposite) Three abiding symbols of Mobile's heritage as an old Southern city—azaleas, antebellum homes, and hoop-skirted maids—come together in a pastel frieze of another era. Beneath this genteel surface, however, beats the heart of a New South city experiencing an exhilarating renewal. *Photo by Steve Goraum/Studio G!*

(left) Two and a half miles south of the Courthouse stood one of Mobile's most popular recreational areas, Monroe Park. Skirting the Western Shore of Mobile Bay along "Garrow's Bend" and serviced by the Bay Shell Road and the streetcar line, this park was the place to go for an afternoon of leisure. With access to the water, amusement rides, a baseball field, food, and entertainment, Monroe Park was the place to have fun. This image shows the outdoor movie screen and visitors relaxing along the bayshore in the park. *Photo courtesy of Erik Overbey Collection/University of South Alabama Archives*

(below) The oldest of the city's parks, Bienville Square encompasses an entire block in downtown Mobile. The property was set aside as a park in the 1830s, and its large fountain was installed in 1890. Filled with giant oaks and colorful azaleas, it's a quiet place to rest from the hustle and bustle of urban life. *Photo courtesy of University of South Alabama Archives*

(above and opposite above) Though tens of thousands of Mobilians drive past Memorial Park on their way to work in downtown, few, probably, are aware of whom it honors. The park, with its classically inspired colonnade, fountain, and reflecting pool, is a serene oasis bounded by three busy thoroughfares. An eagle-topped bronze plaque on one side of the colonnade proclaims: "In honored memory of our heroic dead of Mobile City and County, and to the valor of those who gave their service to their country in the Great World War." The memorial, erected by the Mothers' Army and Navy League of Mobile in 1926, contains the names of sixty-one Mobilians who made the ultimate sacrifice for their country, and honors their memory with a simple poem:

"Oh silent dead in tragic vaults of dust
Revered by all for their unswerving trust
Thy name is sacred and thy cause is just
Rest thou in peace."

Photos by Stephen Savage

(right and following page) Commissioned in 1942, the Battleship USS *Alabama* saw thirty-seven months of active duty during World War II, earning nine Battle Stars in action at Okinawa, the Gilbert Islands, and Leyte. Though she shot down twenty-two enemy airplanes, the *Alabama* suffered no casualties or significant damage from enemy attacks. After surrender documents were signed in September 1945, the "Mighty A" was afforded the honor of leading the American Fleet into Tokyo Bay.

In 1962, word that the USS *Alabama* was going to be scrapped led to a campaign to bring the battleship "home" to Alabama. The U.S. Navy donated the ship to the state, and Alabama school children contributed almost $100,000—mostly in nickels, dimes, and quarters—to help finance the cost of towing the Battleship through the Panama Canal from Puget Sound in Washington State. Today, the ship is the centerpiece of the 155-acre Battleship Memorial Park that also features the Submarine USS *Drum*, an airplane pavilion, and a Vietnam Veteran's memorial. *Photos by Steve Goraum/Studio G!*

60

PLEASE
DO NOT LITTER
THE SEAWALL

A unique Mobile landmark, the former temple of the Scottish Rite, a branch of the Masonic order, is the city's only Egyptian Revival building. Designed by famed architect George B. Rogers in 1920-21, the Temple once boasted a raised rooftop terrace and promenade covered by a brilliant awning. The U.S. Army occupied part of the Temple during World War II. The Aviation Interceptor Center found the 78' x 120' lobby perfect for spreading out maps to track the movement of planes in the Southeast.

(left) *Photo courtesy of Erik Overbey/University of South Alabama Archives*
(below) *Photo by Steve Goraum/Studio G!*

A workman renovates another turn-of-the-century building in the Lower Dauphin Street Historic District for new life as an upscale restaurant. While the first-floor level of most of the structures in the area have been altered over time, the second-story facades beautifully retain many of their original features—like the Victorian slate roof—lending a unique charm to the look of downtown Mobile.
Photo by Dale Moore

(following page) Bienville Square provides a pleasant respite from downtown activities for Mobile residents and nature's creatures, alike.
Photo by Steve Goraum/Studio G!

(left) LoDa, short for Lower Dauphin, is a downtown redevelopment program patterned after similar districts like LoDo in Denver and NoDa in Charlotte. Offering a unique dining, shopping, and entertainment experience, the focus of LoDa is not just to recruit support for businesses, but to attract downtown residents, as well. Upper levels of buildings in the area are being renovated for in-town, loft-style living, and the top floors of Mobile's first skyscraper are being transformed into fashionable apartments and penthouses. *Photo by Steve Goraum/Studio G!*

(below) A rival to the Battle House was the Cawthon Hotel overlooking Bienville Square on the corner of Conception and St. Francis Streets. The Cawthon was known for its fine dining, game room, and "modern" suites. Opened in 1902, the Cawthon was closed in December 1971, and demolished in 1973. *Photo courtesy of Erik Overbey Collection/University of South Alabama Archives*

After dark, Dauphin Street metamorphoses from a pleasant downtown shopping area into a vibrant entertainment district, featuring block after block of restaurants, taverns, and clubs. The lively combination of gracious historic architecture, fine food and drink, and live music have given rise to the LoDa slogan: "Entertainment's oldest address." *Photo by Steve Goraum/Studio G!*

(above) Davis Avenue was for generations the heart of Mobile's black community. It was the center of business, shopping, restaurants, recreation, and entertainment. Dixie Park was on the avenue along with the Pike and Lincoln Theaters, and other entertainment venues. The street was renamed after the death of Dr. Martin Luther King, Jr. to honor the memory of the fallen Civil Rights leader. *Photo courtesy of Julius Marx Collection/University of South Alabama Archives*

(right) For more than fifty years, Besteda Bros. was a mainstay of the business community on Davis Avenue. In addition to being an accomplished tailor, Samuel Besteda (pictured right) was a well-known musician who played trombone in the popular Mobile band, The Melody Masters. *Photo courtesy of Michael Thomason/University of South Alabama Archives*

Neighborhoods are thriving in Mobile. Older sections of the city, like the Martin Luther King Avenue area, are being rejuvenated with new construction. In the western part of the city, subdivisions are mushrooming. *Photos by Steve Goraum/Studio G!*

Mobile has shaken off its old Rip Van Winkle torpor, just like in the fairy tales. We're putting more money and muscle into our public schools. Our biggest public school, the University of South Alabama, is resurgent under new leadership. Downtown is alive with a timpani of jack hammers and pile-drivers as historic buildings are renovating and new foundations laid. We are scraping the rust off our old port facilities and bolting together $200 million worth of new ones. We've worked hard on cleaning up the environment, our shimmering Mobile-Tensaw Delta has never been more accessible, museums and parks are popping up all over. How can a town with that much going for it not live happily ever after?

Mike Marshall
Editor and Vice President/News
Mobile Register

Historic Mobile homes—lovingly preserved over the years—may remain in the family for several generations. *Photo by Stephen Savage*

Oakleigh, Mobile's official antebellum period house museum, is neither plantation nor mansion, but the villa of a prosperous businessman. The Greek Revival home, completed in 1833 using materials found on the property, including bricks made of clay dug from the land—the site today of a sunken garden—lends its name to the Oakleigh Garden Historic District, just minutes from downtown. *Photo by Steve Goraum/Studio G!*

(above) Cool, airy porches furnished with comfortable rockers and swings are a hallmark of Mobile homes built in the days before air conditioning. Originally a necessary survival tool during the city's long, hot summers, porches are still popular spots to relax and greet the neighbors. *Photo by Steve Goraum/Studio G!*

(left) More and more residents are returning to residential living in the downtown area—lured by a lifestyle that includes second-story verandas screened by wrought iron "lace" and lush sub-tropical foliage. *Photo by Steve Goraum/Studio G!*

(above) In the 1900s, middle-income families of the inner city favored Queen Anne-style residences, while wealthier citizens preferred classically influenced mansions. In the city's new western suburbs, contemporary influences were more in evidence. This handsome 1910 Mission-style Spanish Revival home near the corner of Houston and Old Government was built by the Fearn Company, which also developed neighborhoods around Monterey Street and near the corner of Dauphin and Catherine Streets. Present-day Fearnway, which curves from Catherine Street to Old Shell, is one of Mobile's most delightful neighborhoods. *Photo by Steve Goraum/Studio G!*

(opposite) The Tacon-Tissington House, built in 1901, was the last of the great Victorian-Queen Anne mansions constructed on Government Street—the city's main thoroughfare at the time. The beautifully restored home is representative of the growth and prosperity Mobile enjoyed from the last quarter of the nineteenth century into the first quarter of the twentieth century. *Photo by Steve Goraum/Studio G!*

25

CHAPTER TWO

2

A Heritage of the Arts in the Port City

THE ARTS & CULTURE OF MOBILE

Native Mobilian Herbert "Mannie" Pair brings a distinct visual style to the local arts scene. At his gallery in the DeTonti Square Historic District, Pair exhibits his "Fabric of the Past" multi-media collages that pay homage to the Black Experience in American history, as well as his popular series of posters based on Mobile's historic districts. *Photo by Steve Goraum/Studio G!*

Perhaps nowhere is Mobile's renaissance more dramatically evident than in the city's cultural life. Stimulating new initiatives celebrating the city's historic legacy and the visual and performing arts have joined with more established organizations to create a spirited cultural environment.

Two flagship projects—one set amid the pine-shaded expanse of a west Mobile park, the other in the heart of the city's historic downtown district—are reshaping the way Mobile's citizens perceive both the outside world and their own colorful history.

A $15-million expansion of the Mobile Museum of Art at Langan Park has tripled the facility's floor space to 95,000 square feet—with spacious galleries spiraling from an airy glass atrium overlooking the park's lake. Displays from the museum's impressive 6000-piece permanent collection are augmented by touring blockbuster exhibits.

Near the waterfront, in one of the oldest sections of the city, the Museum of Mobile has been reincarnated as an important regional historical center. Recently relocated to the building that once housed the stalls of the old Southern Market, the museum comprises a number of galleries that narrate 300 years of Mobile's history, from colonial days through yellow fever epidemics to modern-day hurricanes. Visitors can squeeze inside a life-size partial replica of the Mobile-built Confederate submarine *CSS H.L. Hunley*, explore the city's active role in the nation's Civil Rights struggle, or take a look inside an ancient Native American temple mound.

The Mobile Symphony—a relative newcomer on the scene—has quickly developed into a premier regional orchestra, enriching the city's music environment. In addition to its six-concert season, the Symphony conducts a variety of educational outreach programs, including youth concerts, in-school performances, and "sneak preview" open dress rehearsals. Sharing a new home with the symphony is the state's oldest performing arts organization, the Mobile Opera. The two organizations share teaching studios, administrative space, and a full-sized rehearsal hall in a handsomely renovated building in the Lower Dauphin Street Historic District. Contributing to the city's lively musical mix are the Mobile Pops, Chamber Music Society, and Jazz Festival.

Mobile's legacy as a theater town—the city hosted such performers as Sarah Bernhardt and Jenny Lind in its role as a regional entertainment center—is carried on today by active, accomplished community theaters as well as area colleges and universities. The Saenger Series brings a dizzying array of talent to its stage each year, with presentations ranging from Shakespearean comedies to lavish musicals.

Regional museums—like the Eastern Shore Art Center in Fairhope, the National African-American Archives & Museum, and the Conde-Charlotte House—offer a diverse range of cultural experiences to area residents and visitors alike.

In accordance with the definition: "a revival of intellectual or artistic achievement and vigor," Mobile's exciting cultural environment is a vivid manifestation of the word "renaissance."

(above) Annual arts and crafts festival. *Photo by Stephen Savage*

(opposite) Highlighting the Mobile Museum of Art's 6,000-piece permanent collection are the works of twentieth-century Southern artists—like this playful Kohlmeyer sculpture. A major expansion recently tripled the museum's floorspace, allowing the city to host blockbuster events. New classrooms and a hands-on interactive gallery are enabling the museum to increase its educational outreach—an essential part of its mission. *Photo by Steve Goraum/Studio G!*

(above) Established in 1987, Mobile Ballet has developed into an outstanding regional dance company, performing such classics as *Cinderella*, *Sleeping Beauty*, and *Swan Lake*, as well as new works like *Dracula*, which was choreographed by Mobile Ballet's artistic director. Through its "Share the Dance" and "Discover Dance" programs, Mobile Ballet reaches out to the community, sharing the beauty of classical ballet with those who might otherwise never experience it. *Photo by Steve Goraum/Studio G!*

(right) Having entertained Gulf Coast audiences for more than fifty years, Mobile Opera is recognized as the oldest performing arts organization in the state. Founded by Madame Rose Palmai-Tenser—a Czech native who fled Nazi oppression in her homeland—Mobile Opera is a vital part of the Mobile arts scene. The company brings together internationally renowned guest artists, area singers, a symphony orchestra, and lavish scenery for memorable productions such as Gilbert & Sullivan's *H.M.S. Pinafore*. *Photo by Steve Goraum/Studio G!*

(above) An integral part of Mobile Opera's mission is educational outreach. Accessible, low-cost programs like "Teen Night At The Opera" and "Young People's Student Matinee" are cultivating a new generation of fans and performers of the 300-year-old art form—among them native Mobilian Chauncey Packer, seen here appearing with the Mobile Opera opposite soprano Carter Scott. *Photo by Steve Goraum/Studio G!*

(following page) One of a chain of seven showplaces built and operated throughout the South by the Saenger Amusement Company, Mobile's Saenger Theatre opened in January 1927, after a year of construction and a half-million dollar price tag. The theater's ornate design paid homage to both classical Greek mythology and Mobile's Gulf Coast heritage, depicting Dionysius above the proscenium and stylized shells, fish, and seahorses throughout the interior.

The Saenger hosted vaudeville shows, dramatic and musical productions, and served as the grand downtown movie palace for generations of Mobilians. Rescued on the eve of demolition in the early 1970s by the University of South Alabama, the Saenger was renovated and served as an early anchor for the renaissance of downtown Mobile.

The theater is home to the Mobile Symphony as well as the Saenger Series—an eclectic season of performances ranging from the Flying Karamazov Brothers and the Irish Rovers to productions by the Alabama Shakespeare Festival. Today, the city of Mobile owns the Saenger, which is undergoing a major restoration and upgrading of its facilities. *Photos by Steve Goraum/Studio G!*

(above) Colleges and universities in Mobile make their own unique contribution to the city's arts scene. Theatre USA, the production arm of the Department of Dramatic Arts at the University of South Alabama, presents a full season of classics, contemporary plays, and original works, as well as children's plays. On-campus productions by the Yenni Players at Spring Hill College and the Upper Room Dinner Theater at the University of Mobile are popular with members of the community as well as students. A respected Mobile theatrical tradition, the Pixie Players mount productions using a full complement of performers, stagehands, costume designers, and technicians—all ages eight through nineteen. *Photo by Courtland W. Richards/University of South Alabama Photographer*

(right) Mobile Theatre Guild presents an eclectic mix of newer, non-mainstream works, and has won numerous awards in regional and national competition. Through its participation in events like the Monaco Festival—an invitation-only competition founded by Princess Grace—the Guild also acts as a cultural ambassador for Mobile to the international arts community.

The Joe Jefferson Players, the state's oldest community theater, presents a season of full-scale dramas, comedies, and musicals. The theater's namesake, who lived in Mobile as a boy, is regarded as one of the great American actors of the nineteenth century. *Photo by Steve Goraum/Studio G!*

(opposite) One of the most prominent members of Mobile's professional visual arts community, Charles Smith has been a full-time ceramic artist for more than twenty years. His wheel-thrown pieces with hand-carved designs routinely attract enthusiastic collectors at area shows such as the Fairhope Arts & Crafts Festival and Mobile's Outdoor Arts & Crafts Show. Topping an impressive list of museums and galleries that have exhibited Smith's work are the Smithsonian's National Museum of American Art in Washington, D.C., the American Craft Museum in New York City, and the Museum of African American Life and Culture in Dallas. *Photo by Steve Goraum/Studio G!*

Mobile welcomes its citizens and visitors from around the world and makes them all feel as comfortable as if they were at home. The quality and availability of world-class arts and entertainment were a pleasant surprise to me. Mobile's symphony, opera, and art museum, along with the city's many parks and historical landmarks, are the equal of their counterparts anywhere in the world. The arts and cultural events in Mobile will impress even the most worldly traveler.

Shoei Yamana
President and CEO
Minolta-QMS

(top) Completed in 1857 as Mobile's main public market on Royal Street, the Southern Market also contained upper floors that housed the offices of city hall. Market stalls and shops below such as "coffee and pastry stands" and "cook stalls" sold fresh and prepared vegetables, meat, hand-made sausage, game, poultry, and fish of all kinds. Above sat the mayor along with the city council, city clerk, assessor, and other officers of city government. City militia units met upstairs in the designated city armory. This complex of buildings is one of two National Historic Landmarks in downtown Mobile.
Photo courtesy of Depuy Collection/University of South Alabama Archives

(above) A gallery of fine horse-drawn carriages helps bring the past alive at the Museum of Mobile. Housed in the old Southern Market building, seen above circa 1910, the recently completed 65,000-square-foot regional historical center features exciting displays of the museum's 50,000-piece collection and a hands-on "discovery room."
Photo by Steve Goraum/Studio G!

(right) Despite a number of volunteer fire departments—including Phoenix Fire Company No.6—Mobile was devastated by infernos in 1827 and 1839 that destroyed most of the city's original French, Spanish, and British structures. The legacy of Mobile's courageous firefighters is honored at the Phoenix Fire Museum, which displays restored steam engines, uniforms, hand pumpers, photos, journals, and antique equipment housed in an 1859 firehouse. *Photo by Steve Goraum/Studio G!*

(below) A commanding multi-story glass-walled lobby welcomes visitors to the Mobile Museum of Art, seen here undergoing a major renovation amid the rolling pine hills of Langan Park. *Photo by Steve Goraum/ Studio G!*

The city honors its multi-cultural heritage at the annual Mobile International Festival—a lively celebration of international cuisine, native music and dance, hands-on art, and cultural displays. Representatives of participating countries—wearing authentic traditional dress—officially open the festivities with the colorful Parade of Nations. *Photo courtesy of Mobile International Festival*

Held annually in September on the grounds of the Mobile Museum of Art in Municipal Park, the Outdoor Arts & Crafts Fair brings together more than 100 artists and craftspeople from across the country. The two-day event, sponsored by the Museum and the Art Patrons' League, features a children's area with hands-on art activities, and entertainment by local singers, actors, and dancers. The juried show offers paintings, sculptures, turned wood, glass, pottery, photography, and other works for sale to festival-goers. Proceeds benefit museum acquisitions.
Photos by Steve Gorum/Studio G!

(above) The Mobile Symphony delights audiences from throughout the Gulf Coast region with a full season of live symphonic performances, a chamber music series, youth symphony productions, and community and educational outreach programs. *Photo courtesy of Mobile Symphony*

(right) A key ingredient in the success of the Mobile Symphony is the dynamic leadership of its music director, Scott Speck. The symphony's first director and co-author of *Classical Music for Dummies*, Speck is uniquely gifted in his ability to bring music to life for both seasoned concert-goers, as well as novices. *Photo courtesy of Mobile Symphony*

Bienville Square is the city's oldest urban park. Originally the site of the Royal Hospital when Mobile was under Spanish rule, the area survived years of neglect in the first half of the nineteenth century when it was used as a horse and cow pasture and for the airing of laundry. The square, dedicated in 1866, has become an intrinsic part of the city's identity. The site of jubilant post-war celebrations, outdoor band concerts, and a speech by President Theodore Roosevelt, Bienville Square weathered the demise of scores of surrounding businesses in the 1970s. Today, the square is the heart and soul of a lively, rejuvenated downtown district, and is a center for such celebrations as First Night, the Lighting of the Trees at Christmas, Mardi Gras, and BayFest.
Photos by Steve Goraum/Studio G!

CHAPTER THREE

3

The Character of the City

THE PEOPLE, PLACES & EVENTS THAT MAKE MOBILE SPECIAL

Sweet, sticky fun is the order of the day at the Watermelon Festival in Grand Bay, in south Mobile County. Patterned after an old-fashioned country fair, the Fourth of July celebration features tractor rides, an open-air market, gospel, rock, and country music, and, of course, watermelon eating contests. *Photo by Steve Goraum/Studio G!*

Remarkable people, extraordinary places, and memorable events—these are the touchstones that help define Mobile as a unique place, and act as a staging ground for the renaissance that's taking place throughout the city.

As with so many other aspects of the community, Mobile's roster of "favorite places" is an intriguing blend of old and new. One of the area's most venerable attractions, Bellingrath Gardens and Home, has been delighting visitors from around the world since opening to the public in the 1950s. Magnificent year-round garden displays—highlighted by spring's explosion of color when a quarter-of-a-million azaleas burst into bloom—are breathtaking for tourists and residents alike. Yet even this grand dame of Southern gardens is enjoying a rebirth. A new master plan is in the works to return Bellingrath to its original splendor, including the renewal of the magnificent tree canopy and forest that once surrounded Mirror Lake—lost to time and hurricanes. With proposed additions including an herb garden, aviary, tearoom, and children's garden, Bellingrath is carefully cultivating its reputation—now and for years to come—as one of the south's most spectacular gardens.

Recent additions to the city's inventory of attractions are taking their rightful places alongside more traditional ones among "Mobile's favorite places." The Exploreum, a hands-on family science center, debuted on the downtown scene in the 1990s, and has matured into a leading regional museum. Thousands of families have explored the world around them through intriguing interactive displays. And nationally renowned touring exhibitions—like the Mysteries of Egypt—draw visitors from all along the Gulf Coast.

Mobilians are coming together as a community to enjoy a variety of exciting new events like BayFest. The weekend festival features appearances by scores of stars—like Gladys Knight, B. B. King, Merle Haggard, and the Doobie Brothers—performing on half-a-dozen outdoor stages. Tempting food, beautiful October weather, and the driving beat of a mélange of musical styles attracts tens of thousands of participants to downtown streets.

But it is the quality of Mobile's people that truly defines the city's character. A few Mobilians live out their lives on the world stage—like Hank Aaron, Jimmy Buffet, and Satchell Paige. Others are local icons of sorts—like the Peanut Man who plies his wares near Memorial Park at the Loop. Regardless of "celebrity status," there is a new sense of appreciation for the diversity found in the half-million people who live, work, and play in Mobile's metropolitan area—Buddhist monks in Fairhope, Vietnamese fisherman in Bayou La Batre, the descendants of the survivors of the slave ship *Clotilda*.

Take a moment and get to know the city's people and their favorite places and pastimes—they're all ingredients in the rich, spicy gumbo of Mobile.

(above) Winston Groom, author of *Forrest Gump*, makes his home on the Eastern Shore of Mobile Bay. *Photo courtesy of Mobile Area Chamber of Commerce*

(opposite) Tucked in a shady niche at the Bellingrath Garden's Great Lawn, the Mermaid Pool has delighted visitors for decades. A part of the garden's original design, its origin is unknown, and is believed to have come from another garden in Mobile or New Orleans. A mystery no one can explain is why the mermaid has two tails instead of one. *Photo by Steve Goraum/Studio G!*

On December 12, 2000, *LST-325* began a 4,350-mile voyage from Gibraltar to Mobile. Manned by twenty-nine World War II veterans with an average age of seventy-two, the LST—or landing ship tank—was herself a veteran of the invasions of Sicily, Salerno, and Normandy. A national audience followed the ship's month-long progress across the Atlantic, and on January 10, 2001, she sailed into Pier D-2 at the Alabama State Docks to a hero's welcome. The ship was the centerpiece of the 6,000-member LST Association's national convention held in Mobile. A drive is underway to turn the ship into a floating museum. *Photos by Steve Goraum/Studio G!*

In celebration of 300 years of maritime history, the Tall Ship *Californian* glides serenely along Mobile River past the convention center. City leaders welcomed the delegation of Tall Ships to Mobile in a special ceremony. *Photos by Steve Goraum/Studio G!*

A family and children's area and mini-stage are part of the fun each year at BayFest, a three-day musical celebration featuring blues, rock, country, gospel, bluegrass, and zydeco—to name a few. One hundred national and local acts—which have included the Doobie Brothers (pictured below), Travis Tritt, Gladys Knight, Percy Sledge, and Billy Preston—perform on seven stages, transforming downtown Mobile into a giant street party on the first weekend of October.

(above) *Photo by Steve Goraum/Studio G!*

(below) *Photo by Catt Sirten*

Giant insects aren't the only creatures that have descended upon the Gulf Coast Exploreum Museum of Science, Mobile's regional science center. Swarms of visitors also have swept through the 65,000-square-foot museum with a Hands-On Hall featuring more than fifty lively, interactive exhibits. The Traveling Exhibit Hall hosts three internationally produced shows each year, like "Mysteries of Egypt"—a dazzling collection of 126 meticulously crafted replicas of artifacts from ancient Egypt. Movie going reaches new heights in the IMAX® Theater with its 70-foot domed screen. The 12,000-watt digital wraparound sound system enhances the awe-inspiring experience. The construction of the Exploreum was a bit of a renaissance in its own right. Part of the museum is located in the historic Matt Sloan Building (named for Mobile's first fire chief), the east facade of which was originally the entrance to the Southern Market complex. *Photo by Steve Goraum/Studio G!*

It's duck season of a different sort when hundreds of the bright-yellow rubber variety of waterfowl, sporting cool wraparound shades, glide across Bellingrath Garden's Mirror Lake. The Great Duck Race raises money for the Boys and Girls Clubs of South Alabama that serve 6,000 youth in Mobile and Baldwin Counties at approximately twenty member locations. The clubs offer a variety of programs, including tutoring, arts and crafts, recreation, and mentoring in a safe, positive environment. *Photos by Steve Goraum/Studio G!*

Cudjo Kazoola Lewis, a resident of the Plateau community just north of Mobile, was the final survivor of the last slave ship to land in America—the *Clotilda*, which arrived in Mobile Bay in 1860 with its illegal cargo of west-African tribesmen. After the Civil War, Lewis and other survivors of the *Clotilda*, joined by fellow tribesmen, settled in the area that came to be known as Africatown. The members of the community continued to speak their native tongue and were largely self-governing, with disputes arbitrated by the tribal chieftain and illnesses treated by an African doctor. Lewis, a leader of and spokesman for the community, died in 1934. *Photo courtesy of Erik Overbey Collection/University of South Alabama Archives*

Mobile has a rich tradition of celebrating the people and places that make the city unique. From citywide festivals that attract tens of thousands of participants to small community and civic fundraisers, folks in the Mobile area love to come together for a good time, a good cause, or simply to enjoy the beauty of our region. We at Mobile Gas are committed to protecting our natural resources so that we may all continue to share that beauty for generations to come.

John S. Davis
President and CEO
EnergySouth, Inc. and Mobile Gas

(above left) Downtown workers can select from a variety of options for weekday lunches, ranging from gumbo and fried crab claws to carry-out deli for a picnic in Bienville Square. Hot dogs, the original fast food, are served up by a vendor from his cart parked in its usual spot in front of Government Plaza. *Photo by Steve Goraum/Studio G!*

(above right) Former Mobile Mayor Joseph N. Langan was an early proponent, among white southerners, for racial justice. His tours of duty in World War II and Korea—where he saw African-Americans give their lives in battle—were key to Langan's decision to fight for equal pay for black and white county public school teachers and voting rights for all citizens. The city's largest park bears his name. *Photo by Steve Goraum/Studio G!*

A ten-kilometer (10k) course that takes runners down oak-shaded thoroughfares past some of the south's most magnificent homes is the hallmark of the Azalea Trail Run that attracts thousands of participants every March. World-class runners like Bill Rodgers, Joan Benoit, Marty Liquori, Joseph Kimani, and Francie Larrieu-Smith have all been able to maintain winning paces despite the distraction of spectacular blooming azaleas, dogwoods, and wisteria lining the course. Race day offers an opportunity for everyone to get in on the fun, with a 10K Racewalk, 10K Wheelchair Race, and One- and Two-Mile Fun Runs. The sidelines make for a lively scene with antebellum-attired Azalea Trail Maids, cheerleaders, team mascots, and radio personalities lending support and encouragement along the way.
(above) *Photo by Steve Goraum/Studio G!*
(below) *Photo by Dale Moore*

(right and below) The America's Junior Miss program—the nation's oldest and largest scholarship program for high school seniors—was held for the first time in March, 1958, in the Saenger Theatre with young women from fifteen states competing. Today, representatives of all fifty states compete for a quarter-of-a-million dollars in cash scholarships at the nationally televised America's Junior Miss National Finals. The program—which recognizes, rewards, and encourages excellence among young people—counts more than 2,000 former high school seniors as honored alumnae, among them Diane Sawyer, Deborah Norville, and Julie Moran. *Photos by Steve Goraum/Studio G!*

(following page) Bellingrath Gardens in the springtime is one of the South's most breathtaking sights. The Gardens' exquisitely landscaped sixty-five acres, set amid a 900-acre semi-tropical rainforest on the banks of Fowl River, come alive with azaleas, dogwoods, tulips, daffodils, hyacinths, lilies, and more.

The 15-room Bellingrath Home, completed in 1935, was the first home in Alabama to be featured on A&E's popular series "America's Castles," and is open to the public year-round. The attractive, surprisingly "livable" home is furnished with fine antiques collected by Bessie Morse Bellingrath. *Photo by Steve Goraum/Studio G!*

CHAPTER FOUR

4

Have the Time of Your Life

MARDI GRAS, FESTIVALS & SPORTS

From its New World origins in the early 1700s in Mobile, Mardi Gras has become an integral part of life along the Gulf Coast. Tens of thousands of revelers line the streets at more than forty parades in Mobile, Dauphin Island, Gulf Shores, and Fairhope during the weeks before Ash Wednesday. Masked members of "mystic societies" ride elaborate floats hurling beads, candy, serpentine, doubloons, and the most-prized catch of all—the Moon Pie. *Photo by Steve Goraum/Studio G!*

American citizens are guaranteed the right to "the pursuit happiness." In Mobile, the people are equally dedicated to "the pursuit of fun." Mobilians love to have a good time. In fact, it's considered a birthright, dating back to the early 1700s, when French colonists in Old Mobile sang and feasted, celebrating Mardi Gras for the first time in the New World.

The celebration rose to a new level in 1830, when the tradition of parading was introduced by Mobilian Michael Krafft and some friends who spontaneously grabbed cowbells, hoes, and rakes and marched noisily through the city. Calling themselves the Cowbellions de Rakin Society, Krafft and friends formed Mobile's first "mystic" society—the organizations that sponsor Mardi Gras balls and parades. A group of Cowbellions and other delegates from the city, journeyed west in the 1850s to help some folks in Louisiana form their own mystic society—giving birth to the world-famous Mardi Gras in New Orleans.

The pre-Lenten celebration all but disappeared during the dark days of the Civil War, but festivities were resurrected in 1866 by a city market clerk, Joe Cain, who dressed up as "Chief Slacabamorinico," and paraded through town on a coal wagon with his friends, singing, beating on tin cans, and waving noisemakers—much to the amazement of federal troops occupying the city.

Mardi Gras has been going strong ever since. And with new mystic societies in Mobile and Baldwin Counties, even this 300-year-old institution is enjoying a modern-day revival. More marching bands and colorful floats fill the streets than ever before, with the regional parade count topping thirty-five.

And the good times keep rolling with a bumper crop of sporting events and games—whether indoor or outdoor, spectator or participant, Mobile has a special love affair with baseball. Long respected as the home of some of baseball's greatest players—including Willie McCovey, Cleon Jones, and Eddie Stanky—the city now has a new love interest. The Mobile BayBears, of the storied Southern League, are the AA affiliate of the San Diego Padres. Playing from April until September, the BayBears regularly draw impressive crowds to Hank Aaron Stadium—named for the city's most famous native son of all.

Mobile's passion for football is equally unbounded. High school games are a fall weekend ritual. And college match-ups arouse almost religious fervor. Fans can cheer on their favorites first hand at the all-star classic Senior Bowl, which for more than fifty years has featured the cream of the crop of college seniors playing in their first professional game. Mobile's renaissance extends to football too, with the city hosting the GMAC Bowl. Less than five years old, the nationally televised game, which kicks off the college bowl season, has earned high marks—and ratings—as an exciting post-season contest.

In the streets and on the playing field, Mobilians love to have a good time, and enjoy sharing it with the world.

When it comes to having fun, this city is dead serious.

(above) Akiko Fukushima (pictured above) and Karrie Webb are among winners of the LPGA's AFLAC Champions Tournament held at Mobile's Magnolia Grove Golf Course. *Photo by Steve Goraum/Studio G!*

(opposite)The character "Folly" rides high on Mardi Gras Day atop a giant champagne glass—the emblem float in the Knights of Revelry (KOR) parade. The oldest daytime parading mystic society, the KORs were founded in 1874. *Photo by Steve Goraum/Studio G!*

ONE

Mobile's tradition of Mardi Gras or Carnival parades began in the 1830s and became a steadfast part of local culture. This parade photograph shows the intersection of St. Francis and St. Joseph Streets with the throngs of people who came out to enjoy one of the many Mardi Gras parades in 1946.
Photo courtesy of S. Blake McNeely Collection/University of South Alabama Archives

Mardi Gras is a family affair in Mobile—with moms, dads, and kids draped in beads thrown by maskers on floats in response to the universal cry, "Throw me something, Mister!"
(right) *Photo by Steve Goraum/Studio G!*
(below) *Photo by Dale Moore*

(above) Confederate veteran and clerk of the Southern Market, Joe Cain revived Mardi Gras in Mobile in 1867 after it lapsed during the Civil War. Cain organized a new mystic society called the Lost Cause Minstrels, dressed himself as the mythical undefeated Chickasaw Chief Slacabamorinico, and paraded with merriment in downtown Mobile. Awe-struck Union soldiers gaped at the spectacle of "Old Slack" but let the procession continue. Mardi Gras now honors the revival by celebrating Joe Cain Day on the Sunday before every Mardi Gras Tuesday. *Photos courtesy of University of South Alabama Archives*

(below) Founded in 1883 by John A. Pope and a group of musician friends who'd gathered to celebrate the birth of Pope's son, the Excelsior Band carries on the proud tradition of marching bands. Clad in their trademark black suits, caps, and white dress shirts, the band is a mainstay of Mobile Mardi Gras parades. *Photo courtesy of Michael Thomason/University of South Alabama Archives*

The most egalitarian celebration of Mobile's Mardi Gras is Joe Cain Day. Begun as a simple procession to lay a wreath on Cain's grave at the Church Street Cemetery, the ceremony has turned into a raucous day-long, city-wide celebration. The official Joe Cain parade, consisting of "homemade" floats built by ordinary citizens (not mystic societies)—winds through downtown streets lined with picnics, parties, cookouts, street dances, and mini-parades.
(above) *Photo by Dale Moore*
(right) *Photo by Steve Goraum/Studio G!*

Mobile is a city of people who love to "get out and do things." Whether they're reeling in a speckled trout, scrambling for moonpies at Mardi Gras, or racing a catamaran across the bay, Mobilians are renowned for enjoying life on land as well as on the water. As a company that services the marine industry, we feel a special bond with the people of Mobile, and share their respect for this very special region of the Gulf Coast.

George W. Gibbs, III
Chairman and Chief Executive Officer
Atlantic Marine Holding Company

Organized and named the "Colored Carnival Association," the Black carnival association later changed its name to the Mobile Area Mardi Gras Association. Their first coronation took place in 1940. Here we see the 1953 coronation of Sidney Weeks and Greta Turner, King and Queen. During the present Mardi Gras Day, King Elexis and his queen reign over the gala.
(above) *Photo courtesy of University of South Alabama Archives*
(left) *Photo by Steve Goraum/Studio G!*

(right) The Order of Doves, the Mobile area's first black mystic society, held its original Mardi Gras ball in 1894, an annual event through 1914. In 1938, the Colored Carnival Association held a parade in the Davis Avenue area. An important milestone for the association was the dedication of its first float warehouse where members could design and build their own floats, rather than renting from white mystic societies. *Photo by Steve Goraum/Studio G!*

(below) The tradition of royalty in Mobile's Mardi Gras dates back to 1872 when white mystic societies formed the Mobile Carnival Association that selected the first male monarch. Originally called "Emperor" and now termed "King," Felix I, the lord of misrule, was joined by his consort, the queen, in 1893. Each year a different king and queen preside over carnival festivities. *Photo by Steve Goraum/Studio G!*

(above) During the nineteenth century and before government assistance, immigrants to Mobile frequently formed associations and benevolent organizations to provide a social safety net for members. One of the most successful was the German Relief Association. In 1896, the Association constructed this large hall on the southeast corner of Conti and St. Emanuel Streets.

After the Association disbanded, the building housed several businesses including the first Morrison's Cafeteria restaurant. It burned in September 1992, and its remains were demolished soon thereafter. *Photo courtesy of Erik Overbey Collection/University of South Alabama Archives*

(left and opposite) Though romanticized images persist of prosperous merchants and the cotton aristocracy in antebellum Mobile, there was a thriving class of shopkeepers, clerks, and artisans, as wells as mechanics and other semi-skilled laborers, including an increasing number of immigrants. Irish immigrants played an active role in local hotel and restaurant businesses.

The Friendly Sons of St. Patrick celebrate their forebears and homeland each year, parading through the streets tossing green beads and plastic shamrocks and medallions. Those who can't claim direct connection to the "old sod" get in on the fun at the "Dauphin to Dublin" Street Party in LoDa—the Lower Dauphin Street entertainment district—where the beer flows green at more than twenty participating restaurants and taverns. *Photos by Dale Moore*

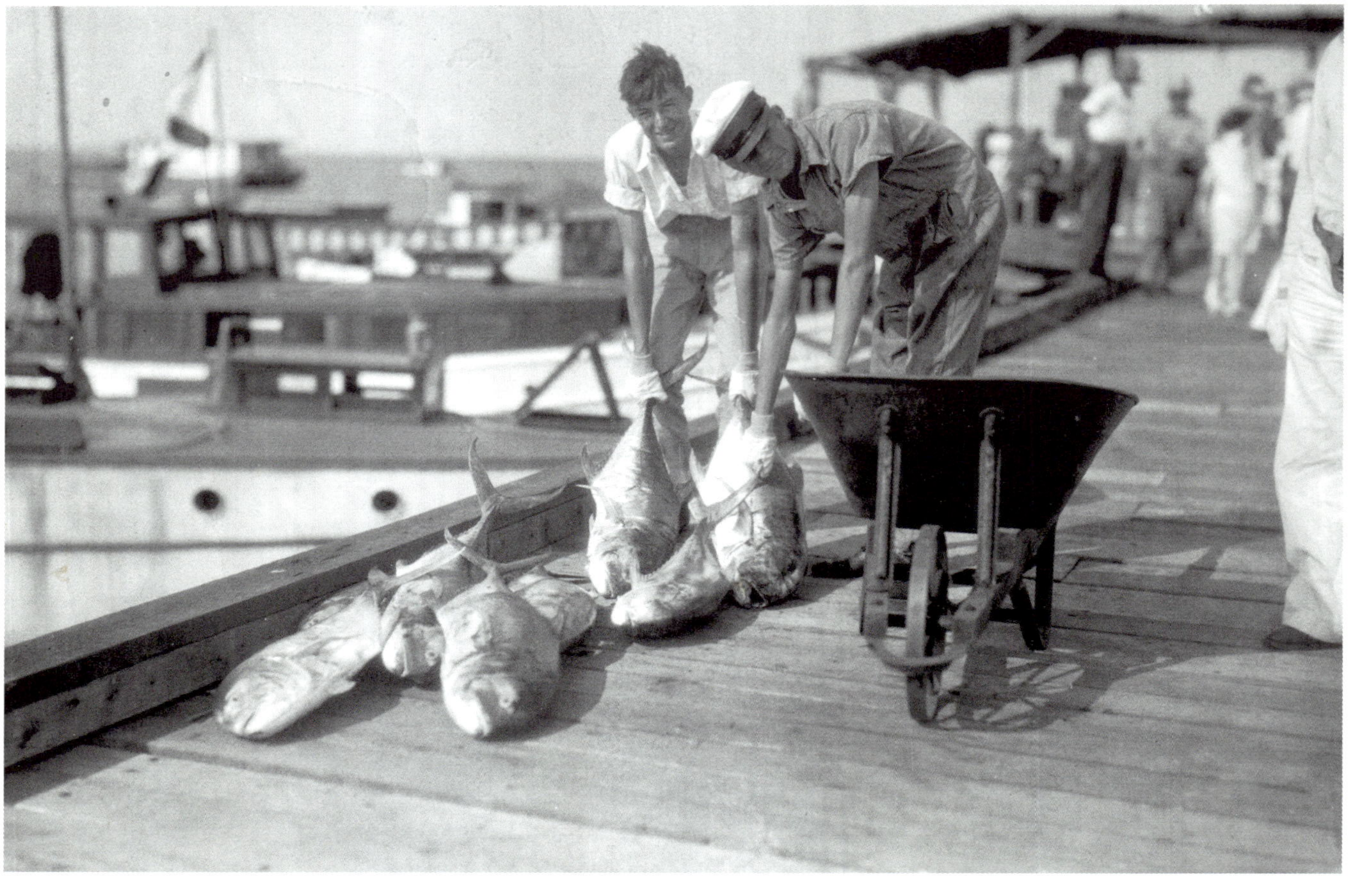

(above) Located at the mouth of three rivers and a bay, Mobile is a popular place for sport fishing and remains so today. Begun in 1929, the Alabama Deep Sea Fishing Rodeo draws thousands of participants each year who compete for a suite of contest prizes. A variety of events and entertainment takes place during the competition. This 1950s image of a big catch at the Alabama Deep Sea Fishing Rodeo on Dauphin Island warms the heart of any fisherman. *Photo courtesy of Erik Overbey Collection/University of South Alabama Archives*

(left) The Alabama Deep Sea Fishing Rodeo is about more than fish—it's about a lot of fun! This image from the 1950s shows the winners of several beauty contest categories chosen to represent several fish types at the Rodeo. *Photo courtesy of Museum of Mobile Collection/University of South Alabama Archives*

Carrier pigeons transmitted news of the daily catch at the first Alabama Deep Sea Fishing Rodeo. Today, the rodeo, a project of the Mobile Jaycees, attracts ample television and radio coverage, as well as more than 50,000 spectators who come to Dauphin Island for events such as the Liars' Contest, official weigh-in of catches, and fresh seafood dinners. More than 2,000 anglers compete for prizes in the inshore, offshore, and big game categories at the three-day event. Rodeo records include a 618-pound blue marlin and a 69-pound, 12-ounce king mackerel. *Photo by Steve Goraum/ Studio G!*

(above) A fisherman's pride shines in the face of this young angler, circa 1895. *Photo courtesy of T.E. Armistead Collection/University of South Alabama Archives*

(opposite) Sailing is a time-honored tradition in the area, with sailboat races on Mobile Bay dating to the 1830s, though the Civil War and fear of the Union fleet briefly interrupted local sailors' passion for the sport. Today, yacht clubs on both sides of the Bay cater to boats ranging in size from 14-foot catamarans to 65-foot luxury vessels—many of which compete each year in the Dauphin Island Sailing Regatta—billed as the nation's largest point-to-point single-day race. *Photo by Steve Goraum/Studio G!*

Gypsy Wind
Cleveland, Ohio

(above) Arlington Fair Grounds just south of Monroe Park on Washington Avenue packed in visitors for race day. Around the track were stands selling food and drink, and there were agricultural and livestock exhibits in the permanent pavilions on the grounds. *Photo courtesy of Erik Overbey Collection/University of South Alabama Archives*

(right) Chartered in the early nineteenth century, Bay Shell Road was a toll road that ran along the edge of Mobile Bay from the foot of Conception Street to near Dog River. Along the road were some of Mobile's finest recreational and amusement establishments, Frascatti and Monroe Parks, Arlington Fair Grounds, Arlington Pier, and the Magnolia Race Course. This image shows a tollgate near where Duval Street once intersected with the road. *Photo courtesy of University of South Alabama Archives*

Swine rule the day at Cathedral Square when the American Cancer Society holds its annual Chili Cook-Off. As many as seventy teams labor over steaming pots, stirring special ingredients into top-secret recipes in an attempt to snare the top prize. To work up an appetite, crowds line the rail to cheer on their preferred porker in the pig races. *Photos by Steve Goraum/Studio G!*

(above) The Mobile Country Club was originally located two miles south of downtown along beautiful Garrow's Bend on Mobile Bay's Western Shore. Here members could play a little golf, relax along the shore, stroll around the grounds, or entertain in the clubhouse (pictured). The site was purchased during World War I by the federal government and converted into the experimental concrete shipbuilding plant that built transports for the war effort. *Photo courtesy of Erik Overbey Collection/University of South Alabama Archives*

(right) Mobile was recently honored as one of the "Top Ten Golf Value Destinations" in the United States by *Golf Digest* magazine. The city is home to a wealth of both private and public golf courses, including Magnolia Grove, the southernmost stop on the nationally acclaimed Robert Trent Jones Golf Trail. Magnolia Grove's three magnificently designed courses have been hailed by the *New York Times* as "some of the best public golf on earth." *Photo by Steve Goraum/ Studio G!*

Mobilians indulge their passion for football at the Senior Bowl, presented by Food World, and the GMAC Bowl, both played at Ladd-Peebles Stadium. A premier showcase for graduating gridiron stars for more than fifty years, the Senior Bowl has offered the nation a first look at the professional games of such NFL standouts as Terry Bradshaw, Dan Marino, and Brett Favre. The roster of the 50th Anniversary Senior Bowl Team reads like a "Who's Who" of the NFL, and includes Joe Namath, Walter Payton, Bo Jackson, Franco Harris, Lynn Swann, "Mean" Joe Greene, Bubba Smith, and Ray Nitschke. *Photos by Steve Goraum/ Studio G!*

With the first drop of the puck in the mid-1990s, Mobilians added such words as "cross-checking," "icing," and "zamboni" to their sports lexicon. A member of the East Coast Hockey League (ECHL), a professional developmental league, the Mobile Mysticks team plays 30-plus home games each season at "The Dungeon," also known as the Mobile Civic Center. The addition of ECHL teams like the Pensacola Ice Pilots and Mississippi Sea Wolves has added a touch of regional rivalry to the season. In association with the Mysticks, the Youth Hockey Association is training the next generation of Gretskys and Lemieuxs, with area youngsters competing in several divisions, including Mites, Squirts, and Pee-Wees. *Photos by Steve Goraum/Studio G!*

Hank Aaron—perhaps Mobile's most famous native son—prevailed over seemingly insurmountable obstacles in the segregated South to become the Major League's all-time homerun leader. Aaron is one of many baseball greats who hailed from Mobile, among them Satchel Paige (pictured left), Ozzie Smith, Eddie Stanky, Billie Williams, Amos Otis, Tommie Aaron, and Tommie Agee.

To honor Hammerin' Hank, the city named its new ballpark after him, Hank Aaron Stadium (above), home of the minor league Mobile BayBears. The AA affiliate of the National League San Diego Padres, the team has sent a number of players to The Show, including Ben Davis, Wiki Gonzalez, and Matt Clement. (above) *Photo by Steve Goraum/Studio G!*
(left) *Photo courtesy of the University of South Alabama Archives*

(opposite) A full complement of mascots entertain the crowds at BayBear's games, making it a top family attraction from April through August. For many fans, it recalls steamy summers spent at Hartwell Field watching players such as Chuck Connors, star of *The Rifleman*, win the Southern League Championship in 1947. *Photo by Steve Goraum/Studio G!*

CHAPTER FIVE

5

The Foundation For Success

GOVERNMENT, TRANSPORTATION & INDUSTRY

Mobile Government Plaza—the nation's first structure to consolidate county government, city government, and court systems in one facility—houses more than half-a-million square feet of operating space in the heart of downtown. A ten-story administration building and a nine-story judicial building are joined by the glass-enclosed atrium—a contemporary interpretation of the traditional town square. Designed to centralize essential services and save tax dollars, the complex symbolizes the cooperative renaissance between the city and the county. *Photo by Stephen Savage*

With a population of 400,000 living in ten municipalities throughout a 1200-square-mile county, the Mobile metropolitan area is an exciting and diverse one. And in a new spirit of partnership, communities are working together to create a sound foundation for future growth.

One of the most concrete symbols of this renaissance of cooperation is the new Government Plaza building that has brought together—under one impressive, distinctively vaulted roof—both the Mobile city and county governments. By consolidating their offices in a single downtown location, the two administrative bodies have made not only municipal services more accessible, but have increased the opportunity for citizen participation in the day-to-day business of government.

A primary focus of the Mobile renaissance is economic development, an area in which Mobile already is making its mark. More than 72,000 net new jobs were created in the Mobile metropolitan area from 1985-1998. And *Entrepreneur* magazine recently ranked Mobile fourth in the Southeast for its excellent small business climate.

An influx of manufacturing plants—ranging from Pacific-Rim companies like Mitsubishi Materials to American corporations such as Johnson & Johnson's McNeil Specialty, has created a wealth of new employment opportunities. IPSCO Steel recently began operations at its north Mobile County-mill, representing a total investment of $395 million and 450 new jobs. Mobile is also fertile ground for technology start-ups—like Chapura, developers of the synchronization software for the country's most popular hand-held computers.

Contributing to the region's stable economy is Mobile's position as a major transportation hub. The Port of Alabama, home to the world's largest forest products terminal, ranks first in the U. S. for wood pulp exports. And the Port's continued importance as an import and export center is being strengthened by a $100-million capital improvement of its infrastructure. Additional plans call for a new, state-of-the-art container handling operation.

Mobile Regional Airport, an all-jet facility served by six airlines, offers competitive fares that attract travelers from throughout the central Gulf Coast area. The Downtown Airport at Brookley Industrial Complex, a former Air Force base, is a regional center for domestic air cargo service.

Ground transportation in the port city is undergoing a renaissance, too. The grand, turn-of-the-century GM&O Railroad terminal is being given new life as a city transportation hub for buses, taxis, trolley, and trains.

Mobile also is reaching out to its neighbors across the bay. One of the most compelling initiatives—"Envision Mobile-Baldwin"—has brought together hundreds of business, civic, governmental, educational, and church groups in a broad-based program to enhance the quality of life for all people in both counties.

Mobile is engaged in an exciting renewal—drawing on the talents and resources of people and organizations throughout the region to forge a dynamic future.

(above) Lobby of Mobile Government Plaza. *Photo by Steve Goraum/Studio G!*

(opposite) The brightly painted facades of historic buildings and the graceful canopy of Bienville Square's oak trees dominate the foreground of this view of Mobile. The handsome art deco building in the center—originally Merchants Bank and now the Mobile headquarters of Regions Bank—was emblematic of the city's prosperity in the 1920s. Though it opened to the public in 1929—just weeks before the stock market crash—the bank, as well as the city, survived the Great Depression, escaping the devastating losses suffered by heavily industrialized cities. *Photo by Steve Goraum/Studio G!*

(above) Before the dominance of the telephone for mass communication, the telegram was the only message medium outside of writing a letter. Telegrams were delivered by couriers such as these lined up outside one of several Western Union offices in downtown Mobile in the 1930s. *Photo courtesy of Erik Overbey Collection/University of South Alabama Archives*

(left) Energized by the aggressive initiatives of the Gulf Coast Technology Council, a coalition of regional tech companies, and programs such as the University of South Alabama's e-commerce major, Mobile is home to dozens of technology companies and poised for explosive growth. One Mobile start-up, Gulf Coast Computer Services, builds custom-designed systems for clients along the Gulf Coast, as well as in Mexico, Venezuela, and Sweden. *Photo by Steve Goraum/Studio G!*

(above) Recently ranked as one of the country's "Best Cities to Start and Grow a Business" by *Inc.* magazine, Mobile is a leader in large metropolitan areas in the South for announced new capital investments. In addition to new construction throughout the area—like the $150-million McNeal Speciality Plant seen here—existing facilities are being reconfigured for new uses. Hertz recently renovated available retail space into an attractive international Reservations Center employing more than 500 people. *Photo by Steve Goraum/Studio G!*

(right) Mobile has had its share of severe hurricanes. Living under the shadow of these storms is a fact of life along the Gulf Coast. A very damaging storm occurred in September 1979. Hurricane Frederick tore across Dauphin Island and through Mobile County leaving a wake of major destruction. Mobile's City Hall was hard hit. Repairs to the building were not complete until 1982. *Photo courtesy of Corps of Engineers/University of South Alabama Archives*

(left) In 1893, Mobile left mule-drawn cars behind to adopt a new mode of transportation—the electric streetcar. Power lines were strung over tracks and the streetcars connected to them via a trailing arm or "trolley." This arm gave them the name "Trolley Cars." The new electric streetcars could carry more passengers, longer distances, more quickly. Soon, an even greater network of tracks criss-crossed the city and brought low-cost mass transit into every neighborhood. The streetcars were abandoned in the early 1940s in favor of the more efficient and flexible gasoline-powered buses. *Photo courtesy of Erik Overbey Collection/ University of South Alabama Archives*

(below) Government Street always has been a busy downtown byway. Businesses of all kinds lined the street and traffic flowed easily along its wide lanes. After the Bankhead Tunnel was opened, the street became even busier due to the increased traffic. *Photo courtesy of Erik Overbey Collection/ University of South Alabama Archives*

(opposite) The gingerbread charm of Victorianism and the sleek authority of contemporary minimalism co-exist harmoniously in the heart of Mobile's business district. *Photo by Steve Goraum/Studio G!*

(above) Flight in the 1920s was still a novelty anywhere. Mobile was no exception. Having your picture taken beside an airplane was quite a thrill, especially if you were a Mobilian and the recently arrived aircraft was named "City of Mobile." *Photo courtesy of Erik Overbey Collection/University of South Alabama Archives*

(right) The bronze sculpture "Family," by the late artist Jo Hess, located at the entrance to the Mobile Regional Airport, perfectly captures a child's excitement about the adventure of travel. Upgraded facilities, increased seating, and enhanced concession services at the airport are helping to make flying a more pleasant experience for families and business travelers, as well. *Photo by Steve Goraum/Studio G!*

Transportation is the foundation to Mobile's economy and the key to our economic future. Mobile's position at the intersection of water, road, rail, and air routes has driven our industry and shaped our character as an international city. Now with aerospace and technology industries rapidly growing, Mobile's airport and seaport system is becoming our greatest competitive advantage.

Mobile's outstanding transportation connects us to friends, family, customers, and suppliers across the globe. It brings the world home to Mobile.

Richard D. Davis
Chairman
Mobile Airport Authority

Aided by aggressive economic development programs, the Mobile area has experienced a surge in industrial growth. Since 1985, more than 222 new businesses and 769 expansions have been reported to the Chamber of Commerce, representing a capital investment of well over $7 billion and a total of more than 25,000 direct new jobs. *Photos by Steve Goraum/Studio G!*

More than half of all the wood chips exported from the southern United States are shipped through the Port of Mobile, which is second only to New York City nationwide in the exportation of forest products. *Photos by Steve Goraum/Studio G!*

The Port of Alabama is a leading importer and exporter of coal. The Port's McDuffie Coal Terminal—the largest facility of its kind on the Gulf Coast—has a through-put capacity of more than twenty million tons per year. The Terminal is the only facility of its kind on the Gulf Coast, with two ship loaders, one ship unloader, single and tandem railcar dumps, three stacker reclaimers, three barge unloaders, and one barge loader. McDuffie also has a 300,000-ton ground-storage capacity for direct reduced iron or other bulk cargo, and is served by three loop rail tracks. *Photos by Steve Goraum/Studio G!*

Shipbuilding on Mobile's waterfront has a long, storied history dating to pre-Civil War days. Today, the area's largest shipbuilding and ship repair companies are counted among the most technologically advanced in the industry with equipment that includes the largest, most powerful production laser for cutting steel plate in use in a U.S. shipyard.

Mobile-built and repaired ships are in operation around the world, including fishing and offshore supply vessels, passenger ships, tugs, push boats, oil spill recovery vessels, casino riverboats, dockside casino barges, drill rigs, double-hull oil barges, and research vessels. Newer ventures include Atlantic Marine's repair and conversion of cruise ships for major lines like Royal Caribbean and Carnival, and Bender Shipbuilding's partnership with the Australian company, Austal USA, to build high-speed passenger and car ferries. *Photo by Steve Goraum/Studio G!*

(left) When the GM&O Railroad decided to build its new terminal on the north side of town, it did so at a time when railroads across the country were constructing new terminals to show off their pride and place in American life. Built in 1905, this ornate passenger terminal was the southern end of a line that once stretched from Mobile to St. Louis. Hundreds of thousands of passengers and millions of tons of freight have passed through this terminal during its lifetime.

Few cities have retained their grand old stations, but Mobile has managed to keep its version in spite of urban development pressures. This image of the terminal is from the 1920s. *Photo courtesy of Erik Overbey Collection/University of South Alabama Archives*

(below) The Bankhead Tunnel was a major construction project financed by the federal government late in the Great Depression. A major technological innovation for Mobile, the tunnel allowed easy access from downtown to the Highway 98 Causeway to Baldwin County. Workers who labored on the Bankhead Tunnel had a dangerous but exciting job. The close quarters, dim light, and complexity of the assignment required extra caution. In this picture, workers are about to install ceiling portions of the tunnel interior.

The Tunnel proved to be a wonderful aid to transportation between Mobile and Baldwin Counties and to travelers moving along the Gulf Coast, as well. Once complete, motorists no longer had to travel north three miles from downtown to cross the Mobile River at the Cochrane Drawbridge and then three miles back to the causeway. *Photo courtesy of Erik Overbey Collection/University of South Alabama Archives*

(opposite) Cars entering and exiting the twin tubes of the George Wallace Tunnel create steady streams of light at rush hour. The Wallace Tunnel, which passes under the Mobile River, was opened in 1973 to alleviate the traffic load carried by the Bankhead Tunnel. *Photo by Steve Goraum/Studio G!*

(above) In 1860, the legislature chartered Mobile's first "street railroad." This early mass transit system conveyed passengers in iron-wheeled carriages or "cars," over railroad-style tracks laid in city streets. Mules pulled the cars in a steady, though temperamental manner, but it was better than walking, and the mule-powered street railroad contributed to a quickening pace of life in nineteenth-century Mobile. *Photo courtesy of University of South Alabama Archives*

(below) As automobiles multiplied on Mobile streets, they began to change the face of the urban landscape. More hard-surface roads were built to accommodate the increasing number of cars, and corner gas stations sprouted up frequently around town, becoming a common sight in every city neighborhood. *Photo courtesy of Erik Overbey Collection/University of South Alabama Archives*

(opposite) Mobile is located at the nexus of major north-south and east-west interstate systems. Interstate 65 connects the upper midwest to the Gulf Coast by way of Mobile. Interstate 10, on its 2,000-mile route from Jacksonville, Florida, to Los Angeles, passes through Baldwin and Mobile Counties—a brief stretch of it in the form of the Bayway—with spectacular views of the bay and lower delta. *Photo by Stephen Savage*

CHAPTER SIX

6

A Choice Lifestyle

QUALITY OF LIFE, EDUCATION & HEALTH CARE

The Visitation Monastery was founded in the 1830s by Mobile's first Catholic bishop, Reverend Michael Portier. As the head of a vast diocese that stretched from the Mississippi River to the Atlantic Ocean, the popular Portier traveled the region on horseback establishing churches and schools. The Chapel of the Sacred Heart (pictured here)—one of the few stone buildings in the city—was built in 1894 with an elongated west arm screened by grilles and shutters to accommodate the cloistered Visitation nuns while they attended Mass. *Photo by Steve Goraum/Studio G!*

Striking architecture, stimulating museums, compelling attractions—all appealing aspects of the city. But what are the qualities that make Mobile more than a "nice place to visit," and transform it into a delightful place to live, work, and raise a family?

Mobile's distinctive quality of life is the product of many factors, among them a commitment to building educational excellence. Home of the oldest and largest public school system in the state—and one of the most populous in the U.S.—Mobile has struggled at times with the enormous demands of serving the needs of 65,000 students attending 100 schools ranging in size from fewer than ninety students to more than 2,000. Yet there is a bright new spirit of rededication to quality education in Mobile. A recent major initiative, overwhelmingly approved by county voters, has ensured a sustained source of funding to continue the city's educational momentum.

One of the city's most promising educational developments is the "magnet school" concept that allows students to attend public schools offering specialized curriculums in advanced academics, communications, college preparatory, creative and performing arts, and math and science. Exciting new partnerships between the business community and the school system have resulted in a variety of effective programs, such as workplace-skills "academies" and job shadowing opportunities.

Mobile is home to several outstanding four-and two-year colleges. Spring Hill College—a Jesuit school founded in Mobile in 1830—is one of the nation's top private liberal arts institutions. The University of South Alabama, with an enrollment of 12,000 students representing forty states and ninety-five foreign countries, is a leading education center.

Served by 850 physicians and nine area hospitals, Mobile is the region's primary health-care provider, with facilities that include a Level I Trauma Center, a Burn Center, aeromedical transport, and neonatal intensive care nursery. Mobile's health-care facilities will soon be augmented by the USA Cancer Institute—a regional academic cancer research institute at the University of South Alabama that will serve a population of 2.5 million in forty-two counties in Alabama, Mississippi, and Florida.

Religious activity is an integral part of life in Mobile, with more than 650 places of worship for major denominations, including Protestant, Catholic, Jewish, and Islamic. Area residents put their faith into action through such groups as the Church Partnership for Habitat for Humanity, which has brought together almost a dozen congregations of different demoninations to provide decent, affordable housing for low-income families.

Climate and natural beauty are key elements of the Mobile lifestyle, as well. The annual average temperature is a mild sixty-eight degrees, with mild winters and pleasant spring and fall seasons. And a movement to protect the area's environment—including an air quality study that will create community standards—is helping to ensure that future generations can enjoy the region's rich resources.

There are many measures of a city's quality index. And by every standard, Mobile is an exceptional place to live, work, and enjoy the good life.

(above) Brilliant blooms tickle the fancy of young and old alike at the Festival of Flowers. *Photo by Steve Goraum/Studio G!*

(opposite) Pediatric health care is a top priority in Mobile, the home of the University of South Alabama (USA) Children's & Women's Hospital—one of only five such free-standing facilities in the country. *Photo by Courtland W. Richards/University of South Alabama Photographer*

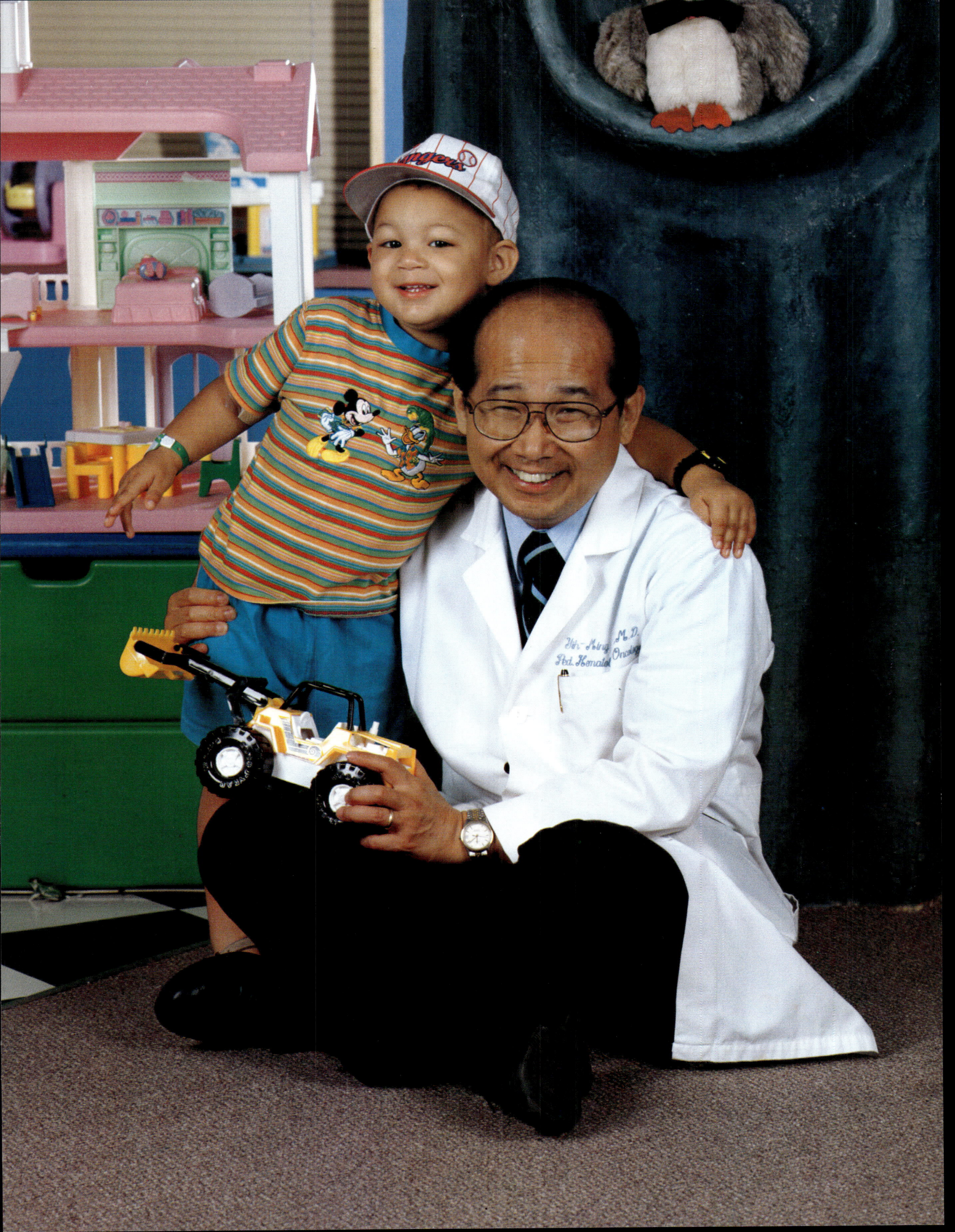

(left) Family reunions, picnics, and festivals are popular Mobile pastimes. An average annual temperature of sixty-eight degrees makes outdoor sports and activities year-round pursuits in the port city. *Photo by Stephen Savage*

(below) Mobile's system of city parks and playgrounds helped earn the city its spot in the Top 100 of *Money* magazine's "Best Places to Live" list. *Photo by Steve Goraum/Studio G!*

(above) In addition to its splendid weather and magnificent natural surroundings, Mobile is famous for its friendly people. The city is a regular on the "Top 10 Most Polite Cities" list issued annually by etiquette maven Marjabelle Young Stewart. *Photo by Steve Goraum/Studio G!*

(following page) The central Gulf Coast is an increasingly popular choice for active retirement living. One Mobile-area community, Fairhope, was named the nation's second-best place to retire in the mid-1990s by *Money* magazine. Perched on the bluffs of the Eastern Shore overlooking Mobile Bay, Fairhope offers retirees an irresistible lifestyle—storybook charm, mild climate, and lively cultural scene—that's high in quality and low in cost. *Photo by Dale Moore*

(above) Hog-calling and goat-milking contests compete with the bright lights of carnival rides on the midway at Mobile's Greater Gulf State Fair. With 300,000 visitors, ninety acres of activities, and 300 vendors, the ten-day event, sponsored by the Mobile Jaycees, is the largest fair in Alabama. Each year, the fair hosts 2,000 physically and mentally challenged children free of charge through the Operation 2000 Program. *Photos by Steve Goraum/Studio G!*

(left) With 460 firefighters and firemedics staffing eighteen fire stations round-the-clock, the Mobile Fire-Rescue Department is able to respond to most calls in the city in six minutes, and reach most other sites in its service areas in six to eight minutes. The department's Emergency Medical teams provide advanced life support measures in emergencies such as childbirth, heart attack, stroke, and trauma injuries. At the Firefigher's Exhibition, held at the Greater Gulf State Fairgrounds, the department presents fire-related demonstrations to area residents. *Photos by Steve Goraum/Studio G!*

(opposite) A Fourth of July celebration erupts in a colorful pyrotechnic display—to the accompaniment of the Mobile Symphonic Pops—at the waterfront convention center. *Photo by Steve Goraum/Studio G!*

ARTHUR R. OUTLAW
MOBILE CONVENTION CENTER

When additional land was needed to bury victims of the yellow fever epidemics, the city bought a small parcel of land outside of the city limits and established Magnolia Cemetery in 1828. Today, the cemetery occupies more than 100 acres and encompasses the Confederate Rest, where 1,100 Civil War dead are buried, and the National Cemetery, final resting place of Geronimo's son. Other notables interred here include Augusta Evans Wilson, author of *St. Elmo* that earned her comparisons with Harriet Beecher Stowe, and Bettie Hunter, an affluent African-American businesswoman of nineteenth-century Mobile. The historic image is of the northside George Street gate that was once the main entrance into the cemetery.

(above) *Photo by Steve Goraum/Studio G!*

(right) *Photo courtesy of Erik Overbey Collection/University of South Alabama Archives*

(left) Mobile is known as "The Azalea City" thanks to a civic beautification project begun by the Mobile Jaycees in the late 1920s. The group planted azalea bushes on major streets, in parks and subdivisions, and around churches and schools throughout the city. Residents were encouraged to plant the flowering shrubs in their yards. The profusion of blooms resulted in the establishment of an annual festival that includes the selection of an Azalea Trail Queen, Ladies-in-Waiting, and Court from competing high school seniors. *Photo by Steve Goraum/Studio G!*

(below) One of the Gulf Coast's premier spring events, the Festival of Flowers offers a breathtaking array of floral and garden displays artfully arranged on 100,000 square feet of rolling green lawn along Spring Hill College's picturesque Avenue of Oaks. Life-size model-garden landscapes are showcased along with exotic "world flower" exhibits and delightful porch and patio settings. Noted flower and garden experts offer entertaining seminars throughout the festival. Visitors can satisfy their shopping bug at The Gardener's Galleria, which attracts vendors from across the U.S. and offers unique patio, garden, and gift items. Best of all, the Festival benefits the Providence Hospital Foundation in its health-care mission. *Photo by Steve Goraum/Studio G!*

(right) The corner grocery, once a fixture in every American city, was a frequent sight in Mobile. The Lignos Grocery once occupied the ground floor on the southeast corner of Government and Royal Streets. From this 1930s image one can almost sense what the store's interior atmosphere must have been like. Above were rooms for rent, hot baths, and other apartments, the occupants of which undoubtedly shopped at the store below. *Photo courtesy of Erik Overbey Collection/University of South Alabama Archives*

(below) Employees of Hammel's Department Store in Mobile prepare to board buses for a company picnic. *Photo courtesy of University of South Alabama Archives*

More than 65,000 children attend the ninety-plus schools in the Mobile County Public School System. With 7,000 employees—more than 4,000 of whom are teachers—the Mobile School System is one of the fifty largest in the United States. Thirty-five languages are spoken in Mobile county schools, reflecting the rich cultural heritage of the area.
(above) *Photo by Steve Goraum/Studio G!*
(left) *Photo by Alan Whitman/Courtesy of Mobile Area Chamber of Commerce*

(left) Students in the Mobile County Public School System are making significant academic gains as measured by the Stanford Achievement Test. The system-wide average on test scores is above the national average. *Photo courtesy of Mobile Area Chamber of Commerce*

(below) The Alabama School of Math and Science, a residential public high school in Mobile, provides an intensive education experience to highly motivated students with a wide variety of backgrounds from throughout the state. The school has ranked eighth in the nation for highest scores on the ACT college-entrance exam. *Photo by Steve Goraum/ Studio G!*

(above) Through partnerships with businesses such as IPSCO Steel, a Canadian firm that opened a manufacturing plant in the Mobile area, Bishop State has developed associate degree programs to prepare local students for jobs in steel manufacturing, as well as other industries, including aircraft, shipbuilding, chemical, and paper. *Photo by Herb Jordan/Courtesy of Bishop State Community College*

(right) Bishop State Community College is a state-supported, open-admission educational institution serving southwest Alabama. With an enrollment of 4,000, Bishop State offers academic, technical, vocational, and career education. Campus life is augmented by a variety of athletic programs, including men and women's basketball, men's baseball, and women's fast pitch softball. *Photo by Herb Jordan/Courtesy of Bishop State Community College*

Mobile is often called the city of trees, and like the large oaks that identify our town, Mobile has deep roots. A port city, Mobile has been influenced by many nations. Our heritage can be found in the wonderful architecture of the downtown and historic districts. We are a city of rich cultural and historical diversity and we have been blessed with an abundance of natural resources. Our rivers, bays, and gulf provide us with inspiring scenery and unlimited recreational opportunities. As an educator, however, I see the true richness of Mobile in the faces of our young people that reflect our city's future and its promise.

V. Gordon Moulton
President
University of South Alabama

(above) Spring Hill, the oldest college in the state and the third-oldest Jesuit college in the U.S., has a reputation as one of the top private liberal arts institutions in the country. The school has a student-faculty ratio of 15:1 and an average class size of seventeen. More than 85 percent of the faculty holds doctorates or the highest degrees in their fields. *Photo by Phillip Gould/Courtesy of Spring Hill College*

(left) The largest of the city's three four-year colleges, the University of South Alabama offers more than eighty undergraduate and twenty-five graduate programs in Arts and Sciences, Business, Education, Engineering, Medicine, Nursing, Allied Health Professions, and Computer and Information Sciences. The University has a $1 billion annual impact on the region and state, and is a key factor in the area's economic development. *Photo by Courtland W. Richards/University of South Alabama Photographer*

(above left) Through its Information Technology Training Institute and Geographic Information Systems training program, Bishop State Community College has put a primary emphasis on building the technology skills of its students. *Photo by Herb Jordan/Courtesy of Bishop State Community College*

(above) Chartered in 1961 as Mobile College, today's University of Mobile was recently named one of "America's Best Christian Colleges" by Institutional Research & Evaluation, Inc. in a survey of more than 1,500 colleges and universities for the fourth consecutive year. *Photo courtesy of University of Mobile*

(left) Approximately 1,400 students from thirty-two states and thirteen foreign countries pursue degrees each year at Spring Hill College. Upon graduation, more than one-third continue their education at select graduate and professional schools across the nation.

The 175-year-old campus is on a naturally landscaped 500-acre site featuring huge oaks, azalea-lined walkways, an eighteen-hole golf course, and several buildings listed in the National Register of Historic Places. *Photo by Phillip Gould/Courtesy of Spring Hill College*

The Wallace Community College Aviation Center, in partnership with Mobile Aerospace Engineering (MAE) and other members of the business community, trains students for high-paying jobs in the aerospace industry. The 45,000-square-foot facility is a state-of-the-art educational and training facility that accommodates 300 students. MAE awards scholarships to select students who then agree to work for the company upon graduation. *Photos courtesy of Wallace Community College Aviation Center*

(above) Established in 1859, the Alabama School of Medicine operated on St. Anthony Street until 1920, when it moved to the University of Alabama. It was Alabama's only medical college for decades. After significant remodeling, the building that once housed the college is now Dunbar Middle School. *Photo courtesy of Erik Overbey Collection/University of South Alabama Archives*

(right) One of two National Historic Landmark buildings in downtown Mobile, the Government Street Presbyterian Church was erected during Mobile's cotton boom in the 1830s. It has a long history of dedicated community service. Today, at a time when many congregations have left downtown, this church is as active and vibrant as ever. This image is from the Historic American Buildings Survey of the 1930s. *Photo courtesy of University of South Alabama Archives*

(opposite) Occupying an entire city block, the Cathedral of the Immaculate Conception has been a striking presence in downtown Mobile for 150 years. The cornerstone was laid in 1835, just a few years after Pope Pius VIII created the Diocese of Mobile. Construction continued for more than sixty years under three bishops. The church was dedicated in 1850, while the facade was built between 1873 and 1890. With the completion of the towers and domes in 1895, the Cathedral assumed the silhouette familiar to generations of Mobilians. The files of the Cathedral contain the record of births, baptisms, marriages, and deaths in Mobile dating back to 1704. *Photo by Steve Goraum/Studio G!*

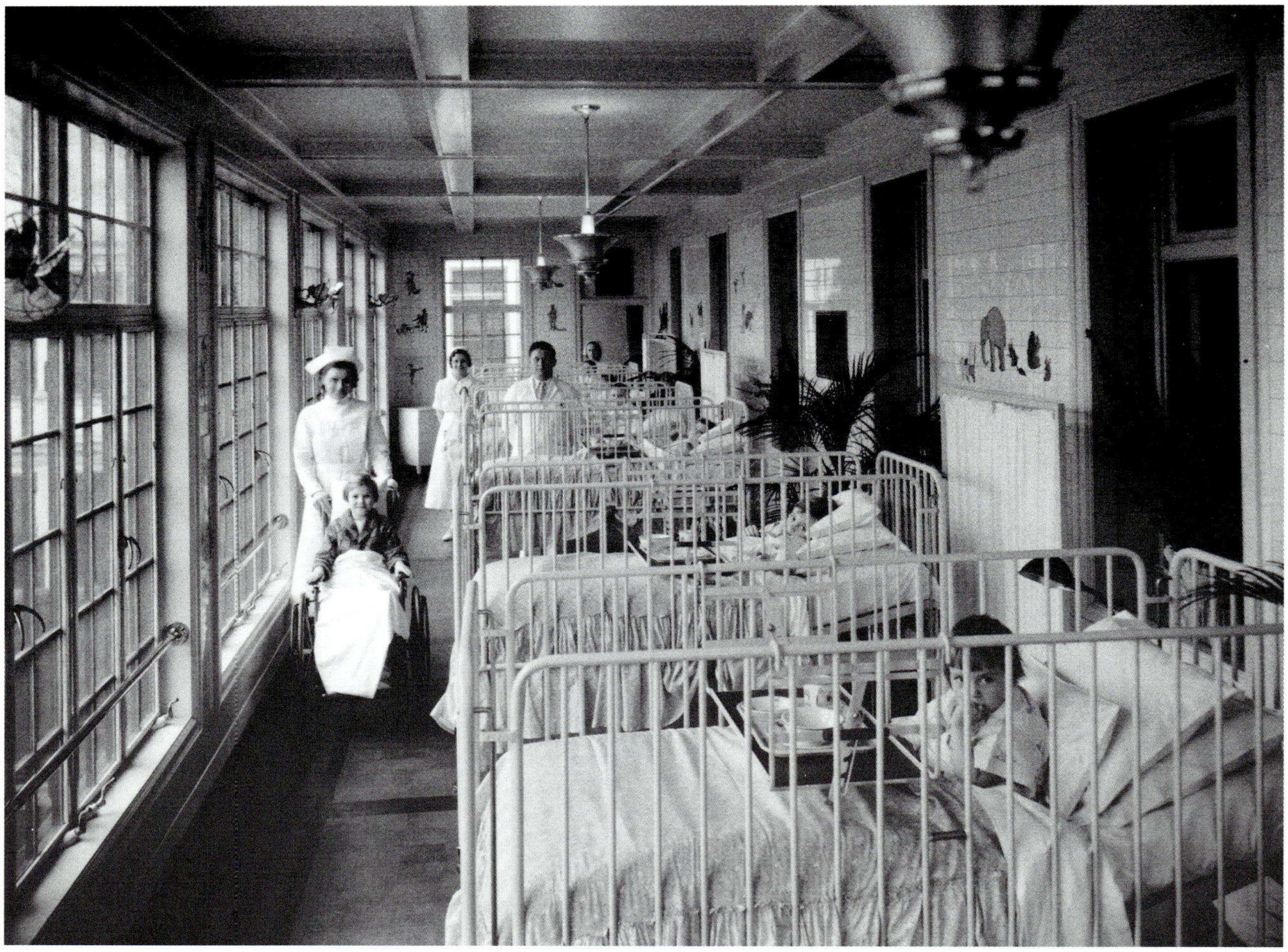

(above) Modern health care has greatly expanded life expectancy and reduced child mortality. Improvements in medical care can be seen in this 1930s photo of a children's ward in a Mobile hospital. *Photo courtesy of Erik Overbey Collection/University of South Alabama Archives*

(below) The Neonatal Intensive Care Nursery at Children's & Women's Hospital, part of the University of South Alabama's health-care system, provides life-saving services for babies born within a 100-mile radius. The unit's nursing staff, respiratory therapists, pharmacists, and social workers are trained to provide expert, compassionate care to their tiny patients. Babies born at other hospitals can be transported to the Nursery in the hospital's specially equipped and staffed Neonatal Transport Unit. *Photo by Courtland W. Richards/University of South Alabama Photographer*

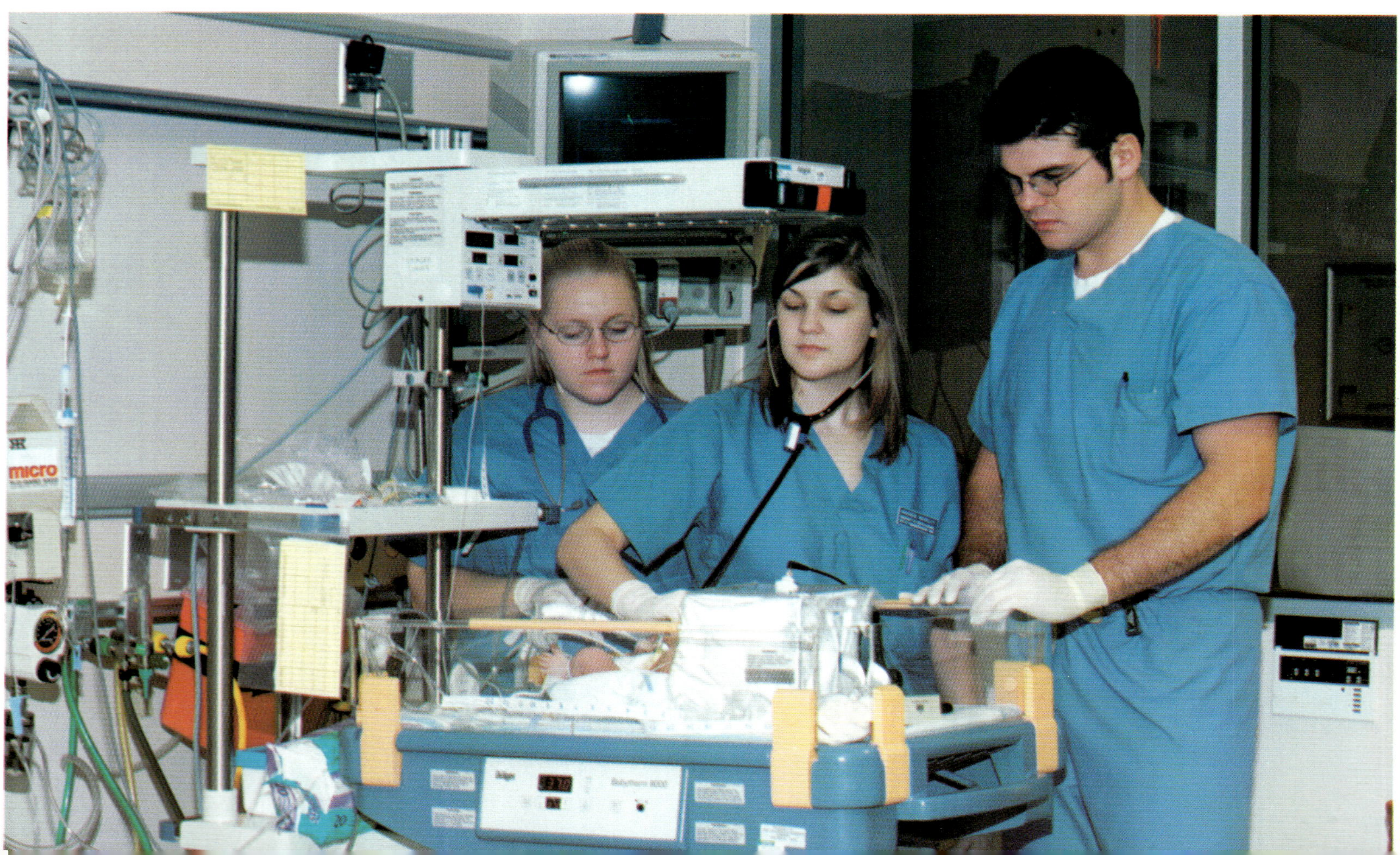

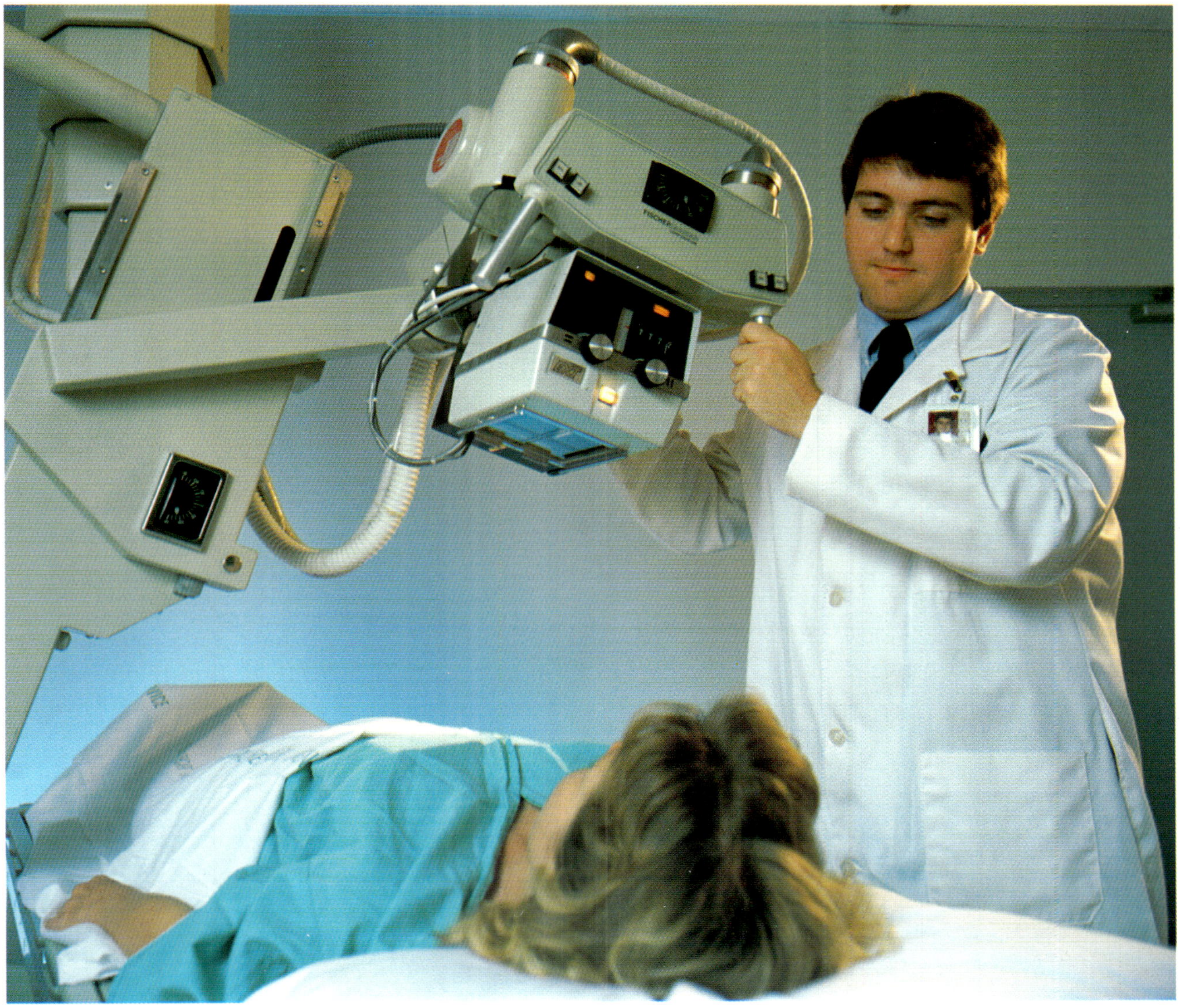

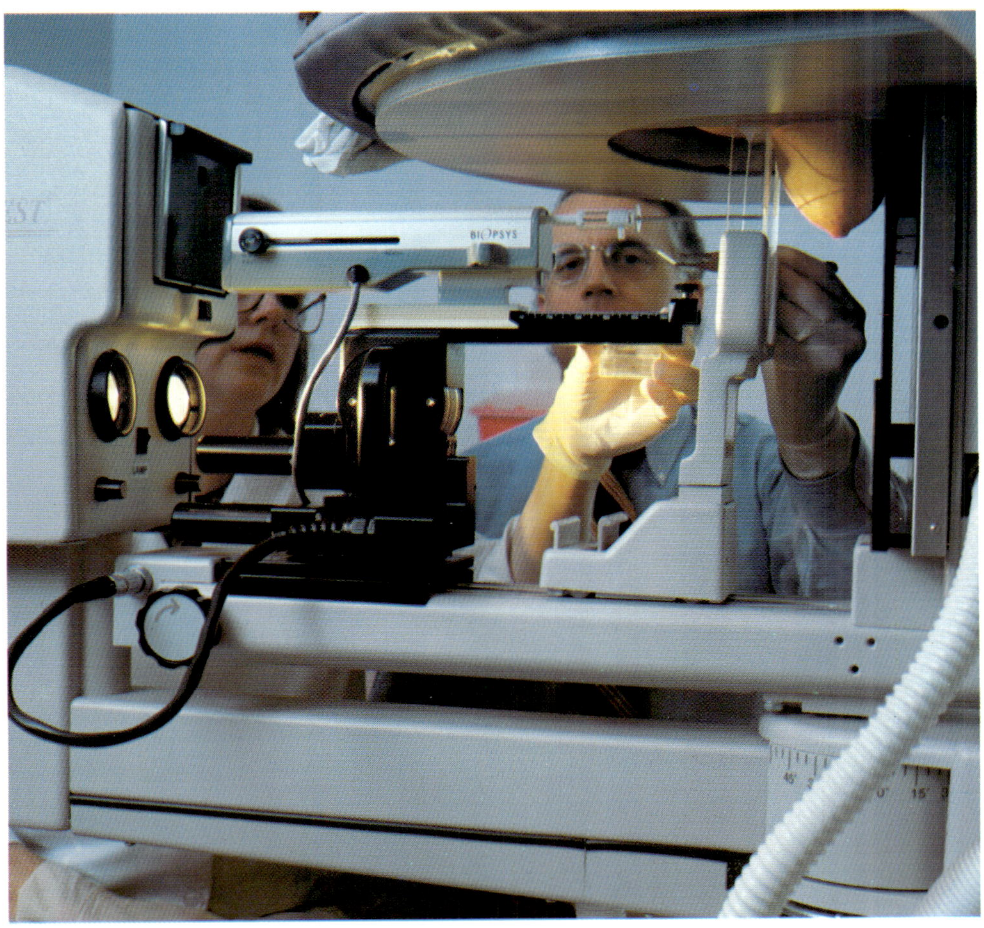

As a regional health-care leader, Mobile is home to a number of top medical facilities.

Springhill Medical Center maintains a family-focused environment with all private rooms, and was the first hospital in the area to establish a Sleep Center and a Chest Pain Clinic.

Providence Hospital offers new technology such as Miraluma imaging—the first FDA-approved nuclear medicine test for detecting breast cancer. The hospital also is participating in a ground-breaking study of stem cell transplantation, in association with Vanderbilt University.

Mobile Infirmary, a 700-bed acute care facility, is the largest non-governmental, not-for-profit hospital in the state. Infirmary Health System serves the needs of residents in outlying areas with Infirmary-Eastern Shore, Thomasville Infirmary, Grove Hill Memorial Hospital, and more than twenty infirmary clinics.

The University of South Alabama Hospitals System—consisting of USA Medical Center, USA Children's & Women's Hospital, USA Knollwood Park Hospital, and USA Knollwood Park Long Term Care Hospital—is the region's largest health-care system. *Photos courtesy of Springhill Medical Center*

(right) SouthFlite USA—the medical transport helicopter of the University of South Alabama Medical Center (USAMC)—brings advanced life support and rapid transit to patients within a 100-mile radius of Mobile. SouthFlite operates in conjunction with the USAMC Level One Trauma Center to provide the region's highest level of emergency care. *Photo courtesy of the University of South Alabama*

(below) The anxiety of hospitalization for children is reduced by the Child Life Program in which certified specialists work with young patients to help them understand their hospital experience. The Star Brite Network provides directed Internet access service to hospitalized youngsters, allowing them to communicate with children in hospitals across the country. *Photo by Courtland W. Richards/University of South Alabama Photographer*

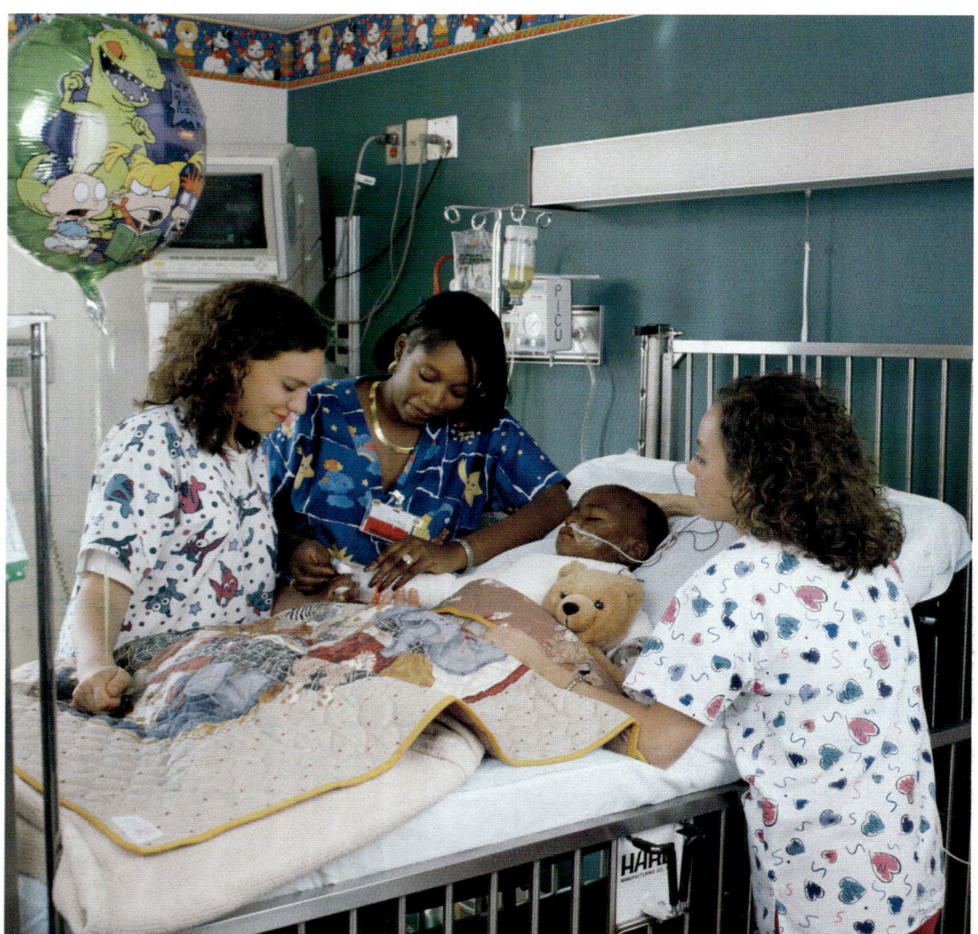

SOUTHFLITE
USA
N911SA

CHAPTER SEVEN

7

Life on the Water

THE MOBILE-TENSAW DELTA, THE BAY & THE RIVERS

Mobile's economy and quality of life are inextricably linked with the area's major bodies of water—the vast Mobile-Tensaw Delta, the Mobile River that drains the Delta, Mobile Bay through which the river flows, and the northern Gulf of Mexico. *Photo by Steve Goraum/Studio G!*

One look at a map, and it's easy to see that Mobile is dependent on water—it defines the region geographically, historically, and economically. As a strategically positioned port, Mobile was a New World outpost for France, England, and Spain in the 1700s. Water propelled the city to greatness as a major exporter in the days when cotton was king. During the 1940s, Mobile shipyards made significant contributions to the war effort, building and repairing more than 3,000 vessels. For the Mobile area, the Delta, Bay, and Rivers are literally the waters of life.

The engine that drives the region's economy and lifestyle is the magnificent Mobile-Tensaw Delta—a 400-square-mile stretch of open waters, marshes, swamps, and bottomlands forest that originates near the confluence of the Alabama and Tombigbee Rivers and extends south for thirty-five miles to the head of Mobile Bay.

It is difficult to overestimate the Delta's importance to Mobile. It purifies and filters the region's water supply, and plays a crucial role in the life cycle of twenty-five million pounds of crabs, oysters, shrimp, and fish hauled in by commercial fisherman in Alabama waters.

An abundance of navigable waterways enabled Mobile to rise to prominence as a major port. Almost 300 private companies are dependent on the Port of Alabama—from stevedoring and towing companies to fuel suppliers and industrial diving operations. Shipbuilding is booming again—with the building of cruise ships, casino boats, and massive tankers under construction on the waterfront.

Because of the ready availability of water, Mobilians have, at times, taken this rich natural resource for granted. But a new appreciation for the delta, rivers, and bay has created a conservation renaissance. The state, in a major public-private partnership, recently bought 47,000 acres of land in the Mobile-Tensaw Delta to protect against development—the single largest land purchase in the history of Alabama. To enhance the public's appreciation of the region's abundance—and thus ensure its preservation—the public and private sectors are cooperating to make the waterfront more accessible to the public. Plans call for the construction of a Maritime Museum of the Gulf, complete with shipwreck artifacts and enormous aquariums displaying fish of the Bay and Gulf. The Museum—and a projected riverwalk project—would join the Convention Center and Cooper Riverside Park in making Mobile's waterfront a vibrant focal point for the region.

For residents, the importance of water to the region's quality of life is more difficult to quantify, but no less vital—a vivid sunset over the river, a moonlight sail on the bay, a tug at a fishing line on the Causeway—essential elements of life in a city born of the water.

(above) The American alligator has found a prime recovery habitat in the Mobile-Tensaw Delta. *Photo by Steve Goraum/Studio G!*

(opposite) With a statewide economic impact of $3 billion annually, the Port of Alabama is an essential component of the region's economic engine. An extensive expansion of port facilities involving a $300-million capital investment is currently underway. *Photo by Dale Moore*

(above) For more than 180 years, the U.S. Coast Guard, or one of its forerunners, has been a strong presence in Mobile. The Aviation Training Center, one of four Mobile-area facilities, is the largest air unit in the Coast Guard, with 400 active-duty and 100 civilian personnel in eight divisions. *Photo by Dale Moore*

(above and opposite) The maritime industry in Mobile is crucial to the region's economy, with almost 300 private businesses dependent on the port. In addition, the jobs of more than 118,000 Alabamians rely on the Alabama State Port Authority, the governing body of the Port of Alabama. Workers representing every county in the state earn more than $3 billion in wages and generate $450 million in tax revenues as a result of port activity.
(above) *Photo by Steve Goraum/Studio G!*
(opposite) *Photo by Dale Moore*

(following page) The Mobile Fire-Rescue Department serves more than 240,000 people in its 210-square-mile jurisdiction. The department provides fire suppression and rescue capabilities to the city's waterfront with a fireboat that can pump water several blocks inland to fire-fighting units. The boat also can pump directly into the fire-protection system of the convention center, supplying both the sprinkler system and manned units inside the building. *Photo by Dale Moore*

(above) The Audubon Society's annual Christmas Bird Count in the Delta usually tallies between 100 and 150 species—not including spring and fall migratory varieties. Among the Delta's inhabitants, at various times of the year, are white pelicans, osprey, great blue herons, and canvasback ducks. *Photo courtesy of* Mobile Register, *© Kii Sato.*

(opposite) The Mobile-Tensaw Delta, one of the last great wilderness areas east of the Mississippi River, is home to dazzling plant life like the shoe-string lily, greenfly orchid, and yellow lotus. *Photo courtesy of* Mobile Register, *© Kii Sato.*

(following page) More than 25 percent of the natural gas produced in the United States comes from the Gulf of Mexico. Since drilling began in the 1940s, more than 120 trillion cubic feet of natural gas has been produced in the Gulf. *Photo by Dale Moore*

Mobile's relationship with the water has, in many ways, defined the city for the past 300 years. As a port city with a strong reliance on the maritime and seafood industries, Mobile also depends on the water for fun and relaxation. The rivers, delta, bay, and gulf all combine to create one of the world's great playgrounds and one of its most valuable natural resources. As a company with a long shipbuilding and repair tradition, Bender is proud to have played a part in shaping Mobile's maritime destiny.

Tom Bender
President
Bender Shipbuilding and Repair Co., Inc.

(above) Marine towing services, ship chandlers and brokers, marine surveyors, fuel suppliers, maritime waste disposal companies, and industrial diving operations are part of the lively commercial scene on Mobile's waterfront. *Photo by Steve Goraum/Studio G!*

(opposite) Built in 1885, Mobile Middle Bay Lighthouse has come to symbolize the spirit of sailing in Mobile and Baldwin Counties. The one-and-a-half story hexagonal cottage was home to a series of lightkeepers, including one whose wife gave birth in the structure in the summer of 1916. When the newborn had difficulty nursing, the lightkeeper arranged for a cow to be brought to the lighthouse and corralled on the deck. Both cow and baby were evacuated a few months later as the great hurricane of 1926 approached.

Middle Bay Lighthouse was built as a replica of the Hooper Strait Lighthouse at Tangier Sound in Maryland. The light was decommissioned in 1967, but is a well-known day marker to area sailors. The tower's massive 54-foot Fresnel lens is on display in the Fort Morgan Museum. *Photo by Dale Moore*

(top) Sand Island Light, completed in 1873, sits three miles south of Fort Morgan on the west side of the entrance to Mobile Bay. A previous lighthouse, built in 1859, was blown up by Confederate forces in 1861 to prevent it from being used by Union forces. At one time Sand Island was more than 400 acres in size, but, today, erosion poses such a dire threat to the 132-foot tall brownstone tower that it is listed on the Lighthouse Digest "Doomsday List" of endangered lighthouses. The Sand Island Lighthouse Preservation Group is actively campaigning to save the structure. *Photo by Dale Moore*

(above) Seafood is plentiful in Mobile. This group of men is enjoying some freshly shucked oysters. *Photo courtesy of S. Blake McNeely Collection/University of South Alabama Archives*

(opposite) A shrimp boat out of Bayou La Batre trawls the waters while seagulls soar and dive after the catch—a common sight on the coast. The seafood industry is the economic mainstay of Bayou La Batre in south Mobile County, providing 85 percent of its gross income. Founded in 1786 on a Spanish land grant, Bayou La Batre is the home of a flourishing Asian-American community of Vietnamese, Cambodians, and Laotians, many of whom work in the seafood processing industry. *Photo by Dale Moore*

CHAPTER EIGHT

8

Beyond the City Limits

BALDWIN COUNTY, DAUPHIN ISLAND & NORTH MOBILE COUNTY

Extending for thirty-two miles from the southernmost tip of Baldwin County, the beaches of Alabama's Gulf Coast are a mecca for sun-worshipping vacationers, as well as retired "snowbirds" in search of the good life. *Photo by Steve Goraum/Studio G!*

As Mobile has prospered and developed in recent years, her citizens and their leaders have grown to appreciate the city's position as part of a larger regional community. The greater Mobile area is truly made greater by her neighbors in Mobile and Baldwin Counties.

At the southernmost tip of Mobile County lies the jewel of the bay's Western Shore—Dauphin Island, a 17-mile long, 3/4-mile wide barrier island that parallels the coastline. Unreachable except by water until the mid-1950s, Dauphin Island still retains its quiet, rustic charm. In addition to mile after mile of white sandy beaches, the Island offers a number of pleasant diversions for visitors—like the Civil War site Fort Gaines, an integral player in the Battle of Mobile Bay, and the Audubon Bird Sanctuary, the first landfall for neotropical migrant birds after the flight from South America across the Gulf of Mexico. On the island's eastern tip is the Dauphin Island Sea Lab and Estuarium, an exciting, interactive marine center featuring a living-marsh boardwalk and giant aquariums that highlight the habitats of coastal Alabama.

Baldwin County, across Mobile Bay on the Eastern Shore, is geographically the largest county in Alabama, and one of the fastest growing. For years, the area was a resort community—accessible only by bay boats that ferried people and goods across the shallow waters. When the region was connected to Mobile County by the Causeway in the 1920s, the world began to discover the treasures that lay on the Eastern Shore.

Today, a booming economy and rapid growth not withstanding, the communities of Baldwin County retain their easy-going resort appeal. One of the best known is a utopian settlement founded in the early 1900s. Idealistically named "Fairhope," the town lives up to its name as a progressive artist's colony with flower-lined streets that are home to shops, galleries, boutiques, cafes, and restaurants. The town's "meeting place" is the delightful bayfront park and quarter-mile-long pier. Here locals and visitors gather to feed the ducks, enjoy the sunset, and cast their fishing nets.

In south Baldwin County, all roads lead to Pleasure Island, home of Gulf Shores and Orange Beach. Thirty-two miles of sugar-white sand and clear, emerald waters have turned this area into one of the nation's favorite beaches. Though the site of explosive development in the 1980s and 90s, with restaurants, condominiums, and entertainment mushrooming to cater to the growing tourist trade, Pleasure Island is still a peaceful haven with long stretches of beautiful, isolated beaches.

Recognizing that the whole is greater than the sum of its parts, Mobile and Baldwin Counties are coming together in a renaissance of cooperation to meet the challenges of development, and to share and protect the region's resources. It's what being a good neighbor is all about.

(above) Seagulls perched on pier. *Photo by Steve Goraum/Studio G!*

(opposite) With brightly colored flags fluttering in the May breeze, a column of fishing boats, shrimp trawlers, and pleasure boats parade slowly down the bayou—the culmination of a day full of activities at the Blessing of the Fleet in Bayou La Batre. For more than fifty years, this close-knit community of 2,500 in south Mobile County has gathered to ask God's blessing for a bountiful harvest and a safe return from the sea. The festivities begin with Mass, and continue through the day with seafood dinners, oyster-shucking and shrimp-cleaning contests, and a land parade.
Photo by Steve Goraum/Studio G!

Mobile's adjoining waters always have been a source of recreational fun. Although swimsuit styles have changed since those worn in this 1930s photograph, what better way to cool off on a hot summer's day than with a refreshing dip. *Photo courtesy of Erik Overbey Collection/University of South Alabama Archives*

(above) Fishermen try their luck from a pier on the Causeway that crosses Mobile Bay, while the downtown area looms in the background. Within half an hour, it is possible to be in the midst of a cypress swamp in the magnificent Mobile-Tensaw Delta, whose watershed accounts for about 20 percent of the nation's fresh water supply. Encompassing more than 300,000 acres of marshes, islands, bays, creeks, and bayous, the Mobile-Tensaw Delta is second in size in the lower forty-eight states only to the Mississippi Delta. *Photo by Steve Goraum/Studio G!*

(right) One doesn't have to own a boat or beachfront property to take advantage of nature's bounty in Mobile Bay. On a casual drive across the Causeway any time of year, fishermen can be seen along the road dropping lines or fishing from the water. Three hundred species of fish pass through the Delta and Bay during the course of the year. The Delta cuts a swath through Baldwin County, sustaining more species of fish than any county in Alabama, while the state supports more fish species than any other in the nation. Favorite catches include speckled trout, redfish, and flounder. *Photo by Steve Goraum/Studio G!*

Former Secretary of the Interior Bruce Babbit is one of a growing number of visitors to tour the Mobile-Tensaw Delta. Largely inaccessible to the general public until recent years, the Delta is experiencing an upsurge of interest in and appreciation for its importance to the Mobile area. Wildland Expeditions' 22-passenger vessel "Gator Bait" meanders through twenty-six miles of waterways, giving landlubbers an up-close and personal look at alligators, brown pelicans, cypress trees, and other denizens of the delta. *Photo by Dale Moore*

Located across the street from the Exploreum and the Museum of Mobile, Cooper Riverside Park is one of the "beads" in the city's "String of Pearls," which represents a series of projects that have spurred the rejuvenation of the downtown area. The park is named for Ervin S. Cooper (1911-1982) whose life's work was devoted to the maritime industry in Mobile. *Photo by Steve Goraum/Studio G!*

(above and left) At the "back door" of the Arthur R. Outlaw Convention Center, visitors can board the historic sternwheeler *Cotton Blossom*, one of only four boats featured on the National Register of Historic Places, for sight-seeing, discovery, and sunset dinner cruises. *Photos by Steve Goraum/Studio G!*

(following page) In addition to new construction and repairs, a number of Mobile shipbuilders also specialize in converting old vessels for new uses. One of the port's more dramatic conversions involved the *Glomar Explorer*, a 23-story high salvage vessel built by the CIA and Howard Hughes during the cold war. More than twenty years later, Atlantic Marine successfully converted the super-secret vessel for use by major oil companies as a drill ship in water depths up to 7,500 feet. *Photo by Dale Moore*

CAPT. JOHNNY

(above) The Battle of Blakeley, considered the last major battle of the Civil War, actually occurred several hours after Lee's surrender at Appomattox. Several hundred people take part in a "living history" re-enactment each year, including African-American re-enactors representing the 6,000 black Union soldiers who fought in the Hawkins Division. Historic Blakeley State Park on the Eastern Shore of Mobile Bay is the largest National Historic Register site east of the Mississippi. Created in 1981, the sprawling 3300-acre park preserves five-and-a-half miles of breastworks and offers visitors fifteen miles of nature and hiking trails. *Photo by Steve Goraum/Studio G!*

(left) "Damn the torpedoes. Full speed ahead." With this now-famous order, Admiral David Farragut steamed forward into Mobile Bay and onto the pages of history. The last confederate port of note on the Gulf Coast, the city of Mobile was protected by the bay, whose only entrance was through the narrow channel running between Fort Morgan to the east and Fort Gaines to the west, on Dauphin Island. The Battle of Mobile Bay lasted only hours, but echoes of the Civil War can be heard today at the annual three-day "Thunder on the Bay" event at Fort Gaines, which is highlighted by a re-creation of the naval battle. Living history weekends explore not only Civil War history, but colonial times as well, with demonstrations of hawk throwing, blacksmithing, and open-hearth cooking. *Photo by Dale Moore*

(opposite) A black battalion of Alabama volunteers served the nation during the Spanish-American War—the Capital City Guard of Montgomery and the Gilmer Rifles of Mobile, which included H.W. Parlee (pictured). *Photo courtesy of Erik Overbey Collection/ University of South Alabama Archives*

(following page) Arching high over the mouth of Perdido Bay as it empties into the clear, warm water of the Gulf of Mexico, Perdido Pass Bridge connects the pristine white beaches of the Alabama Gulf Coast with those of Florida. *Photo by Steve Goraum/Studio G!*

(above) Visitors to Dauphin Island's Fort Gaines can get a double helping of Civil War history by riding the auto-passenger ferry across the mouth of Mobile Bay to Fort Morgan. On the 40-minute trip, the ferry plies the same waters as the Union warships that led the attack on the two confederate forts during the Battle of Mobile Bay. *Photo by Steve Goraum/Studio G!*

(left) Mild temperatures, affordable prices, and Southern hospitality make Alabama's Gulf Coast a major winter destination for "snowbirds." Each fall, retirees from northern states head south for a winter of fishing, golfing, and fine dining. *Photo by Dale Moore*

(right) Despite its reputation as one of the South's favorite playgrounds, Gulf Shores is a vacation haven with long stretches of quiet, secluded beach. *Photo by Dale Moore*

The Gulf Coast of Alabama has experienced explosive growth since Hurricane Frederick devastated the area in 1979. High-rise condos, large national hotels, and magnificent private homes have joined the simple beach cottages of an earlier era. *Photo by Steve Goraum/Studio G!*

Dauphin Island's year-round population of 1,200 swells in the summer with vacationing families. But because of its non-commercial nature, the island serves as a sanctuary—for people as well as their feathered friends. Dauphin Island was recently selected as one of the top four locations in North America for viewing spring migrations by *Wild Bird* magazine. The Audobon Bird Sanctuary—with 164 acres of maritime forest, marshes, dunes, lake, and swamp—provides a variety of habitats for migrating species. *Photo by Dale Moore*

The delightful community of Fairhope is the center of cultural and commercial activity on the Eastern Shore. More than eighty colorful boutiques, galleries, and shops—many featuring works by resident artists and craftspeople—line the beautifully landscaped streets of the quaint shopping district. *Photo by Dale Moore*

(top) Hundreds of rose bushes encircle the sparkling fountain that marks the entrance to Fairhope's bayfront park and pier—a focal point of the town's relaxed lifestyle. *Photo by Dale Moore*

(above) The pier at Fairhope on the Eastern Shore was a very popular recreational spot as this 1930s image confirms. A Bay Boat stop, many people from Mobile visited the pier to swim, fish, go to the bathing casino, to walk about, or to see and be seen. Others commuted via Bay Boat from this pier on a daily basis to work in downtown Mobile. *Photo courtesy of Erik Overbey Collection/University of South Alabama Archives*

The quarter-mile-long pier at Fairhope's bayfront park is a prime lookout for an Eastern Shore phenomenon—Jubilees. A jubilee occurs when an unusual combination of tides and weather conditions cause blue crabs, flounders, and other fish to crowd towards shore due to lack of oxygen. As the cry of "Jubilee" rings out up and down the beach, locals are roused from their sleep (jubilees almost always occur before sunrise) by the prospect of gigging hundreds of flounders and catching tubs full of crabs to stock the freezer for months to come. *Photo by Steve Goraum/Studio G!*

The Grand Hotel at Point Clear always has been a major Eastern Shore attraction, and it continues to be today. Located south of Fairhope on a secluded point of land, its fine beaches, grounds, and service are a hallmark of Southern hospitality. Guests who want to get away from it all, yet still be in touch with Mobile have stayed at the hotel, known today as Marriott's Grand Hotel Resort and Golf Club, from the mid-nineteenth century up through the present.
(above) *Photo courtesy of Museum of Mobile Collection/University of South Alabama Archives*
(right) *Photo courtesy of Erik Overbey Collection/University of South Alabama Archives*

The "sport of kings" reigns on Mobile Bay's Eastern Shore as the Point Clear Polo Club hosts an annual match to raise money for charity. Tailgaters sip wine and feast on catered picnics under large, colorful tents then stroll out onto the field between chukkers to flatten divots. Proceeds benefit the University of South Alabama's fight against cancer. *Photos by Steve Goraum/Studio G!*

While the city of Mobile celebrates its tricentennial, her sister communities around the bay play a large role in this historic occasion. Part of what makes a metropolitan area great is a strong relationship with other cities and towns throughout the region. Mobile has learned this lesson well and will grow and prosper as she continues to reach out to her neighbors. Degussa is proud to have been a part of this community since 1973, and shares in the regional celebration.

Drew Burke
President
Degussa Corporation

Gulf State Park—with 2.5 miles of sugar-white beaches, an 825-foot fishing pier, beachfront hotel, and lakefront cabins—is the crown jewel of Alabama's State Park system. Other accommodations on Alabama's Gulf Coast range from full-service resort hotels and luxury condominiums to secluded beach homes and campgrounds. *Photos by Steve Goraum/Studio G!*

(above) With more than thirty miles of beach fronting the Gulf, along with assorted bays, rivers, and bayous, it's easy to see why watersports reign supreme on Pleasure Island. Cabin cruisers, catamarans, jet skis, and small outboard motor boats are all at home in the clear, sparkling waters. *Photo by Steve Goraum/Studio G!*

(following page) Gulf Shores is a regular on *Southern Living* magazine's annual list of the "Top Five Beaches of the South." *Photo by Steve Goraum/Studio G!*

PART TWO

Photo by Steve Goraum/Studio G!

MOBILE GIANT

CHAPTER NINE

9

Networks, Energy & Transportation

Photo by Steve Goraum/Studio G!

ENERGYSOUTH, INC.

Founded in 1836 with a mission to light the city streets of Mobile and provide gaslight for private homes and businesses, Mobile Gas Light & Coke Company today is known as EnergySouth—a company with a rich history as a reliable and economical energy services provider and committed corporate citizen.

EnergySouth is the holding company for a family of energy businesses: Mobile Gas Service Corporation, Bay Gas Storage Company, MGS Marketing Services, Southern Gas Transmission, and EnergySouth Services. Together, these companies are dedicated to a corporate mission to be the energy and services provider of choice for customers in every market they serve.

Mobile Gas Service Corporation

For Mobile Gas Service Corporation, location is everything. The company is strategically positioned at the gateway through which vast reserves of natural gas flow to market through the Gulf of Mexico. Major gas producers, such as Exxon, Shell, and Chevron, pump natural gas directly to Mobile Gas from on-shore processing plants in south Mobile County. From there the gas goes either to a storage facility or directly to Mobile Gas Service's customers in Mobile and surrounding areas. A steady, dependable supply of gas is always available to the company's 100,000 residential, commercial, and industrial customers, without reliance on outside sources or third-party pipelines—a status unique in the industry.

(above) John Davis, president and CEO of EnergySouth and Mobile Gas.

(right) EnergySouth is now expanding into nearby Baldwin County.

To further meet the demands of its residential customers, Mobile Gas sells, services, and finances related merchandise. Top-name appliances in the newest decorator colors, with the latest conveniences and energy-saving features, are available including five locations throughout the city. And Shop-at-Home representatives meet customers in their homes to help them make their selections. In addition, Mobile Gas repairs all makes and models of gas appliances, furnaces, ranges, water heaters, clothes dryers, outdoor grills, gas lights, patio heaters, and gas space heaters—even if the appliance was purchased elsewhere. Through the company's convenient financing program, customers can arrange easy monthly payments.

While Mobile Gas is a familiar name as a supplier of natural gas to residential areas, the company also serves a thriving industrial market—a market that has increased significantly in the past decade, including such customers as Alabama Power, McNeil Specialty Products, and Degussa Corporation.

Bay Gas Storage Company

Gas that is not directly routed to Mobile Gas' customers through the company's 2,000 miles of lines is piped to the Bay Gas Storage facility in McIntosh. With this gas-storage capability, EnergySouth can keep an ample supply in reserve for Mobile Gas customers during peak demand times—such as extremely cold weather.

Bay Gas Storage is also perfectly located to serve other developing markets throughout the southeast, particularly the growing gas-fired electric generation industry. Major customers include the Southern Company, Alabama Power, Western Gas Resources, Alabama Electric Co-operative, Olin Corporation, and Sonat.

At the storage facility 40 miles north of Mobile, gas is stored in a large underground cavern created by leaching salt. The area is historically significant as a major source of salt—an essential component of gunpowder—for the Confederacy during the Civil War.

Bay Gas began construction in late 2000 on a second storage cavern at its McIntosh location. Cavern #2, like the first, will be located between 4,000 and 5,000 feet below the surface. These caverns are created by circulating water under pressure in a salt dome measuring one-and-a-half miles in diameter and five miles in height. Gas is then injected into the storage caverns at pressures up to 3,000 psi using large compressors.

(above) Discriminating builders and home buyers choose gas for their new homes.

(left) Chefs prefer the precise cooking control of natural gas.

(above) Energy systems—a promising market.

(right) Customer Service is our top priority.

MGS Marketing Services

MGS Marketing Services assists existing and potential customers of EnergySouth in purchasing natural gas. As a subsidiary of EnergySouth, MGS serves utilities and industrial customers throughout the southeast, including several in the Mobile area.

Southern Gas Transmission

Southern Gas Transmission, a majority-owned subsidiary of EnergySouth, is engaged in the intrastate transportation of natural gas to one of the world's largest producers of pulp for the paper industry.

EnergySouth Services

As an industry leader in gas distribution and storage, EnergySouth provides a number of ancillary services to support and enhance its core business. EnergySouth's Training Services Division provides Operator Qualification Training to employees of other natural gas systems and contractors. EnergySouth's team of instructors represents more than a century of industry-related experience.

EnergySouth Corrosion Services designs, installs, and maintains cathodic protection ground beds and related corrosion-control systems for natural gas utilities and other customers who have metal structures in contact with soil or water.

Employee Involvement

A key component of EnergySouth's success is the contribution of its employees. The company not only encourages, it solicits employee participation in corporate activities through the Company Suggestion Program. The program awards cash prizes to staff members whose suggestions have been implemented with measurable benefits to the company. Recent awards have been given for suggestions relating to the company's computerized gas-control system and its computer-aided dispatch system.

In addition, company-sponsored training of key system operators and customer-contact and service personnel has resulted in the professional development of valued employees, as well as improved customer response times and increased customer satisfaction.

Community Commitment

As one of the few major corporations headquartered in Mobile, EnergySouth, Inc., bears a unique and enthusiastic sense of responsibility to the community. "Having the 'home office' located in Mobile gives us both the freedom and the incentive to take an active role in working for the community," says Davis.

For many Mobile-area residents, Mobile Gas is synonymous with involvement in the community, Davis says. "And we rarely have to ask for volunteers. Our people seek us out, bring their ideas to us. Our volunteers really do volunteer." He points to Mobile Gas' annual team participation in the Chili Cook-off as an example, as well as one-on-one involvement in programs like the Mobile Public Library Summer Reading Program and the Boy's and Girl's Clubs.

Mobile Gas makes its auditorium available for public forums and meetings that benefit the community, such as: Red Cross, which uses the auditorium to teach CPR classes to the public, the Mobile Pops Symphony, Volunteer Mobile, Power Squadron, and many others. "The auditorium is used almost daily by the community," says Davis.

One particular community investment is paying big dividends today in the form of cool, green, leafy shade. As a result of the company's ambitious tree-planting program, hundreds of oak trees have been planted throughout the city of Mobile.

Looking To The Future

As EnergySouth approaches the 175th anniversary of the founding of Mobile Gas Light & Coke Company, it continues to explore new markets and new technologies. Projected future growth areas include the offering of a broader range of energy and related services, such as distributed electric generation, energy control and management services, and home warranty service.

To prepare for this growth, EnergySouth has already begun investing in cutting-edge technology, such as a computerized facilities-management system that improves coordination among all corporate divisions—engineering, operations, planning, marketing, and customer service—and allows for more precise measurement of gas flow from suppliers to customers.

The company also foresees an active role in e-commerce, selling products via the internet—perhaps even EnergySouth-manufactured products—opening up national and international markets.

In planning for the future, Davis looks to EnergySouth's Corporate Vision for guidance: To employ our resources effectively to improve the quality of life for our customers, investors, employees, and the community.

"To re-coin a phrase," Davis says, "What's good for Mobile is good for Mobile Gas.' This is our home. Anything that improves this community ultimately benefits this company. It's good business as well as good citizenship."

(above) Mobile Gas sells, services, and finances top-name appliances in the newest decorator colors, with the latest conveniences and energy-saving features.

(left) For many Mobile-area residents, Mobile Gas is synonymous with involvement in the community.

MOBILE REGISTER

Although the *Mobile Register* is the oldest newspaper in Alabama—and one of the oldest in the country—in many ways it's one of the newest. Since 1992, the paper has been on a mission—to reinvent itself as one of the most well-written, high-profile news sources in the South.

The *Register* began its renaissance when Howard Bronson became Publisher, President, and Chief Executive Officer. Since then, the number of newsroom employees has increased from 87 to 126, which makes the *Register* one of the more generously staffed dailies, according to industry standards. Overall employment has jumped from 399 to 522.

The increase in personnel has helped transform the daily paper's substance and appearance. From 1992 to 1999, the "newshole"—the amount of space devoted to news rather than advertising—jumped by a daily average of 43 percent. The newshole in the flagship Sunday edition grew 35 percent.

The larger newshole has translated into more and better local news coverage—the *Mobile Register*'s bread and butter. While providing more local coverage than most other papers its size, the *Register* also travels more—with reporters covering stories throughout the U.S., and, occasionally, abroad.

The paper was able to further refine its focus when the *Mobile Press* ceased publication in 1997. Says Bronson, "We took all of the resources of the afternoon paper and put them into the morning edition." Standard afternoon features such as the comics and syndicated columns were merged into the *Register*, as were the *Press* employees, so no jobs were lost.

On the production side, the paper has made big investments in the physical plant, upgrading the old letterpress equipment to provide better print quality and the ability to reproduce color photos and graphics on the front page of every section. The distribution system was revamped, increasing the number of carriers and reducing route sizes, which means earlier and more dependable delivery service for the customer.

Most important of all, the paper has made a big investment in its people—increasing employee pay and benefits, allowing the paper to attract and hold the industry's best writers, reporters, and staffers.

(above) *Mobile Register's* 220,000-square-foot office space and printing facility, located at the corner of Water and Beauregard streets, will house the latest generation printing press and distribution equipment. Depicting a true feel of Mobile with its old-style DeTonti Square architecture, the $75-million project should be completed in early 2002. Everyone is invited to schedule a time to tour the new facility and view the 30 locally produced works of art that chronicle Mobile's colorful and rich heritage.

(right) Howard Bronson—President, Publisher and CEO.

The Measure of Success

One measure of the *Register*'s success in transforming itself is the esteem with which it is held by colleagues. The paper's major investigative reporting projects have won top state and national awards, including the nation's preeminent award for environmental reporting, in both 1993 and 1996. The *Mobile Register* has also been recognized for its commitment to public service and was a 1995 finalist for the Pulitzer Prize in editorial writing for a series of pieces highlighting the need for constitutional reform in Alabama.

Perhaps the best indicator of the paper's renaissance is public approval. Circulation is at an all-time high, notes Bronson.

But according to Michael Marshall, editor, the changes have just begun. The *Mobile Register* will be celebrating Mobile's 300th birthday in a new home. Scheduled for completion in early 2002, the new 220,000-square-foot *Mobile Register* building will be located at the corner of Water and Beauregard streets, in the heart of the DeTonti Square District, across from the historic GM&O railroad terminal—a sign of the *Register*'s commitment to downtown revitalization.

One of the major features of the new facility is a state-of-the-art printing press that will give readers the clearest reproduction available in the industry. With the ability to print 75,000 copies per hour—a 50 percent increase in speed over the old press—the paper will have later deadlines, meaning more late-breaking news and West Coast sports scores.

The facility's generously proportioned newsroom will allow for future expansion, indicative of management's bullish attitude on the future of printed news.

At the same time, the *Register* is exploring alliances with other media to provide the best news product possible. The paper maintains a lively online presence at Alabama Live, www.al.com, with comprehensive news, sports, weather, editorials, and features. Without the space constraints of the traditional print medium, the *Register* will be able to provide more in-depth coverage of the news online—publishing entire transcripts of documents such as depositions, minutes of city council meetings, official government documents, and more. The paper is also partnering with Alabama Public Television and plans to provide studio space to the station inside the *Register*'s newsroom.

Leadership and Advocacy

The *Register* is an active participant in the community, working with Calloway Smith Middle School to help develop a student newspaper. The paper sponsors such events as the state fair and the 4th of July Fireworks celebration, and is a major contributor to the United Way.

Perhaps the most important community contribution the *Register* makes, however, is its leadership role in the civic arena—editorially promoting an agenda for the public good, while offering fair and impartial reporting on the issues. The *Register* has identified four major areas for advocacy: constitutional reform, education, state tax reform, and the environment. By focusing its efforts on these crucial issues, the *Register* seeks to improve the quality of life for all citizens—guaranteeing equitable treatment under the law, the right to a quality education, freedom from unfair taxation, and proper stewardship of natural resources.

When Marshall assumed editorship of the *Register*, he wrote a column about the qualities of "a good newspaper," promising to "involve the community, reflect the community, illuminate its problems, help work through those problems."

In light of the paper's metamorphosis in recent years, consider it a promise kept.

(above) Michael Marshall—Editor and VP/News

(left) Weighing over 500 tons and costing over $19 million, *Mobile Register*'s new printing press will ensure quality printing of its award-winning coverage for decades to come. The new press will allow more late-breaking news and better graphics with more than 75,000 copies printed per hour as opposed to the 45,000 per hour the old press is capable of printing. The new press affords three times the number of color positions that the current press offers and will be visible to the public through a 70-foot-tall glass wall.

MOBILE AIRPORT AUTHORITY

From chief executives to avionics technicians, nearly 5,000 people work at 125 businesses located at the Mobile Regional Airport and the Brookley Complex. With a total of 3,700 acres, these two premier facilities are owned and operated by the Mobile Airport Authority. The authority is a group of community leaders committed to being a leading catalyst for economic growth and air service development in the region. The five members of this locally appointed board serve staggered six-year terms, bringing new perspectives while maintaining continuity and stability. Receiving no local tax dollars, the authority internally funds its work of making Mobile an international center for trade, tourism, and transportation.

Mobile Regional Airport

Mobile's economy is built on transportation. Its deep-water port is the 12th largest in the nation, interstates run non-stop to Jacksonville, Los Angeles, and Chicago, and railroads connect it to all of North America. As railroads were to the 19th century, air service is to the 21st—and Mobile is uncommonly well suited to explore that opportunity. Five airlines fly nearly a million travelers a year through Mobile Regional Airport—home to 25 companies employing 500 people. The central Gulf Coast's only all-jet airport, Mobile has more non-stop service to major hubs than any other airport in the region. And with a parallel runway and new international concourse in the works, Mobile is uniquely positioned for the future.

Along with adding new air service, the authority is also dedicated to improving the customer experience at Mobile Regional Airport. W. H. Smith, international book, news, and gift shop chain, operates more than 180 stores at major airports in North America, including Chicago O'Hare, Atlanta Hartsfield, and Los Angeles. Usually found only in larger cities, W. H. Smith selected Mobile Regional Airport as the location for one of its stores.

One of the world's largest food and beverage concessionaires, The Compass Group provides all food and beverage services for Mobile Regional Airport travelers and visitors, bringing the quality

Kathy Groth, Customer Service Representative, United Express.

and variety sophisticated air travelers have come to expect. To make airport life more comfortable for the frequent flier, the airport developed the Executive Club. Members have access to a comfortable, quiet, private setting in which to conduct business or simply relax. The club provides work stations with data ports, phones, fax, and copy machines, as well as a television, magazines, newspapers, and complimentary snacks and beverages.

An ambitious program of remodeling and renovation, including a new elevator, expanded seating, improved signage, and interior decor emphasizing regional charm ensures that airport customers will continue to enjoy a first-class travel experience for years to come. Planned limited-access highways from the airport to Interstates 65 and 10 will make the region's leading airport even more convenient.

Brookley Complex

A former U.S. Air Force base near downtown Mobile, the Brookley Complex is a major corporate/industrial facility specializing in aviation and aerospace. The 1,700-acre complex houses more than 100 businesses with 4,500 employees. Occupying most of its 3.5 million square feet of office, warehouse, and hangar space, such tenants as ST Mobile Aerospace Engineering and Teledyne Continental Motors enjoy immediate connections to two interstate systems and quick access to air, rail, and deep-water transportation. Major employers draw from a skilled, well-trained work force. The Aviation Center at the Brookley Complex is one of only two schools in the state for aviation and aerospace professionals. And the Alabama Industrial Training and Development Center, also at Brookley, delivers customized programs for specific industrial needs.

Located at Brookley, the Mobile Downtown Airport, with its 8,600-foot and 9,600-foot runways, is a regional center for domestic air cargo. Both FedEx and UPS maintain full-service operations, while Emery and Airborne operate sorting centers at Brookley. With U.S. air cargo trade to Central and Northern South America passing $5 billion yearly, Mobile is poised to be a vital link in a more efficient and cost-effective international air-trade corridor. The scores of acres available for development, and the facility's status as a Foreign Trade Zone, mean Brookley will remain a major force in the region's economic development.

An Integrated Approach

The Mobile Airport Authority combines superior air, road, rail, and water transportation with the resources required to create unique solutions for major manufacturers and shippers worldwide. As the Mobile Airport Authority enters its third decade, it looks ahead to exciting new opportunities. Efficient, cost-effective air transportation between Mobile and locations around the world isn't simply important, it's a key to the area's economic future. In focusing on this goal, the Mobile Airport Authority fulfills its mission to create jobs, promote travel, and improve the region's quality of life.

(top) Ronnie B.T. Koh, President, ST Mobile Aerospace Engineering.

(middle) Paul Brown Maintenance, Mobile Airport Authority.

(left) David Stewart, Aircraft Mechanic, United Parcel Service.

ALABAMA POWER COMPANY

Alabama Power's low prices, reliable service, and community development make Alabama a better place to live. As a Southern Company subsidiary, Alabama Power is part of one of the most successful, fastest-growing, and exciting companies in the electric-utility industry.

You name it; electricity makes it work. Lights, air-conditioning, computers . . . . Alabama Power is the power source for so many things Alabama residents and businesses use every day. And the prices the company's customers pay for that energy are among the lowest in the nation.

Best of all for the state's communities, low prices and world-class customer service are bolstered with a sense of community as old as the company itself.

Development from the Start

Alabama Power was founded in 1906 by William Patrick Lay, a steamboat captain. In 1907, Congress gave Lay approval to build a dam and power plant on the Coosa River. To raise the necessary money for the project, Lay teamed up with hydroelectric pioneer James Mitchell and Montgomery attorney Thomas Martin.

With the help of English and American investors, the three men underwrote an ambitious 20-year plan for hydroelectric development in Alabama. The original plan also called for extensive efforts to bring new businesses and residents to Alabama.

Alabama Power employees collect water samples to help gather data to further environmental research studies.

"Company founders such as William Patrick Lay and Thomas Martin knew that community and economic development for this state would have a profound and positive effect on the company's business success," says Alabama Power Chairman and CEO Elmer Harris. "We continue to focus on their vision because thriving communities and growing businesses improve the state's economy. And a strong economy helps education, culture, and the overall quality of life in Alabama."

The company established its corporate headquarters in Birmingham in 1912. Since then, the company has developed a reputation as the state's leading corporate citizen. Alabama Power's long-running commitment to economic development and community enhancement adds value to the reliable electric service it provides.

Economic Growth

Alabama Power was the first electric utility in the United States to establish its own economic-development department. If you think about it, Alabama Power's commitment to economic and community development makes a lot of business sense. New and growing businesses locating in the company's service territory mean new customers and more profits.

But company leaders say that there are other, more broad-based, motives at work.

"Our company recognizes the importance of vibrant, growing communities," says Alan Martin, an executive vice president at Alabama Power. "We believe that the health of our company and society depends on helping all citizens share in the nation's economic growth. To this end, we must encourage and support the growth of all business—large and small."

Community

Because strong communities are sure-fire business incubators, Alabama Power puts a lot of time, energy, and resources into community activities.

"Through programs related to education, the environment, and social involvement, Alabama Power and its employees continually work to strengthen our communities," Harris says.

The company, the Alabama Power Foundation, and the Energizers contribute millions annually to community programs, education initiatives, and environmental programs throughout the state.

Environmental Stewardship

Alabama Power is safe, responsible, and committed when it comes to the environment. It either meets or exceeds the standards set by state and federal agencies for protecting human health and the environment. Over the last several years the company has made major reductions in its air emissions and

Lay Dam is one of Alabama Power's 14 hydroelectric facilities that produce electricity for its customers and create recreational waterways and wildlife habitats.

continues to support initiatives that help address air quality issues. One of every 50 employees at Alabama Power has direct, full-time environmental responsibilities. Alabama Power ranks in the top 10 of all investor-owned utilities for its investment in equipment and technology to improve the environment, according to the U.S. Energy Information Agency. Its commitment to the environment goes beyond its business. By sponsoring, supporting, and running a variety of programs, Alabama Power is helping to teach the public, students, and teachers about environmental responsibility.

A True Corporate Citizen

Alabama Power offers affordable electricity to customers, superior customer service, and is a leader in the community. Those are the hallmarks of being the state's leading corporate citizen.

"We've been doing business this way for 95 years now, and our business keeps getting stronger," Harris says. "And as our business gets stronger, we'll continue to invest in the overall health and success of the community and our state."

BELLSOUTH

BellSouth is an integrated communications services company headquartered in Atlanta, Georgia serving more than 41 million customers in the United States and 16 other countries. In Mobile, BellSouth is the leading provider of telecommunications, online and directory advertising, internet, data, and e-commerce solutions. "Our objective," says Gigi Armbrecht, regional manager for Southwest Alabama, "is to enable people to communicate whenever, wherever, and however they want."

To accomplish this ambitious goal, BellSouth Corporation offers telecommunications services through three companies: BellSouth for wired services; Cingular Wireless, a joint venture between SBC Communications and BellSouth which handles wireless services; and BellSouth Real Yellow Pages.

(above) BellSouth technicians use the latest technology to deliver the company's DSL product—BellSouth® FastAccess® Internet service—to Mobile homes and businesses.

(right) Cingular employees express themselves by making a human formation of the company's new logo.

BellSouth in Mobile

BellSouth's heritage in Mobile dates to 1879, when the city became the first in Alabama to have a telephone exchange—only three years after Alexander Graham Bell filed his patent.

Throughout its history, the company has been committed to providing state-of-the-art communications services in the Mobile area. In a recent five-year period, BellSouth invested more than $75 million—more than $1 million per month—on technology and infrastructure enhancements. The company provides the highest quality voice and digital data services utilizing more than 200 sheath-miles of fiber-optic cable containing 7,500 miles of fiber-optic lines. "Such innovations," says Armbrecht, "help people communicate better, faster, and easier."

One example of the company's leading-edge technology is BellSouth FastAccess DSL, a service that turbo-charges existing copper phone lines, making internet downloads up to 50 times faster than with conventional modems.

A hallmark of BellSouth service is dependability, even during hurricanes and other catastrophes. The company takes disaster planning very seriously, and has placed 70 percent of the Mobile District's network underground and all area switching offices on redundant fiber-optic rings.

Cingular Wireless

In October 2000, the wireless divisions of BellSouth and SBC Communications joined forces to form a new company, Cingular Wireless. Cingular provides wireless voice and data service to more than 19 million customers in 38 states, the District of Columbia, and two U.S. territories. SBC and BellSouth share control of Cingular Wireless which operates in 42 of the top 50 markets in the U.S., and—originally under the name of BellSouth Mobility—has provided wireless service in Mobile for 14 years.

A single-source provider for nationwide wireless voice, internet, and data services, Cingular is dedicated to simplifying the wireless industry and offering new and personalized services targeted to the needs of the individual customer. With an approach that treats each customer as unique, Cingular is the fresh alternative to wireless service. As the single solution for people and businesses looking to make their own special mark on the world, Cingular celebrates every individual's innate ability to communicate and express themselves.

The Real Yellow Pages

Throughout the years, The Real Yellow Pages' focus has been to provide the consumer with ideas and information to make a good purchase decision. This process of putting buyers and sellers together has been the key to The Real Yellow Pages' success. Its competitive edge has been the accuracy and completeness of the directory—making it the phone book of choice.

A hallmark of The Real Yellow Pages is its responsiveness to the needs of consumers and advertisers. As a result of extensive surveys and focus groups, the Mobile directory has implemented a number of changes, including an expanded community interest section in an updated format. The Real Yellow Pages' sales reps specialize in specific markets, making them an even more valuable source of marketing expertise for advertisers.

In addition to the traditional printed directory, The Real Yellow Pages is available online with advanced search capabilities.

Though it may lack the glamour of other types of media, The Real Yellow Pages offers advertisers the most important advantage of all—results.

BellSouth and the Community

With a rich tradition of supporting the community, BellSouth donates time and money to a variety of projects—from health and human services to public education. "We're especially committed to education programs," says Armbrecht, pointing to the more than $1.3 million in cash and in-kind services BellSouth has donated to public education during the past 10 years. In the interest of student safety, the company installed wireless phones in all Mobile County school buses. BellSouth sponsors the premier middle school academic tournament in the county. And the Groundhog Day job-shadowing program allows hundreds of students to partner with BellSouth employees for a unique day-long, on-the-job learning experience.

Another school-friendly program, SafeLine, enables students to anonymously call a voice-messaging system to report fights, drug activity, and gun sightings. A school official is instantly alerted via pager. The company is also the community partner for the State Board of Education's Alabama Reading Initiative, a program in which BellSouth employees are granted time off during the workday to tutor second graders.

BellSouth and the Future

"We're on the edge of something new and exciting," says Armbrecht, referring to the rapidly evolving telecommunications industry. She foresees an era of great challenges, and even greater opportunities.

One constant in the tidal wave of change is BellSouth's clear, singular focus: To be a one-stop shop for all the communication needs of its customers, at home or work or play, every day.

(left) BellSouth technician Ken Worthen (right) helps Timothy Stone practice his reading. Active supporters of the Alabama Reading Initiative, BellSouth employees tutor second graders from Westlawn Elementary School. BellSouth donates thousands of dollars and hundreds of hours of company time to help struggling young readers improve their skills.

MOBILE AREA WATER AND SEWER SYSTEM

From artists' renderings of Mobile Bay, to the deep-water port that has enriched the city and helped establish it as an industrial power, abundant water resources have virtually defined Mobile during the past 300 years, both culturally and economically. An understanding of Mobile's water resources is vital to understanding its rich history, as well as its future success.

Publicly owned and operated by the Board of Water and Sewer Commissioners under a deed of trust from the City of Mobile, the Mobile Area Water and Sewer System (MAWSS) has served the vast majority of the Mobile area's homes and businesses with clean water and water disposal since 1951. And, with a commitment to build on the past and plan for the future as a faithful steward of this essential natural resource, MAWSS is working to fuel sustainable growth for Mobile well into the 21st century.

Water Resources

Past and current decisions are key to the promising futures of MAWSS and its customers. The Converse Reservoir (previously known as Big Creek Lake) has been the most valuable of MAWSS' water resources for the past 50 years and will continue to be an important part of a growing supply capability for the next 50 years. The 3,600-acre reservoir, which supplies water for 70 percent of Mobile County's population, has a 103-square-mile watershed that is continually fed by springs, streams, and rainfall.

Just as residents may take for granted the bountiful bays, streams, and rivers with which the Mobile area is blessed, because of the vision of MAWSS, they have also had the luxury to take for granted an ample water supply, while others struggle over this vital resource. The Converse Reservoir is unusual in that its watershed lies completely within Mobile County. Most major municipalities, like New Orleans, draw from sources such as the Mississippi River, where the water quality, and sometimes quantity, is affected by circumstances beyond their control. Because of MAWSS' reliance on the Converse Reservoir, it avoids the risks of more easily contaminated or depleted wells and groundwater. Water from the reservoir undergoes a rigorous, multi-stage treatment and purification process, ensuring that the water that reaches Mobile homes and businesses is clean and pure. Because of the investment MAWSS made 50 years ago to ensure an abundant water supply, the Mobile area controls its own water destiny, with the power to protect and conserve this vital resource for the future.

MAWSS is not content to rest on the successes of the past, however. Recognizing that more than 50 percent of the U.S. population now resides within 50 miles of its coastal areas, and that the Mobile area is one of the fastest growing regions in the Southeast, MAWSS is developing a source-water assessment as the basis for a master plan to protect the reservoir and its watershed well into the 21st century. The plan will also address regional considerations of alternative water supplies and increasing wastewater needs so that these resources can support sustainable growth along the Gulf Coast.

(above) "Essie" was sculpted by the former Harry Myers, Sr., under commission by MAWSS for its Myers facility, named for the artist.

(right) Converse Reservoir is the Mobile area's primary drinking water supply.

Water Disposal

While MAWSS builds on the solid foundation of the past, new management is charting a course for the system's second fundamental directive: the safe

disposal of wastewater that protects the health of the community and environment. The abundant rainfall that replenishes the Converse Reservoir also poses many challenges to the safe disposal of wastewater by an aging system in need of rehabilitation. Having earned a reputation for maintaining low rates and ample supply for customers, in the 1990s the system faced the reality of raising rates to implement improvements necessary for quality service and the protection of the environment. System managers credit MAWSS customers for supporting the rehabilitation effort, allowing MAWSS to make major progress in a short period of time. Between 1995 and 2000, $96 million in improvements were completed or under construction with another $22 million committed for future work.

Because of a shift in management's focus, MAWSS acknowledged the importance of ensuring the integrity of the system to help provide a sustained quality of life for this and future generations. Consequently, the system is looking further out, from 30 to 50 years, to solutions for the regional needs of water and water disposal, and balancing these needs with environmental protection. Among the many new initiatives that the system is taking are to: explore alternative decentralized wastewater treatment systems capable of serving smaller numbers of customers in more remote areas with reduced environmental impact, review ways to better reduce the threat of water runoff to the environment, develop partnerships with other area utility interests, and monitor the levels and reasons for improper disposal in order to provide better alternatives.

These initiatives are but a snapshot of how MAWSS is committed to building on the past and bettering the future. MAWSS recognizes, along with area citizens, that the Mobile area's water resources have been fundamental to its history, growth, and quality of life, and the system is committed to preserving, protecting, and conserving those resources as a faithful steward, ensuring the long-term viability of the community's wealth, health, and welfare.

(above) MAWSS employees work around the clock to implement a record number of improvements in record time.

(left) The Mobile area's water resources are fundamental to its future quality of life.

WKRG 5

From its earliest days as a CBS affiliate, WKRG-TV has been synonymous with television broadcasting in Mobile. With an impressive series of "firsts" to its credit, WKRG, founded in 1955 by Kenneth R. Giddens, has established itself as a powerful force in the community. Counted among the station's ground-breaking achievements are: first local color broadcast, first local on-location color broadcast, first local morning news show, first local noon show, first electronic news gathering (live remote), and first station with satellite uplink, live doppler, and helicopter.

The station's local personalities—from Connie Bea Hope to Mel Showers—have been touchstones for generations of Mobilians. Says Robin De Laney, director of marketing and creative services, "WKRG is a reflection of the community itself. The word 'communication' comes from the Latin 'communicare' which means to make common, to bring together, to provide a common experience. That is what we as a station do."

The Community-Minded Station

WKRG-TV remained under the ownership of the Giddens family until 1998, when it was sold to Spartan Communications. Spartan subsequently sold the station to Media General of Richmond, Virginia—an independent publicly owned communications company with interests in newspapers, television, interactive media, and diversified information services. The change in ownership was necessary for the continued growth and leadership position of the station, says De Laney. "The Media General relationship is a good one. It is a leading communications company with strong southern roots." Media General owns 26 network-affiliated television stations throughout the southeast, as well as 25 daily newspapers, and almost 100 weekly and other periodicals.

Media General, says De Laney, is making it possible for WKRG to develop key technologies that will enhance its broadcast capabilities for years to come. "Together we're laying the foundation for digital distribution of content," he says. "As television and the Internet continue to converge, WKRG will be in the forefront of this interactive, participatory community." The station is already making its online presence strongly felt, with a lively Web site which incorporates live doppler radar and continuous news updates.

WKRG has long been respected for its strong sense of responsibility to the community. A key way the station has demonstrated this commitment is in its tireless coverage during times of emergencies, such as hurricanes. "After we were knocked off the air by Hurricane Frederick in 1979," says De Laney, "we continued broadcasting from the transmitter in a concrete building at the base of our tower in Baldwin County. During Hurricane Georges, we broadcast for 54 hours straight. No one stayed on the air as long as we did covering the breaking news of the storm."

It was because of its community spirit that WKRG first became involved with the Mobile Tricentennial Commission's video project. "As our contribution to the celebration of the city's three-hundredth birthday," says De Laney, "WKRG produced the official tricentennial video, *We Are Mobile: The Spirit of a Place and Its People*."

"We Are Mobile"

As a starting point for the two-hour documentary, De Laney, an NYU film school graduate student, taped interviews with more than 100 people—historians, writers, artists, civic leaders, musicians, librarians, photographers, including well-known Mobilians like Joseph Langan, Winston Groom, Robert Battles, and Emily Hearin. "It became apparent that the definition of 'Mobilian' was not who was born here, but who loves it here," he said. "What we have tried to do is discover the underlying spirit of the city. What do we all have in common, and, at the same time what makes us unique?"

In researching the written records of more than 300 years of history, the documentarians found one description of the area to be particularly meaningful. De Laney quotes the words, from 1558, of Spanish explorer Tristan de Luna: "The bay is very healthful and has the climate of Spain, both in recurrence of rain and cold. The country to the east of the bay is higher than that to the west side. In the bay and its vicinity are many fish and shellfish…there are pines suitable for making masts and yards . . . oaks, live oaks, nut trees, cedars, junipers, laurels . . . palmettos and grapevines . . . streams of fresh water which flow into the bay."

The video project was under the direction of Ann Bedsole, president of the Mobile Tricentennial Commission and the Tricentennial Executive Committee. Essential guidance came from historian Michael Thomason, director of the archives at the University of South Alabama, who provided many of the historical images used in the production of the video.

While working on the video, De Laney discovered parallels between his hometown, Mobile, and his workplace, WKRG-TV. "We're both facing a new future," he says. Such issues as regionalism, technology, and the digital revolution will have an immense impact on the city and the station, according to De Laney. "How we respond now is what determines that future."

Reflecting on the experience of crafting the two-hour documentary, De Laney concludes: "TV captures a snapshot of the city as it changes, and change is as natural as the tides of Mobile's rivers. Ultimately, the documentary is just another day in the life of Mobile, a place fighting to keep a special identity as a place and a people."

10M
9M
8M
AP
CW
7M
6M
5M
4M
3M
ER
BW
BH

CHAPTER TEN

10

Manufacturing, Distribution & Forestry

Photo by Dale Moore

MINOLTA-QMS

QMS's merger with Minolta in 1999 marked the beginning of a dynamic new era in the business's 25-year history, and the emergence of a revitalized company positioned to become a global leader in the color laser printer market. In the mid-1990s, QMS found itself increasingly unprepared to compete in a worldwide marketplace. Although it held an industry-wide reputation as a respected developer, manufacturer, and supplier of innovative document printing solutions, the company lacked the capital to invest in the engineering necessary to revitalize its product line. Attempts to build brand awareness and leverage its proprietary Crown® architecture had met with only limited success.

A strategic alliance with the Minolta Corporation proved to be the catalyst for growth that both QMS and Minolta were seeking.

A Strategic Alliance

From the coalition of QMS—with its traditionally strong position in the color laser market—and Minolta—with its superb print engine capabilities and global network—came a new partnership, Minolta-QMS. Incorporating the strengths of each company, the new business offers faster time to market and a broader product line. With an established global distribution and service network already in place, Minolta-QMS is making a serious bid for an even greater share of the market.

The highly recognizable "Minolta" name allows QMS to leverage a strong identity into the company's new co-branded product line. And through its agreement with IBM to be the global service provider for its printers, Minolta-QMS has gained access to a world-class service organization, enabling it to provide true quality customer service.

A Technological Alliance

For consumers, the Minolta-QMS convergence is a winning combination. Minolta's world-class engine technology fully utilizes QMS's outstanding research and development department, software design capabilities, and controller technology to create the broadest range of color and monochrome printers on the market.

As market preference continues to shift from monochrome to color printers, and from self-contained printers to sophisticated printer/copiers with finishing features, the need for the faster, truer color printers of Minolta-QMS has never been greater.

The move away from mainframe to distributive computing means an increased demand for network printing capabilities—a specialty of the company's Crown architecture. Crown technology's "first in, first out" priority-printing mode enhances the speed at which jobs are taken from the network, thus freeing up local network resources, enhancing network capability, and allowing faster overall throughput.

In the coming years, Crown technology will have an even greater impact on the industry. Minolta-QMS printers will be Web enabled, allowing end users to download applications and third-party solutions directly to the printer from the Internet. Sophisticated and powerful multi-function products with web-management software will allow customers to print directly from a Web site—without having to process the job through their CPU.

(above) Mike Dow, mayor of Mobile, welcomes the president of Minolta Co., Ltd., Yoshikatsu Ota, as QMS announces its merger with Minolta.

(right) Among the many charity activities that Minolta-QMS supports is the inclusion of special guests from the community, including residents from a children's shelter, at the company's holiday party.

Satisfying the Market

Due to a major initiative to meet consumer demand and increase its market share, Minolta-QMS is turning its focus on "consumables"—replacement items, such as toner. Now customers will be assured of a high-quality printing experience throughout the life of the product. It is projected that consumables—with their higher profit margin—will soon constitute 50 percent of corporate revenues annually.

Before the merger, 60 percent of the company's business was done overseas. In fact, QMS ranked second—at 26 percent—

in European market share. However, Yamana points out that QMS was "international, not global. QMS printers were manufactured domestically then shipped overseas. But issues such as exchange rates and different market requirements and distribution methods were not managed with a global perspective. We, as a company, must now realize that only 25 percent of our business is in North America. The other 75 percent is based in Western Europe, Japan, Eastern Europe, and Asia."

Utilizing Minolta's international distribution and service network, the company is on track to make great inroads in the global color laser market—a market that is growing at the rate of 30 percent annually. The company projects that by 2005, 70 percent of corporate revenues will come from the overseas market.

Another avenue of growth the company plans to explore, according to Yamana, is consulting. Minolta-QMS will help businesses manage their document flow more effectively and efficiently, assisting clients in leveraging technology to enhance productivity, increase profitability, and reduce costs.

The Importance of E-commerce

"To make e-commerce work," observes Yamana, "you need three things: a sales force calling on corporate clients to establish demand, a highly interactive Web site that enables users to configure purchases to suit unique environments, and a back-office infrastructure to effectively and profitably handle the transactions." The Minolta-QMS alliance has resulted in a convergence of these three abilities that Yamana predicts will soon constitute 30 percent of the company's overall sales. The remaining 70 percent will be divided between the traditional dealer/distributor network, at 40 percent, and the Minolta copier sales staff, at 30 percent.

Award-Winning Products and Industry Firsts

Minolta-QMS has a long-standing record of industry "firsts" including: the first PostScript laser print system in 1985, the first color PostScript print system in 1988, and the first desktop color laser printer in 1993.

The company continues to demonstrate its technological superiority in both monochrome and color printers. The monochrome family ranges from low-priced small office-home printers, to systems for workgroups, departments, and high-volume production. The color family includes affordably priced print solutions for graphics applications, small business, and mid-to-large corporations.

(above) The company's full range of color and monochrome printers delivers solutions for both home office and business applications.

(left) Sign at the entrance of Minolta-QMS property.

Minolta-QMS has garnered more than its share of industry recognition over the years, earning spots on *PC World's* "Top 10 List," and being named a MacUser Award Winner and a *PC World* "Best Buy."

Yamana foresees continued development in Minolta-QMS's monochrome and color product lines, with an emphasis on multi-functioned, networkable printer/copiers.

Community Leadership

Although Minolta-QMS concentrates on a global market, it possesses a strong commitment to the local community. Company-wide programs have resulted in strong employee support for organizations such as the United Way. Minolta-QMS is a sponsor of the Azalea Trail Run and participates in events put on by March of Dimes, Red Cross, and other volunteer organizations.

(above) Consulting may play a bigger role in the future profits of Minolta-QMS.

(right) Consumable sales are an important component in both domestic and offshore markets.

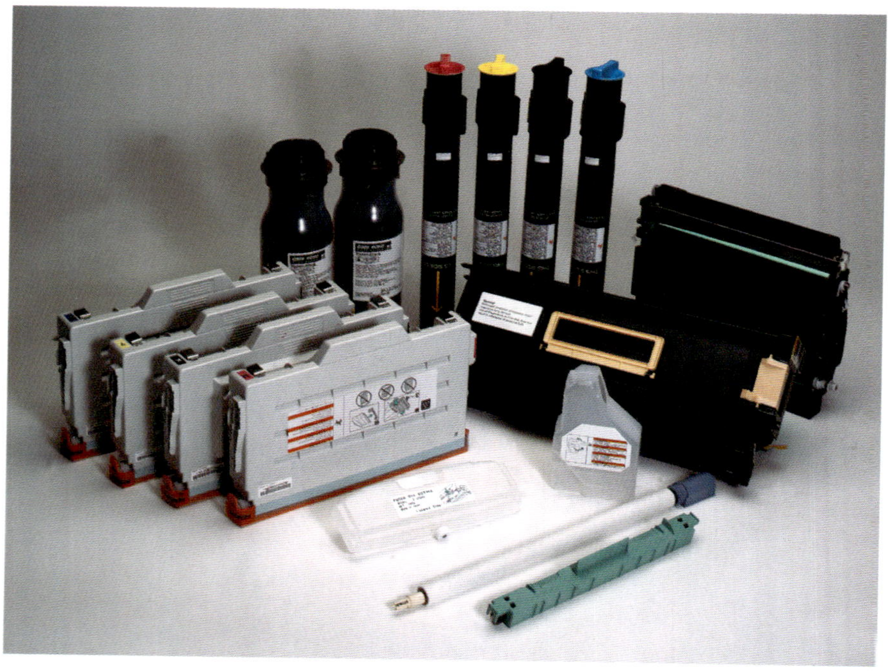

Minolta-QMS actively supports and encourages employee volunteerism, granting paid time off for participation. The company's commitment to service is so strong that "community involvement" is one of the benchmarks for evaluating senior-level management in performance reviews.

One area in which Minolta-QMS has made a significant impact is the arts. "I believe companies like ours need to support the arts," says Yamana. "While it is important to underwrite charities and similar community services, support for the arts is also needed and is vital to the development of a great city. With that in mind, our Contributions Committee maintains a balance among charities, services, and the arts."

QMS is a major contributor to the expansion fund of the Mobile Museum of Art. The Museum of Art has the potential

The Future

As Yamana looks ahead, he foresees a bright future for Minolta-QMS. Specific goals have been established in five areas to measure the company's progress: revenue growth, growth with specific earnings targets, managing assets in the e-commerce world with specific rate of return objectives, improved customer satisfaction with a survey-driven "customer-satisfaction index," and improved employee morale with specific morale-index goals.

While the competition—Xerox, HP, and Lexmark—is formidable indeed, Yamana believes that the synergy of QMS's strength in printers, combined with Minolta's preeminence in copiers and digital imaging, leaves the company perfectly positioned to meet the challenges of a changing marketplace. "Minolta-QMS," he predicts, "will play a major role in the implementation of the fully digital office of the future."

of becoming a "center of gravity" for the western section of town, says Yamana, "much the way downtown development has revitalized the eastern section of Mobile."

Though he is not an artist himself, Yamana says he derives a great deal of "pleasure and emotional nourishment" from attending the symphony, opera, and similar events. "We have tremendous potential in this area," he says, "and there seems to be a general awakening to the importance of the arts in our community."

(above) Minolta-QMS, Inc., President and Chief Operating Officer Shoei Yamana.

(left) Minolta-QMS products consistently win the highest honors from magazines such as *PC World*.

ATLANTIC MARINE AND ALABAMA SHIPYARD DIVISIONS OF ATLANTIC MARINE, INC.

Since the late 1800s, the shipbuilding and ship repair industry has been a powerful presence on Pinto Island. Alabama Drydock and Shipbuilding Company (ADDSCO), founded in 1916, maintained operations on Pinto Island for decades. By 1943, as many as 40,000 men and women worked there, turning out ships in record numbers for the war effort—2,800 naval and merchant ships, 20 liberty ships, and 102 T-2 tankers. Today, Atlantic Marine and Alabama Shipyard continue the tradition.

Atlantic Marine, Inc., a Jacksonville, Florida, company founded in 1964 by George W. Gibbs III, established Atlantic Marine-Mobile and Alabama Shipyard in Mobile in 1989, after acquiring ADDSCO. The two companies are strategically located on the Mobile River adjacent to a 42-foot-deep ship channel leading to Mobile Bay with unobstructed access to the Gulf of Mexico and major shipping lanes.

Atlantic Marine Mobile and Alabama Shipyard jointly occupy 650 acres on Pinto Island under the Alabama Shipyard bridge crane of the Mobile skyline. The companies offer their customers a full range of shipbuilding and repair services. Atlantic Marine specializes in ship repair and conversion for the domestic and international commercial market. Alabama Shipyard focuses on new construction, with an emphasis on deep-sea, ocean-going commercial ship construction, and the fabrication needs of the offshore oil industry.

Strategies for a Dynamic Future

Because of major investments in plant and equipment throughout the 1990s, Atlantic Marine and Alabama Shipyard together offer technologically advanced ship repair, conversion and construction facilities to a global market. In addition, both of the two companies operate on a continuous, seven-day-a-week production schedule that enhances quality and contributes to on-time, on-budget delivery. A sophisticated, computerized schedule of events and costs for every project allows Atlantic Marine and Alabama Shipyard to track each project component in detail, monitoring the project's progress and budget from design through completion.

The investment isn't in just brick, mortar, equipment, and electronics. Atlantic Marine and Alabama Shipyard employ a quality-management approach that involves every employee. Both yards are ISO-9000 certified, offer extensive job training, and make available the opportunity for formal education to every employee who chooses to participate. A corporate emphasis on safety has resulted in one of the best records in the industry. Sound environmental practices have made Atlantic Marine and Alabama Shipyard leaders in environmental awareness, proactive building projects, and compliance programs.

(right) Carnival Cruise Lines' *Sensation* is one of the many cruise ships repaired and refurbished at Atlantic Marine.

Atlantic Marine-Mobile

Because of their close proximity, Atlantic Marine and Alabama Shipyard together offer an unparalleled package of services to customers. One of the most high-profile ship conversions in history was successfully undertaken by Atlantic Marine in conjunction with Alabama Shipyard.

In 1974, a Soviet submarine exploded under mysterious circumstances and sank in the Pacific. The CIA initiated a project to recover the sub for intelligence purposes, hiring Howard Hughes and Global Marine to build a one-of-a-kind salvage vessel, the Glomar Explorer, a technological marvel two football fields in length and twenty-three stories high. The mission, however, met with only limited success.

But the innovative design of the Glomar Explorer led to a second, less clandestine mission. In 1996, Global Marine decided to convert the Glomar Explorer into a deep-water drill ship. The final phase of the $180-million project was awarded to Atlantic Marine because it had completed more such conversion and drill package installations than any other shipyard in the world. Working in conjunction with Alabama Shipyard, Atlantic Marine successfully completed the mammoth task—installing the full drilling package and making additional modifications to the ship. The converted Glomar Explorer was dedicated and put into service on schedule. Atlantic Marine's knowledge of and experience in the offshore oil industry was instrumental in the company's successful completion of this challenging project.

With two docking facilities, 6,000 feet of pier space, and quality production facilities, Atlantic Marine is equipped to offer repair and conversion services ranging from routine dry-docking and inspection of cruise ships, bulkers, and tankers, to constructing and

(above) The combined facilities of Atlantic Marine-Mobile and Alabama Shipyard.

(left) The *Marine Chemist*, owned by Marine Transport Lines, is an example of the large tankers that come to Atlantic Marine for repair.

(above) The *Nicole Leigh Reinauer* and the *RTC 135*, an articulated tug/barge (ATB) unit was built for Reinauer Transportation Companies of New York and delivered in 1999. An additional ATB unit is being built for this customer to be delivered in 2001.

(right) Global Marine Drilling's *Glomar Explorer* on drydock *Alabama* during the conversion of the Navy ship to an ultra-deep-water drillship.

fitting complex offshore conversions. The emergence of the rapidly expanding cruise ship industry in the Caribbean offers Atlantic Marine the opportunity to periodically augment Mobile's skyline with the large cruise ships that regularly occupy dry dock Alabama. Atlantic Marine-Mobile's reputation for quality workmanship and on-time delivery has made it the shipyard of choice for major cruise lines. Royal Caribbean, Holland America, Carnival Cruise Lines, and others rely on Atlantic's fast turn-around schedules.

The pier area has a water depth of 30 feet, a 75-ton derrick barge, and three cranes with lifting capacities of 30, 50, and 150 tons. The full-service shops include hull, paint, pipe, electrical, carpentry, insulation, rigging, and outside and inside machinery. Machine shop equipment includes overhead cranes, a full complement of machine tools, presses and portable boring equipment, lathes for material up to 41 feet long, and vertical mills handling 16-foot by 10-foot components. Major renovations have resulted in many machines being reconditioned to original factory tolerances. Storage space is plentiful with two large warehouses, as well as extensive outside storage capability.

The *Alabama,* one of the largest floating dry docks in the country, is a self-contained dry-docking and repair facility for vessels up to 160 feet wide. It has an overall length of 854 feet, a lifting capacity of 50,000 long tons displacement, and can accommodate ships capable of transporting up to 125,000 tons of cargo. Dry Dock 17 serves vessels up to 90 feet wide with a lifting capacity

of 14,200 tons for cargo vessels that can transport up to 35,000 tons of product.

Alabama Shipyard

Alabama Shipyard has gained global attention for the construction of chemical tankers for international trade, bluewater construction of commercial ships, and satisfying the fabrication needs of the off-shore oil industry. The company's Accuracy Control Program and enhanced capabilities in critical areas yield unparalleled precision throughout the shipbuilding process, ensuring final product compliance. Staff designers and engineers essentially "build" the ship on computer before it is constructed on the building ways, incorporating structural, piping, ventilation, and electrical designs in a 3-D virtual model.

After nearly 10 years of major investment in plant and equipment, Alabama Shipyard has emerged as one of the most technologically advanced ship construction facilities in the United States. The massive Steel Erection Area, which occupies a quarter-of-a-million square feet, handles ship sizes up to 600 feet by 160 feet and has a 275-ton bridge crane and two 150-ton gantry cranes. The Pipe Fabrication Facility uses automatic and semi-automatic systems to cut, bend, and weld pipe and fittings to exacting tolerances. The completely enclosed, environmentally safe Unit Blast and Coat facility handles modules and sub-assemblies up to 270 tons. CNC plasma- and oxy-fuel-cutting machines handle 3/4-inch plates up to 12 feet by 53 feet. The Panel Line Facility encompasses more than 39,000 square feet of covered floor space and uses a state-of-the-art one-sided welding system. The Steel Storage Area, supported by a 35-ton magnetic crane system, is accessible to ground and rail transportation.

When Alabama Shipyard delivered two single-decked, single-screw, double-hull chemical tankers to a Danish owner in 1998, it became the first American shipyard in more than 40 years to deliver an ocean-going vessel for export. The company has also established a reputation for constructing articulated tug barges (ATBs) featuring double-hulls and the patented Intercon Coupler System.

In little more than a decade, Atlantic Marine-Mobile and Alabama Shipyard have evolved into two of the world's most highly regarded names in marine construction and repair, delivering quality work that is competitively priced and on-schedule, while laying a solid foundation for the future.

(above) Ships are constructed in modules at Alabama Shipyard, then the sections are joined together.

(left) This overhead view of the erection area shows the *Amalienborg*, a 16,000 dwt chemical tanker under construction. When it was delivered to a Danish shipowner in 1998, it was the first self-propelled ocean-going vessel built for export by an American shipyard in over 40 years.

DEGUSSA CORPORATION

As the largest plant in Degussa Corporation's North American operation, the Mobile facility in Theodore Industrial Park employs more than 1,400 area residents, and has a combined payroll in excess of $70 million. Founded in Mobile in 1973, the plant has a total impact of more than $200 million each year on the local economy. Corporate investment in the local plant exceeds $1 billion—five times the original projected figure of $200 million.

Its parent company, Degussa AG, based in Frankfurt, Germany, has a 125-year history of providing superior chemical products to the European economy and employs 46,000 on five continents with worldwide annual sales of $12 billion.

One of the 10 largest employers in Mobile County, Degussa is particularly proud of two remarkable statistics—in the company's 25-plus-year history there has never been a layoff and the annual employee turnover rate is less than one percent.

Hire The Best

"Our people are our lifeline," says Charles E. Story, Vice President of Government and Public Affairs, "and we've made a significant investment in job training." Degussa sponsors the Pre-Hire School in conjunction with the Alabama Industrial Development Training Department. The curriculum, taught during an intensive 14-week period, consists of more than 70 hours of classroom time. Offered free of charge to those who qualify—primarily those with some college or technical training—the school is an excellent means for those who are "underemployed" to realize their full potential in the marketplace. It has also proven to be an exceptional source of well-trained, highly qualified workers for the company.

Pre-Hire School is just the beginning of a rigorous training regimen for Degussa workers. When employed, they go through another eight weeks of instruction. In fact, 25 percent of their working hours in the first two years are devoted to training; then, 40 to 80 hours per year.

With the exception of a few tech employees, Degussa is entirely staffed with workers from the Mobile area. The company also employs a strong "promotion from within" policy. Summing up the company's philosophy, Story observes, "It just makes sense to hire and keep the best people."

(above) Degussa's Hydrogen Peroxide Unit produces an environmentally friendly replacement for bleach in the pulp and paper industry. Hydrogen peroxide breaks down into water and oxygen after it is used.

(right) Degussa emphasizes training for all employees. New employees receive over 250 hours of training followed by an annual refresher.

An Extensive Product Line

Degussa manufactures more than 200 product lines serving markets as diverse as the automotive, building materials, pulp and paper, poultry, and mining industries in the U.S., Mexico, Canada, South and Central America, Europe, and Asia.

From everyday goods like toothpaste and car tires to specialized items like poultry feed additives and adhesives, and caulk and joint compounds, Degussa products enhance the quality of life for people on four continents.

Environment

As one of the earliest residents of Theodore Industrial Park, Degussa has worked long and hard to be a responsible corporate citizen and a good neighbor in south Mobile County. The company's environmental protection control equipment, an investment of almost $100 million, includes an innovative biological wastewater treatment system that handles half-a-million gallons daily. The Rock Reed Filter System, an artificial marsh containing indigenous plants, is the result of a collaboration between Degussa personnel and NASA's National Space Technology Laboratories. In operation since 1988, the artificial marsh system polishes the water before it enters the Theodore Barge and Ship Canal. Closely monitored by a staff of environmental chemists and marine biologists, the system exceeds some of the most stringent discharge criteria in the state. A beneficial by-product of the Rock Reed Filter System is that it has become a natural habitat for wildlife, including nesting waterfowl and turtles.

The company has an aggressive air pollution control program that uses thermal oxidizers as well as chemical and mechanical scrubbers. In addition to water and air pollution control, Degussa has undertaken an ambitious recycling program that stresses waste minimization and reduction.

With a 25-person staff representing more than 200 years' experience in the environmental field—including two former EPA officials—Degussa is committed to operating its facilities in a manner that preserves the integrity of the environment and protects the health and safety of its employees and the surrounding community. Says Story, "We're not satisfied unless we exceed permit requirements."

Giving Back To The Community

Degussa is an active supporter of a variety of community projects. The company has been recognized by the Mobile Area Education Foundation for its 25-year commitment to the improvement of education in Mobile County. A long-time participant in the Partners in Education program, Degussa employees volunteer at nearby schools, like Theodore High School, and take part in the Rolling Readers program, a grassroots children's literacy program targeting students in kindergarten through third grade, which receives enthusiastic employee participation.

The company funded the "Writing to Read" labs at Hollinger's Island Middle School and Burroughs Elementary, completely outfitting the labs with the necessary computer equipment. In addition, Degussa underwrites higher education by funding programs like the United Negro College Fund and the Marine Environmental Sciences study center on Dauphin Island.

The company also champions such causes as the United Way, Ronald McDonald House, and a number of civic clubs, as well as partnering with the Mobile Area Chamber of Commerce and the Alabama Development Office in promoting economic development locally and statewide.

Concludes Story, "Our philosophy has always been to give back to the community. I think we're living proof that with a good labor market, as we have in Mobile, and a commitment to training, as we have at Degussa, you can get the job done—whatever it is."

Environmental efforts are of paramount concern. Degussa operates a four-stage water treatment process. The highly acclaimed "Rock-Reed" filter is an adaptation of NASA technology.

BENDER SHIPBUILDING & REPAIR, CO., INC.

Since its founding in 1919 as a machine and blacksmith shop, Bender Shipbuilding & Repair Co., Inc., has been known as a company with a firm commitment to quality. Today, as a full-service shipyard that builds, converts, and repairs vessels for commercial and government owners and operators, Bender has forged a reputation as one of the most innovative shipyards in the United States.

Located along more than a mile of Mobile River, Bender fronts more than 7,000 feet of water with depths up to 42 feet. More than 800 people—welders, construction workers, marine architects, engineers, designers, draftsmen, and administrators—are employed at the company's 54-acre facility.

As economic trends have shifted over the years, Bender has been quick to apply its resources and experience to meet new challenges in the marketplace. The company's rapid response to continuous change has helped make Bender one of the most successful and versatile shipbuilding and repair companies in the world.

A Leader in Shipbuilding and Conversions

More than 1,000 Bender-built vessels are in operation around the world—including fishing and offshore supply vessels, passenger ships, tugs, push boats, and dry docks. Bender first established its name in shipbuilding by supplying fishing vessels to the Pacific Northwest and overseas. With the decreasing demand for these vessels, Bender turned to new markets, such as oil spill recovery vessels, drill rigs, double-hull oil barges, research vessels, and shrimp boats for export. Bender was one of the first Gulf Coast shipyards to convert and build vessels for the fast-growing casino riverboat market, including the first such vessel used in Louisiana. When Illinois river waters opened to gaming, Bender's swift 90-day conversion launched the Alton Belle Casino in record time, far ahead of its competition. On-site construction of a 400-foot casino riverboat in Elgin, Illinois, earned the company the prestigious "Distinguished Ship of the Year" award presented by *Maritime Reporter*. Today, Bender is considered the nation's leading builder of casino riverboats and dockside casino barges.

In a recent joint venture with Austal Holdings Ltd. of western Australia, Bender has begun building 300-foot aluminum catamaran ferries. The newly formed company, Austal USA, LLC, is located in a completely enclosed, state-of-the-art facility on Mobile River.

Bender is an industry leader in conversions, having converted more vessels to new uses than any other U.S. shipyard. After the collapse of the oil industry in the late '70s, Bender converted more than 30 offshore vessels to trawlers for the Alaskan fishing industry—lengthening and widening the existing vessels into at-sea factories for processing freshly caught fish. Conversions will continue to be an important part of Bender's market mix, as more and more companies realize the economies of re-fitting seaworthy vessels for new uses.

Round-the-Clock Ship Repair

As one of the leading ship repair operations on the Gulf of Mexico, Bender has master repair contracts with all branches of the Defense Department, U.S. Army Corps of Engineers, and U.S. Coast Guard. A complete in-house staff of estimators, naval architects, engineers, designers, and draftsmen, coupled with access to

(above) Aerial view of Bender Shipbuilding & Repair Co. Inc., on the West Bank of the Mobile River.

(right) Bender-built fireboat for the Port of New Orleans showing off in front of the Mobile Convention Center.

the Gulf Coast's largest concentrated shipyard workforce enables the company to provide round-the-clock full-service repair and conversion service to vessels up to and including Panamax size—the largest vessel able to go through the Panama Canal.

The company also frequently performs off-site pipe, mechanical, and structural work in Florida, Mississippi, and Louisiana, as well as industrial work at customers' facilities along the entire Gulf Coast.

Efficient, Technologically Advanced Facilities

Bender's reputation for innovation and efficiency in every step of the building and repair process is due in large part to the company's impressive facilities. The fully equipped yards can handle any size or type repair or conversion to any classification society. The company's four steel floating dry docks have lifting capacities ranging from 4,000 to 24,350 tons. Cranes include a 65-ton floating derrick crane; 15 hydraulic, crawler, and rubber tire cranes with lifting capacity up to 250,000 tons; and 11 overhead cranes with 5 to 80 tons lifting capacity servicing 234,500 square feet of covered work area. One hundred twenty thousand square feet of covered warehouse space contains complete machine, electrical, and carpenter shops, as well as the First Operations Shop.

The First Operations Shop is recognized as the most efficient and technologically advanced steel plate processing facility in the U.S. shipbuilding industry. The focal point of the First Operations Shop is the Tanaka LMXIII—the largest, most-powerful production laser for cutting steel plate in use in a U.S. shipyard. The laser can cut 13-foot-by-1.5-foot steel plates up to 1.75 inches thick, with the ability to handle continuous cutting of three 40-foot-long plates.

With the laser, Bender can achieve accuracy to within four-one-thousandths of an inch, leaving no dross or slag along the cut. When two laser-cut plates are fitted together, the seam is almost imperceptible, and no post-processing is necessary. Speed is another benefit of the Tanaka laser. Jobs that used to take four hours to complete with traditional machining can now be accomplished in less than 20 minutes. The laser creates no gases and very little smoke or heat, so it's far less polluting than torch cutting. Increased accuracy by this new laser technology means less scrap material is created. Bender offers laser-cutting services to area shipyards and to other industries for applications such as bridge and building construction.

A Standard of Quality

Throughout its 80-year history, Bender Shipbuilding and Repair has measured its worth by one standard: to provide the finest marine products and services safely, on time, at competitive prices. With its commitment to quality, leading-edge technology, and a prime central-Gulf Coast location, Bender lives up to that standard everyday.

(above) Bender's dry dock, "Pete B," which is capable of lifting vessels up to 24,000 tons, including Panamax size—the largest vessel able to go through the Panama Canal.

(left) Plate cutting is done with a fully computerized 6,000-watt Tanaka LMXIII laser on a 145-foot-long cutting table in the First Operations Shop.

THE FINCH COMPANIES, INC.

A reputation for flexibility and the ability to move at a moment's notice has paid off in a big way for The Finch Companies—a respected name in Mobile business circles for more than 65 years.

In 1933 Tom and Genevieve Finch, defying all odds, began a warehousing operation that not only survived the Great Depression, but went on to become one of the southeast's leading logistics companies. Operating out of a 60,000-square-foot building on flood-prone Commerce Street, the family, according to Tom and Genevieve's grandson, and company president Tommy Fulton, first demonstrated their renowned ability to respond swiftly when rising water from Mobile's frequent torrential rainstorms would force them to relocate the warehouse's contents from the first floor to the second with little advance warning.

Providing top-notch service to clients like Dole Pineapple, Kellogg's Cereal, and Diamond Matches, the business thrived and eventually outgrew its original home. In 1956, Finch Warehousing and Transfer Co., Inc., opened its doors at the current location on Telegraph Road. In the years since, Finch has evolved into one of the southeast's leading logistics companies—a dynamic organization comprising five divisions: Warehousing, Trucking, Packaging, Fulton Realty, and Interiors Now. Grouped together as Finch Logistics, the Warehousing, Trucking, and Packaging divisions are the keystone of the business.

Finch Warehousing

A crucial link in any manufacturer's operation is distribution—the ability to move goods from production to profit. Finch—with more than 830,000 square feet of warehouse space—is strategically located to help businesses distribute and market their products as efficiently and profitably as possible. Situated in the heart of the city's transportation and industrial district, the Finch warehouses—with three private tracks—are serviced directly by the Illinois Central and Burlington Northern railroads. In addition, Alabama State Docks' interchange yard offers open switching to the major railroads servicing the port.

Just minutes from I-10, I-65, and I-165, Finch warehouses regularly accommodate almost 100 truck lines yearly—in addition to its in-house trucking operation. Deepwater access is available through the Port of Mobile, one of the Gulf Coast's busiest.

Having served customers in industries as diverse as paper, pulp, chemicals, steel, clothing, and food, Finch is expert at handling products with exceptional care as few times as possible. Due to a specialized plant design allowing uncongested operation and lift maneuverability, Finch is unmatched in its ability to handle shipments regardless of configuration—packages, pallets, or pieces.

(above) A dream fulfilled.

(right) Newsprint ready for shipment quickly and efficiently.

The latest materials-handling equipment and computer tracking programs enable Finch to handle each and every product in its care with the same attentiveness given by its manufacturer.

Finch Trucking

Quickly responding to a request from one of its customers to provide distribution assistance at competitive prices, Finch established its trucking division in the early 1980s. Offering local drayage as well as regional transportation within a 350-mile radius, Finch has the resources to coordinate and maintain tight distribution schedules. Because of its flexibility, Finch can customize its distribution services to fit each customer's individual needs. The team of drivers, operating a fleet of 15 power units and 40 trailers, provides skilled transport for both warehouse and non-warehouse customers alike.

Finch Packaging

One of the company's newer—and fastest growing—divisions has evolved from its founding in 1995 into a major component of the Finch Logistics enterprise. Proving once again its responsiveness to customer needs, the Packaging Division was established in direct response to a major customer's need for non-standardized containerization. The division's strength lies in its ability to provide fast turnaround on even the most labor-intensive, high-volume projects.

Finch offers a complete line of services including: shrink wrapping, cartonning, cello-wrapping, display assembly, and heat sealing. In addition, the company can fold, pack, bundle, sort, poly-bag, and stretch wrap a variety of diverse products.

An important service offered by Finch, known as "reconfiguration," is critical to a company's ability to supply its products in a packaged form that complies with the end user's requirements. Many discount and warehouse-style stores demand unusual sizing, packaging, or bundling of products. To meet these demands, Finch uses state-of-the-art technology—such as heat-tunnel shrinking and L-bar sealers—allowing the company to meet such unusual requests as packaging grits by the case rather than the box, and bundling and palletizing paper towels in a jumbo 12-pack size.

Another specialty is "reverse logistics," the management of store-returned products. Finch handles the pick up and disposal, or reconfiguration—including repackaging and relabeling—and return to market. In addition, the company designs and manufactures end-of-aisle displays for a variety of products and store environments.

(above) From casual to elegant, Interiors Now can make it happen.

(left) The newest addition to our family—Interiors Now—wow!

(above) From homes to offices to reception areas, Interiors Now is ready with a phone call.

(right) Rest easy—same day delivery is usually available.

The STAR System

The overriding concern of Finch Logistics—whether warehousing, shipping, or packaging a product—is to treat that product with the same care the manufacturer used in making it. For this reason, Finch instituted its own in-house quality process—The STAR System. Representing Strategy, Training, Assessment, and Results, the STAR System is Finch Logistics' guarantee of systematic quality service on every job.

For Finch, quality is an on-going process. As a member of the Southeastern Warehouse Association, Council of Logistics Management, the Warehousing Education and Research Council, and the International Warehouse Logistics Association, Finch demonstrates its commitment to excellence on the industry level, as well as on the corporate level.

Fulton Realty

Customers requiring comprehensive warehousing—from 10,000 to 500,000 square feet—rely on the commercial real estate division of Finch Logistics. Tailored to meet the needs of commercial and industrial clients, Fulton Realty can handle the job from site location to lease management. A Fulton specialty is the ability to custom design and build warehousing to meet the unique requirements of each customer.

Interiors Now

Having been active in the business since she was 12, helping parents Tom and Genevieve in the warehouse business, Betty Jo Fulton is more than qualified to run The Finch Companies' newest division, Interiors Now, founded in 1997.

A full-service furniture sales and leasing business, Interiors Now is located in the company-owned Fulton Square shopping center at the corner of Grelot Road and Knollwood Drive—the heart of the city's westward apartment and housing expansion. From elegant bedroom sets to contemporary living room arrangements, the 4,000-square-foot showroom is filled with all the handsome, comfortable pieces needed to completely furnish even the largest home or apartment.

In addition to its thriving retail sales business, Interiors Now offers retail and commercial rental as well. Students, interns, and others temporarily residing in the city—a growing segment of the market—are among those taking advantage of these services. Whether a single dining room set is needed, or a full decorated home, Interiors Now can handle the job with same-day service if needed. Drawing from an extensive line of attractive accessories, the store's designers can add inviting personality to newly furnished homes.

With the addition of the store's Housekeeping Package, an apartment or

Looking Ahead

The Finch Companies can boast of a long, impressive history. But Tommy Fulton has his eyes steadfastly trained on the future. Even though Finch is a "single-city" warehouse—one of the nation's largest—its interests are global, already conducting business with Latin American and South American concerns. E-commerce will strengthen the companies' standing in the international arena.

Finch's expansion plans are operational as well as geographic, involving order fulfillment, strategic partnerships with larger corporations, and import/export activities.

"When my grandparents started this business more than 65 years ago," says Fulton, "no one used words like 'logistics' or 'third-party provider.' But they knew that first-class service and customer satisfaction would always be the key to our success. And we strive to live up to that, every day."

home is instantly—and completely—ready for comfortable living. From bed linens and dinnerware to salt and pepper shakers, Interiors Now takes care of the details, large and small.

Through its Corporate Apartment Leasing program, Interiors Now offers short-term housing for a variety of clients, such as corporate executives and families displaced by fire or other catastrophes. With accommodations in Mobile and Baldwin counties, the corporate apartments of Interiors Now provide everything needed to create a comfortable, temporary home including: utilities, cable, and housekeeping supplies, as well as furnishings and accessories.

In living up to its full-service reputation, Interiors Now offers same-day delivery and purchase-option plans. Rental furniture returns are also available for purchase.

For the perfect temporary housekeeping solution, Interiors Now is the place to go.

(above) In the heart of the paper-producing area order fulfillment is the key to customer satisfaction.

(left) Our corporate apartments fill the need for temporary housing on a month-to-month basis. Prestigious locations available.

COOPER/T. SMITH CORPORATION

Cooper/T. Smith is one of America's oldest and largest stevedoring and maritime related firms. Headquartered in Mobile, Cooper/T. Smith has operations on all three U.S. coasts encompassing 38 ports, and has foreign operations in Venezuela, Brazil, Colombia, and Mexico. The company also maintains ownership in numerous satellite companies, complementing the multi-faceted maritime objectives.

The story of the Cooper family is as interesting as a saga out of the Old West. It begins right after the Civil War when Henry Harrison Cooper and his two brothers came to the New World from Scotland and settled in South Carolina. They soon immigrated to Alabama and settled in Baldwin County in an area later appropriately named Rosinton. They were rosin farmers securing rosin for naval stores from the plentiful Baldwin County pine trees. Each of the three brothers married one of the McKenzie sisters, homesteaded 160 acres each, and put their roots down to establish ties that would link their descendents firmly to Alabama over the next century and more. Henry Harrison Cooper and his wife, Matilda McKenzie Cooper, had 14 children; the next to the youngest was named Angus Royal Cooper. It was this son who established the waterfront tradition that the family would follow for generations. Angus was born in 1877, and at an early age he went to work on the Mobile docks as a tally man (one who counts the ships' cargoes). His early days on the docks prepared him to build a strong stevedoring company in America. It was on February 5, 1905, that he established what has now become Cooper/T. Smith Corporation through various name changes and acquisitions over the years. In 1925, Angus Cooper and his family moved to New Orleans where he would expand his stevedoring business and manage the Munson Line's gulf-wide operations. The Munson Line prospered so well that Munson built one of the first true skyscrapers in New York City. However, hard times hit when the bottom fell out of the economy in 1929, and Munson Line fell into financial difficulty. Angus Cooper continued handling stevedoring for one of Munson's allies, Alcoa Steamship Company, and as a result, the Munson Line surrendered all of their equipment to him in lieu of pay. This was the next big step in building a significant family-owned stevedoring company.

Meanwhile, Angus Cooper's youngest son, Ervin, who was born in 1911, graduated from Tulane University in 1933 and joined Alcoa Steamship in New Orleans and in New York, then later joined his family business. After he married Margaret Folmar of Troy, Alabama, had two sons (Angus II and David), he went on to personally direct the firm's expansion to ports throughout the U.S.

Management and Advisors gather at the statue of Ervin S. Cooper at Cooper Riverside Park.

Both sons, Angus II and David, graduated from the University of Alabama, joined their family's company, and set out on a seemingly impossible mission. This mission was to grow the business worldwide and compete internationally in the global market with the biggest maritime firms in the world.

Today's Cooper/T. Smith is a progressive and innovative organization employing thousands worldwide. Its subsidiaries include warehousing, insurance, terminal operations, tugboats, push boats, barging, barge fleeting, floating terminals, and the most recent acquisition of Kimberly Clark's Marine and Timberlands Division, now renamed Cooper Marine and Timberlands Corporation. In fact, the company impacts an astonishing array of industries throughout the country, from agriculture and energy to chemicals and construction.

Stevedoring is still a central part of Cooper's business. The company's state of the art equipment and automation provide customers with fast and cost-effective movement of cargo to and from ships at port. Cooper/T. Smith prides itself on its ability to operate globally. "We have huge barge-mounted cranes that can be transported anywhere a customer needs the service," says David Cooper. "The company's barge-mounted cranes can be sent virtually anywhere in the world in 45 days or less. Our people can also help clients adapt or modify their own equipment and facilities to significantly enhance their performance."

Ervin S. Cooper (1911-1982). Dedicated to the maritime industry throughout the world, the city of Mobile built a riverside park to honor the accomplishments of Cooper/T. Smith.

One hundred years earlier in Rosinton, Alabama, the Coopers were drawn to the waterfront by producing rosin for naval stores. Each generation had made their contribution, and the legacy was left in the hands of the younger Coopers with a dream. Today, at the foot of Government Street in Mobile, Cooper Riverside Park honors the memory of Ervin S. Cooper (1911-1982). There, a bronze statue of Ervin Cooper presides over the area. Within, he is immortalized sitting on a Waterman Steamship Company bench gazing over the Mobile River which has meant so much to the Cooper family. Cooper/T. Smith has grown from a modest beginning to a complex, multifaceted maritime giant in the last one hundred years. Earning a worldwide reputation for lasting partnerships and high-quality service, Angus Cooper II and David Cooper plan to make the next century of the business just as exciting.

KIMBERLY-CLARK CORPORATION

For more than 125 years, Kimberly-Clark has made products that make people's lives better. Providing a multitude of benefits—including better health, comfort, convenience, and an enhanced quality of life—these products bear some of the world's most trusted brand names, such as Kleenex, Huggies, Kotex, Scott Tissue, and Depends.

Since its founding in 1872, Kimberly-Clark has grown to become the second-largest household and personal-care products company in the United States, and the leading tissue manufacturer in the world. As one of the 400 largest companies in the world, Kimberly-Clark employs 55,000 people worldwide, with manufacturing facilities in 40 countries and sales of more than $13 billion annually in more than 150 countries.

In 1995, Kimberly-Clark merged with Scott Paper Company and has transformed itself from a paper manufacturer into a global consumer products company, organized in three divisions: Personal Care, Tissue and Towel, and Health Care and Other. Personal Care products include diapers, training pants, feminine care, and incontinence care products. The Tissue and Towel division manufactures facial and bathroom tissue, wet wipes, and paper towels for both in-home and away-from-home use. The Health Care and Other category encompasses such diverse products as surgical masks and gowns, and technical and specialty papers.

The Mobile Mill: Vital To Company and Community

The Mobile Mill is a key member of the Kimberly-Clark family, specializing in the manufacture of "away-from-home" tissue and towel products, as well as Scott Tissue and Scott Towels for home use. Kimberly-Clark's "away-from-home" product category is an essential part of the company's product mix, and includes high-performance tissue and towel products for commercial, industrial, and institutional customers such as hotels, restaurants, schools, and hospitals.

In 1999, Kimberly-Clark shut down the local pulping operation, allowing the mill to focus on its core business of manufacturing tissue and towel products. The Mobile Mill operates one of the largest and fastest tissue machines in the country. Running at a mile a minute, the machine produces approximately 63,000 metric tonnes of paper per year for the manufacture of bath tissue and paper towels.

With almost 1,000 employees and an annual payroll of $49 million, the Mobile Mill has a total economic impact of $350 million, most of which goes back into the local economy.

(right) Personal care products.

Kimberly-Clark is renowned for its good citizenship; it and its employees actively participate in the community. The company encourages and supports its people who make a difference for others outside the workplace.

The company's Bright Futures program has awarded more than $9 million in scholarships to the children of Kimberly-Clark employees. Of this, more than $600,000 has been awarded to students in southwest Alabama.

Through the Matching Gifts program, the Kimberly-Clark Foundation matches employee contributions to qualified charitable and educational institutions in the United States on a dollar-for-dollar basis, up to $10,000 per person each year. The Community Partners program provides for corporate grants to charitable and educational organizations based on employee volunteerism and participation in the organizations' activities. Nationwide, Kimberly-Clark has donated more than $4.5 million dollars to communities through the Matching Gifts and Community Partners programs.

Kimberly-Clark and its employees are strong supporters of the United Way of Southwest Alabama, with employee contributions in recent years of $300,000. Through matched employee contributions and donations, the company has contributed almost $1.5 million over a two-year period. In addition, Kimberly-Clark, on many occasions, has contributed significantly to the Red Cross and the United Way to help offset expenses associated with natural disasters in Gulf Coast communities.

Environmental Responsibility

Environmental responsibility is a key element of Kimberly-Clark's success. A four-part policy shapes the company's decision making: protection of the biosphere, sustainable use of natural resources, use and conservation of energy, and reduction and disposal of waste. As a result of these guidelines, Kimberly-Clark has upgraded wastewater treatment standards at all facilities and has improved energy efficiency by 10 percent. Kimberly-Clark is serious about environmental responsibility because it benefits everyone—the company, its employees, and the community.

A Corporate Culture of Trust and Respect

Kimberly-Clark's corporate philosophy is based on succeeding through hard work and fair play. The result is an atmosphere of cooperation and communication that makes working at Kimberly-Clark more than just a job, and has helped earn the company the honor of being named one of Fortune magazine's "Most Admired" corporations since 1983. Kimberly-Clarkers thrive in a corporate culture founded on trust and respect. The spirit of teamwork allows each employee to focus on individual strengths as well as common goals.

With a commitment to quality products, innovation, and technology leadership, Kimberly-Clark is well on the way to achieving its primary goal—to become one of a small handful of companies recognized as "best in the world" in terms of people, products, and return to shareholder.

(above) Family care and away-from-home products.

(left) Tissue manufacturing process.

ST MOBILE AEROSPACE ENGINEERING, INC.

ST Mobile Aerospace Engineering, Inc. (MAE), was established in September 1990 as a company under the Aerospace Sector of Singapore Technologies Engineering. As part of its strategy to diversify into commercial aircraft maintenance and to meet worldwide demands for third party aircraft maintenance and modification work, Singapore Technologies Engineering founded MAE as the foothold in the United States to serve the growing North and South American markets.

MAE, a Federal Aviation Administration (FAA) approved Aircraft Repair Station, specializes in undertaking heavy maintenance, inspection, repair, refurbishment, and modification of narrow and wide body aircraft ranging from Boeing B717, B727, B737, B747, B757, B767, B777, DC9, MD80, DC10, MD11, and Airbus A300, A310, and A320.

MAE is strategically located at the Brookley Airport and Industrial Complex in Mobile on the southern coast of Alabama. The airfield at Brookley has a 9,600 foot runway complete with an Instrument Landing System (ILS). In addition to the existing facilities, MAE has undergone a controlled level of growth not only in new facilities but also in the amount of work. However, one of the most important factors about the Mobile area is the warm weather that allows greater flexibility to work all year round.

MAE's main facility consists of eight hangars, 527,000-square-feet hangars, 100,000 square feet of support shops and administrative offices, a 34,000-square-foot, dedicated aircraft wash/strip rack, a new state-of-the-art Super-Nose Dock, and additional new equipment to enhance its range of services. The maintenance hangars can easily accommodate six wide-body aircraft (up to B747) and ten narrow-body aircraft simultaneously. Also the Super-Nose Dock can house two wide-body aircraft for interior and avionics modifications and upgrades.

(above) The conversion of the Boeing DC-10 passenger aircraft to the MD-10 freighter is performed at MAE.

(right) MAE's 10th anniversary celebration.

The Aerospace Sector of Singapore Technologies Engineering is comprised of a group of companies that together provide a worldwide level of unique offerings. These include a wide range of products and services including heavy aircraft maintenance, structural modification and refurbishment, aircraft engine and component overhaul and repair, aircraft and avionics system design and integration, and manufacture of engine and aircraft parts and subassemblies. MAE brings along with it, the reputation and commitment of the Aerospace Sector of Singapore Technologies Engineering to

provide its customers with quality, reliability, and service excellence.

Within the past 10 years of operation, MAE has emerged from its start-up status to establish itself as one of North America's leading third party repair stations. Among its customers are airlines and chartered operators, freight carriers, and leasing companies.

The type of work MAE performs includes heavy maintenance inspection and checks, life extension work on aging aircraft, corrosion prevention and control programs, major structural work and modification, passenger-to-freighter conversions, complete interior refurbishment and/or reconfiguration, avionics modifications and fleet standardization, and aircraft stripping and painting.

Starting from scratch and growing steadily, MAE maintains a work force of about 1,000 technical, engineering, and administrative personnel, comprised mainly of licensed Airframe and Powerplant (A&P) aircraft mechanics.

Together with the Singapore Technologies Engineering group, MAE is committed to meeting the long-term needs of the aviation industry and is continually strengthening its capabilities to remain at the forefront of the aerospace technologies. MAE has developed a work force that is highly skilled, technically competent, and extremely motivated. The company takes special pride in maintaining the highest possible standard of quality, workmanship, and reliability that has won many satisfied customers.

(above) Aerial view of MAE's eight-hangar facility.

(left) Boeing 757-200 passenger aircraft undergoing conversion to a freighter at MAE.

ALABAMA STATE DOCKS

With a statewide economic impact of $3 billion annually, Alabama State Docks is an essential component of the state's economic engine. "Our reason for existing is to sustain and fuel continuous growth in the state," says James K. Lyons, State Docks director and chief executive officer. "Our sole 'profit motive' is to pay our own bills and help grow the business and industrial base in Alabama."

Lyons is the first director in the Docks' 73-year history to serve under the newly created Alabama State Port Authority—a nine-member governing board with representatives from throughout the state. A key benefit of the revamped organizational structure is a new sense of continuity and stability that is crucial to long-term strategic development. "We are now able to plan effectively for a future that's beneficial to the whole state," says Lyons.

(far right) The Alabama State Docks maintains the public seaport complex at the deepwater Port of Mobile, one of the nation's busiest ports.

(right) Forest products are the leading general cargo moving through the State Docks. Alabama's seaport handles more woodpulp than any other port in the nation.

A 300-Year Tradition

Building on a sea-faring heritage that dates back to the early 17th century, the state authorized construction of the Docks with a $10 million investment on 548 acres of swampland and marsh. Since receiving its first cargo ship in 1927, Alabama State Docks has grown to become a major American port, ranking 11th in the nation in exports.

With five miles of waterfront facilities and 10 inland docks, the Alabama State Docks' total acreage exceeds 3,000 acres. Channel depth ranges from 40 to 45 feet and cargo-handling area encompasses 4 million square feet. Annual revenues are in excess of $60 million, with total annual tonnage at the 18 million mark.

Nationwide, the Docks ranks at or near the top in several export categories—including first in wood pulp and second in forest products. Other top exports include coal, lumber, linerboard, and paper. The Docks is increasingly making its presence felt in imports, with impressive numbers in coal, aluminum, and steel. Top trading partners include Japan, Venezuela, Canada, the United Kingdom, and Mexico.

Gateway To The World

Two key factors in the success of Alabama State Docks are its prime location on Mobile River and excellent facilities. The river offers easy access to the Gulf of Mexico and international shipping, and acts as a gateway to the extensive river system of the Tennessee/Tombigbee Waterway for inland commerce.

General cargo operations cover almost two miles of waterfront, encompassing 27 berths and a 16-acre container yard served by a rail-mounted, 45-ton lift capacity Paceco crane and a 110-ton lift capacity harbor crane. The Docks' general cargo includes forest products, heavy metals, pipe, aluminum, project cargo, and bagged goods.

With an annual throughput capacity of 23 million tons, the terminals on McDuffie Island offer two bulk operations. McDuffie Coal Terminal is the largest such facility on the Gulf Coast, with two ship loaders, one ship unloader, single and tandem railcar dumps, three stacker reclaimers, three barge unloaders, and one barge loader. McDuffie Terminals has a 300,000-ton ground-storage capacity for direct reduced iron or other bulk cargo, and is served by three loop rail tracks.

Alabama State Docks operates two state-of-the-art facilities serving the Theodore Industrial Complex. Middle Bay Port's 200 acres of prime waterfront property includes 13 buildings and a two-sided 600-foot pier. The Marine Liquid Bulk Terminal, located on the turning basin of Theodore Ship Channel, accommodates ships up to 850 feet in length and allows one vessel and two barges to dock at the same time. The laser approach system makes docking safer and more accurate.

A waterfront landmark, the Terminal Railway—which connects to five mainline railroads—operates on 75 miles of track, using eight locomotives to transport cargo to and from piers, warehouses, and terminals, and to move railcars to and from local industries outside the main docks complex.

Alabama State Port Authority also operates 10 inland docks on 376 acres in Bridgeport, Claiborne, Columbia, Cordova, Demopolis, Eufaula, Montgomery, Phenix City, Selma, and Tuscaloosa-Northport.

Competing in the 21st Century

While Alabama State Docks continues to break records for total tonnage handled, there is still much room for expansion and development, says Lyons. Previous building plans were geared to the export needs of the state—grain elevators, lumber handling facilities, and coal terminal. Lyons stresses the importance of meeting the needs of the shipping industry as a whole in planning for the future, for example by building wider aprons to accommodate larger ships and expanding warehouse space to store more cargo. Lyons foresees a shift from bulk materials to containerized cargo.

"Containerization is growing at the rate of six to seven percent annually," he says. "And with the location of Mercedes and Honda in Alabama, we have a much greater need for containerized shipping." Lyons also anticipates the increasing prominence of Mexico and the Central American nations as trading partners. "Because of our proximity to the Caribbean basin and our extensive interior river system," he says, "we're strategically located to make major gains in that market."

The important thing for Alabamians to understand, Lyons says, is the value of Docks to the state as a whole. More than 118,000 Alabama jobs depend on the Alabama State Docks, with more of those jobs in the northern part of the state than the Mobile area. In addition, the Docks generates more than $450 million in tax revenues each year.

Lyons foresees a bright future for Alabama State Docks. A major expansion involving a $300-million capital investment is on the drawing board, with plans for completion in three to five years. "Because of the steps we're taking now," he says, "we will be in a strong position to compete internationally well into the 21st century."

(above) Aluminum is the leading imported general cargo handled by the Alabama State Docks.

(left) The State Docks handles a number of different bulk cargoes and can accommodate both import and export movements of coal, iron ore, and other bulk commodities.

AMERICAN TANK & VESSEL, INC.

American Tank & Vessel, founded in 1982, is a Mobile-based company specializing in the design, engineering, fabrication, installation, repair, and reconstruction of tanks, vessels, spheres, digesters, and distillation columns. The company offers complete turnkey service—both in-house and in the field—to clients in the petrochemical industry, as well as paper mills, the U.S. Army Corps of Engineers, and the U.S. Navy and Air Force.

The company has 275 U.S. employees, and is a global concern with offices in Houston, Texas; Baton Rouge, Louisiana; and Birmingham, Alabama. Corporate headquarters are in Mobile, and the company's fabrication plant is located in Lucedale, Mississippi.

Fabrication Facilities At Home and Abroad

American Tank & Vessel's main manufacturing plant is located in a Free Trade Zone, and offers comprehensive services including forming, fabrication, welding, normalizing, PWHT, third-party radiographic work, testing, lining, and painting. The plant includes separate designated facilities for API and ASME work, machine shops, painting facilities, maintenance and repair shops, material storage, trucking and rail service, and access to deep-water shipping. American Tank & Vessel's plant equipment surpasses that of most others in the industry, with a 6,500-ton hydraulic press capable of cold-forming a 4-inch steel plate, a 3,000-ton hydraulic press, and automated welding processes for carbon steel and alloys. The plant has the capability of rolling a pipe six inches in diameter, can form extra heavy walls, can form four-inch-thick carbon steel plates into spherical sections, heavy wall columns, and towers, and can fabricate fuel tanks up to 300 feet in diameter.

Among the company's more high-profile projects were the fabrication of a wind tunnel in Tullahoma, Tennessee, for the Corps of Engineers, and the design and construction of a continuous digester with a stainless steel liner for export to Brazil. The digester was 30 feet in diameter and stood more than 200 feet tall.

American Tank & Vessel also offers comprehensive field services with on-site design, fabrication, assembly, and construction for vessels and towers including the erection of flat bottom tanks, internal and external floating roofs, vessels, pressure vessels, and spheres of every size and configuration. Field service is crucial for installation at congested sites, for fast-turnaround, and for on-site modifications and repairs.

American Tank & Vessel's Special Services

Fast-track emergency projects—those that are critical to a customer's day-to-day operation—are a specialty of AT&V. Using its existing service facilities that are not at a peak load, American Tank & Vessel is able to deliver unequalled speed and value. Such projects include the design, fabrication, radiography, and ASME stamping of 22 vessels, each 10'6"x30'—in less than 60 days.

American Tank & Vessel engineers, constructs, and modifies internal and external floating roofs in existing or new tanks, and assists in emission considerations, service application, and economic evaluation.

The company holds the ASME "R" stamp for repair of ASME pressure vessels, including the design and construction of the tank, foundation, cathodic protection systems, leak detection, painting and liners, and insulation.

With American Tank & Vessel's Digester Replacement Option, it is often possible for a client to completely replace a digester more quickly and for the same cost as repairing it with a weld overlay.

Quality, Safety, and an Emphasis on Excellence

Quality control and safety are of paramount concern to American Tank & Vessel. The company's Quality Assurance/Quality Control audit, which includes not only required items, but also non-code issues and construction, yields the highest degree of quality in standards and customer specifications. American Tank & Vessel maintains a consistently low EMR and is 100 percent compliant with each client's safety requirements.

American Tank & Vessel provides added value to its customers, offering:

- a $10,000,000 pollution insurance policy;
- a $10,000,000 errors and omission policy;
- a $25,000,000 umbrella policy (except for the limits listed above);
- an EMR of .52;
- a construction record with no fatalities; and
- an acoustical test, in addition to the code requirement for vacuum box and hydrostatic testing of the tank bottom.

With unsurpassed performance in engineering, fabrication, and construction, American Tank & Vessel provides innovative solutions to clients worldwide with a reputation based on a four-part corporate philosophy: to offer superior quality, competitive pricing, rapid response time, and dependable delivery on every project it undertakes.

PHENOLCHEMIE, INC.

Phenolchemie is the world's largest producer of phenol and acetone—the building blocks of some of the most in-demand products on the market today. From a pair of prescription eyeglasses to the compact disc featuring the latest hits, many of the items we use every day would not exist without these two key chemical components.

Look in the medicine cabinet, on the kitchen counter, or at any automobile or house, and Phenolchemie's presence is felt—with phenol or acetone as essential parts for Aspirin®, counter tops, plywood and oriented strand board, or acrylic glass for tail lights on cars.

A leader in the industry for more than 40 years, Phenolchemie established its U.S.-based affiliate in 1998 to serve its customers in North and South America. Joining production plants in Gladbeck, Germany, and Antwerp, Belgium, the facility in the Mobile area is a primary provider to the world's single largest market for phenol and acetone.

A key reason for the location of Phenolchemie's newest production facility in the Theodore Industrial Park is the deep-water canal and turning basin. The basin allows for the expedited loading and transport of the plant's products by the industry's over-sized cargo carriers—the largest vessel allowed through the Panama Canal. "Our business, in a way, is tied to the water," said Greg Oakes, Director of Engineering, "so what better place to locate than Mobile?"

Because of this link to the water, Phenolchemie has a vested interest in protecting the quality of the region's natural resources and has demonstrated its commitment by setting industry standards in environmental protection. The company, by engaging in an ongoing program to reduce its use of resources and the creation of waste, lives up to the stringent requirements of the chemical industry's Responsible Care® guidelines and the tenants of sustainable development. Phenolchemie continuously strives to exceed national, state, and local regulations.

With a work force of more than 100, drawn mostly from the local market, and a $250-million investment in the area economy, the company has had a strong, positive impact on the community. Dr. Peter Bickert, president and CEO of Phenolchemie, Inc., stresses the corporate commitment to the community: "We value the long-term perspective, based on honest and fair relationships with our customers and vendors as well as our employees and their families. We are dedicated to the continuous development and well-being of our employees, enabling them to achieve and maintain the highest level of customer satisfaction, safety, and occupational excellence."

As members of management point out, the company manufactures and markets only two products: phenol and acetone. "It's all we do, so we better do it right," they say. And Phenolchemie, Inc., proves they're doing business the "right" way, every day.

(above) Front view of the Phenolchemie plant.

(right) Aerial view of the Phenolchemie plant.

MOBILE PAPERBOARD CORP.

As the oldest continuously operating mill in Alabama, Mobile Paperboard Corporation takes great pride in being part of an industry with strong historic ties to this region, as well as in being a member of the Newark Group—one of the largest manufacturers of recycled paperboard in the U.S.

The second-largest mill in the Newark Group, Mobile Paperboard is a leading supplier of recycled paperboard in the southeast, with exports to the Caribbean, Latin and South America, and the Pacific Rim.

Of the 12,000 plus tons of recycled paperboard the company manufactures each month, about 70 percent is used by other Newark Group affiliates to manufacture book covers and sturdy spiral tubes and cores—essential to carpet, paper, fabric, film, and tape manufacturers. The company maintains a strong allegiance to independent converters, supplying paperboard to furniture makers, the filter industry, and for general industrial packaging.

Mobile Paperboard uses 100 percent recycled material. This, according to Vice President and General Manager Chris Conrad, is a key statistic, since paper recycling has come to be recognized as a critical part of the world's manufacturing base. "Until there is a market for recyclables," he points out, "the recycling loop isn't closed. Mobile Paperboard provides the market and closes the loop, making recycling a viable option for both business and consumers."

Conrad also points out the impact of the company's organizational structure. "Our corporate culture emphasizes maintaining local identity," he says. "Each location is run with a high degree of autonomy." The structure gives the Newark Group subsidiaries the power of a large company with the entrepreneurial qualities of a small independent business.

Mobile Paperboard's autonomy is seen in its community involvement, and its support of charities and events of particular importance to employees and the local community. The company is also an active participant in the Mobile Area Chamber of Commerce, Envision Mobile, the Millennium Fund, Mobile Area Education Foundation, and other programs.

As a responsible employer of more than 190 workers, Mobile Paperboard is especially concerned with safety in the workplace. Major initiatives have resulted in outstanding records in the reduction of lost-time accidents. The company also maintains a good relationship with local unions.

In addition to its role in the recycling movement, Mobile Paperboard is committed to being a good corporate citizen on the environmental front.

Though a national leader in the manufacture of recycled paperboard, Mobile Paperboard does not seek the spotlight, letting its accomplishments speak for themselves. "We're not a very 'high-profile' company," says Conrad, "but we're extremely proud of our company's reputation for manufacturing a quality product in an environmentally friendly manner."

(above) Mobile Paperboard Corporation recycles over 160,000 tons of cardboard, newspaper, magazine, and other grades of recovered fiber annually.

(left) Mobile Paperboard's #2 Paper Machine produces high strength products used in the manufacturing of tubes and cores for the paper, textile, film, and carpet industries.

MITSUBISHI POLYSILICON

At the heart of every computer in the world is a chip made from silicon. Silicon is the most abundant element in the earth's crust next to oxygen, but only in its most pure form does it have the properties necessary to serve in electronics. That's where Mitsubishi Polysilicon of Mobile, Alabama, enters the picture.

Mitsubishi Polysilicon produces polysilicon that is 99.999999999 percent pure. Those are scientifically accurate numbers, not hyperbole. The company's product is the purest, most stringently fabricated silicon available in the world.

Mitsubishi Polysilicon is a wholly owned subsidiary of Mitsubishi Materials Corporation of Tokyo. Mitsubishi Materials has taken a leading position in the high-tech arena as a supplier of advanced electronic products, silicon wafers, and related products. The company is a prominent process manufacturer specializing in the smelting, refining, and fabrication of metals, as well as the production of cement and aluminum cans.

In 1995, continuing demand for polysilicon and a customer presence in the United States, created a need for a polysilicon production facility in the U.S. The Mobile site was selected for several reasons, such as the Alabama Industrial Development Program. This program helped ensure the company has a qualified, excellent workforce available. Mitsubishi Polysilicon employs 125 skilled personnel to perform the precise measurements and chemical processes necessary to purify the polysilicon. Alabama's affordable electricity rates were also important because of a large power consumption in the reduction process.

The presence of Degussa Corporation in Mobile is also a benefit to Mitsubishi. The two companies already have side-by-side facilities in Yokkaichi, Japan, that allowed them to share products. Degussa manufactures a substance used in the production of polysilicon, and a by-product of Mitsubishi's plant is used by Degussa to make fumed silica. Mitsubishi built its Mobile operation on property right next door to Degussa.

The raw material for Mitsubishi Polysilicon is purchased from a supplier in Norway. This 98 to 99 percent pure metallurgical silicon is first processed in a chlorination and distillation process to remove the remaining impurities. The silicon from this process then goes to a reduction process, where it is deposited on the surface of electrically heated silicon rods. After four or five days, the rods are grown to the desired diameter. The rods are then sent to a finishing process, where they are first sized and then put through an acid solution to remove any remaining impurities. The polysilicon is then rinsed in ultrapure water and vacuum dried, inspected, and then carefully packaged for shipping to customers. Customer applications for its polysilicon are silicon wafers, photovoltaic cells, silicon targets for glass coatings, and silicon parts for semiconductor fabrication equipment.

Mitsubishi Polysilicon is committed to being a responsible corporate citizen. It has done this by participating in and contributing to community functions and organizations through the donations of its time, talents, and resources. The company is committed to environmental responsibility as well. Air emissions from the facility meet or exceed all local, state, and federal standards, and no process water is discharged into area waterways.

"We have found a wonderful home in Mobile," says Mike Hashimoto, who was the project manager and was later named president and CEO. "The citizens and the business community here have made us feel very welcome. We have found a fantastic workforce here—absolutely dedicated to getting the job done." Hashimoto says that Mitsubishi Materials corporate leaders in Japan have noted the quality of the employees in Mobile and plan for future growth at this site.

(above) Aerial View of Mitsubishi Polysilicon Plant.

(right) Reduction Process.

MASLAND CARPETS

As the corporate headquarters of an internationally respected leader in design-oriented carpets and rugs, Masland Carpets in Saraland has made a significant impact in the global marketplace, as well as on the Mobile economy.

Founded in Pennsylvania in 1866, Masland's association with south Alabama dates back to 1968, when all the company's carpet production was relocated to Atmore. A few years later, Masland opened a distribution center in Saraland. In 1992, headquarters were moved to the Saraland facilities where they remain today.

The company's products are marketed to two different audiences, Commercial and Residential. The brand "Masland Contract" is marketed to corporate, hospitality, retail, institutional, and health-care designers and architects. The Residential brand, "Masland Carpets and Rugs" targets better-brand department stores, upper-end rug and carpet stores, and is specified through professional designers and architects.

Since relocating headquarters to the Mobile area, Masland Carpets has experienced dramatic growth. From 1992 to 1999, the company's rapid expansion created 550 jobs—increasing the number of Masland associates from 350 to 900, while more than tripling sales, from $47 million to $160 million. The two south Alabama facilities combined give Masland more than one-million square feet of production space, and with the favorable position of continuing growth, the physical plant will expand again in 2001.

Masland's strength in the marketplace is founded upon the company's commitment to style and design. With one of the industry's widest selections of distinctively different carpets and rugs, Masland is a consistent award-winning specialist in complex, sophisticated textures and patterns.

Masland's clientele includes upscale retail establishments such as Nordstrom, Saks Fifth Avenue, and Neimann-Marcus. Masland also has a long list of prestigious installations such as ProPlayer Stadium in Miami; the historically registered Hotel Dupont in Wilmington, Delaware; the Georgia Dome in Atlanta; and the San Francisco City Hall in California.

Though international in scope, Masland is a concerned corporate citizen on the local level and actively supports America's Junior Miss, the United Way, Mobile Museum of Art, Mobile Area Education Foundation, and the Chamber of Commerce's Millennium Fund. In addition, Masland partners with Robbins Middle School in Prichard. Having established itself as one of the region's fastest-growing companies, Masland is committed to excelling as the foremost supplier of design-oriented carpets and rugs in the floor covering industry, while remaining a corporation with a strong sense of environmental and civic responsibility.

(above) Masland's commercial Chicago showroom.

(left) Masland offers an extensive area rug line.

DUPONT AGRICULTURAL PRODUCTS

DuPont Agricultural Products in Axis, Alabama, is a division of one of the oldest continuously operating industrial enterprises in the world. Specializing in the manufacture of crop protection products for farmers, the plant is a leader in developing a new generation of "selective" products that target only insects harmful to crops, leaving "beneficials"—like bees and predator insects—unharmed. The plant also manufactures specialty chemicals used in the manufacture of DuPont Lycra®, Kodak film, and other popular products.

In keeping with its tradition of social responsibility, DuPont is renowned for its rigorous company-wide safety program—a part of the corporate culture rooted in the company's 1802 founding as a manufacturer of gun powder. The du Pont families, who lived at the plant site on the banks of the Brandywine River, outside Wilmington, Delaware, worked in the mills alongside employees. Family members initiated all new procedures themselves, asking no employee to perform work they would not do themselves. The DuPont plant in Axis, built by Shell in 1968 and purchased by DuPont in 1986, has not had a "lost workday case"—an on-the-job injury that caused an employee to miss work—since its purchase.

DuPont is also proud of its excellent environmental record, with plant-wide recycling programs for paper, aluminum, wooden pallets, and some metals. The plant, located miles inland from the Mobile River, treats waste water onsite to diminish any impact on area waterways. And the company's air emissions are low, consistently exceeding regulatory requirements.

Through its involvement with the LeMoyne Industrial Park Community Advisory Panel, DuPont has developed a strong relationship with the surrounding community. The plant and its neighbors maintain an ongoing dialogue on issues relating to business progress, new products, and process changes, as well as adherence to air and water regulations.

A unique feature of the DuPont plant is its location on the original site of "Old Mobile." The company has set the area aside in perpetual easement to the Archaeological Conservancy—a national non-profit organization dedicated to preserving important archaeological sites for research. DuPont is committed to ensuring the site is protected for future generations, and helps fund research by the University of South Alabama.

DuPont is respected worldwide for its community involvement, and the Axis plant is no exception, generously supporting the United Way, Mobile Symphony, and Mobile Art Museum. With a strong commitment to education, the company participates in the Adopt-A-School program, partnering with Calcedeaver Elementary in Mt. Vernon, tutoring and reading to students, giving financial support, and helping maintain the facility. The Mobile plant annually awards a scholarship to Bishop State Community College's Process and Instrumentation Technology Program.

Since 1986, DuPont Agricultural Products has been proud to be a member of the Mobile-area community and to fulfill its corporate mission of delivering science-based solutions that make a difference in people's lives.

(above) Production facility for Steward®, a new crop protection product that targets only harmful insects leaving beneficials unharmed. *Photo by Aaron Tesney*

(right) Employees of the DuPont Site who work daily to insure safe operations and quality products. *Photo by Aaron Tesney*

CHAPTER TWELVE

12

The Professions

Photo by Steve Goraum/Studio G!

LYONS, PIPES & COOK

(above) The offices of Lyons, Pipes & Cook are located at 2 North Royal Street in the downtown business district. The firm offers a wide range of legal services, representing local, regional, domestic, and international clients.

(right) Long-term relationships have been the key to the firm's success and the basis for its growth.

Lyons, Pipes & Cook, one of the South's leading law firms, was founded in 1899 by Joseph H. Lyons, a Harvard law school graduate. Initially, the firm was comprised of two partners—Mr. Lyons and Thomas Stevens, a renowned trial lawyer. For years, the firm was located on the fifth floor of the original First National Bank building. In 1967, the firm moved to the newly completed First National Bank building, now known as the AmSouth Bank building, where they occupied the 25th floor. In 1979, Lyons, Pipes & Cook completed construction of its present offices at 2 North Royal Street. At the time, downtown Mobile was in a decline and businesses were relocating to west Mobile. By constructing its new offices at this corner, the firm helped to pioneer the revitalization of downtown Mobile.

Today, Lyons, Pipes & Cook has 25 attorneys practicing in nearly every area of law. Now in its second century of providing sound, experienced counsel and representation to local, regional, national, and international clients, Lyons, Pipes & Cook continues to be respected for its unquestionable integrity, outstanding client service, value, and quality.

Lyons, Pipes & Cook was originally known for its insurance defense practice, representing most of the major insurance carriers in the United States. Today, the firm offers representation in the following areas: alternative dispute resolution, appellate law, corporate law, criminal defense, domestic and family law, employment law, environmental law, estate planning, personal and commercial litigation, maritime, oil and gas, professional liability defense, real estate, tax law, and worker's compensation.

One of the keys to the firm's success is its ability to attract top legal talent—attorneys who not only have the knowledge, experience, and sound judgment needed to be successful, but who combine these attributes with care, compassion, and community involvement. These skills are nurtured and rewarded at Lyons, Pipes & Cook, resulting in exceptional service and a high degree of loyalty from its clients. Many of the firm's clients have been with the firm for over 50 years. Long-term relationships have been the key to the firm's success and continue to be the basis for its growth.

While Lyons, Pipes & Cook is proud of its heritage and service,

it is firmly committed to meeting the challenges of the future as well. Its attorneys and staff are supported by state-of-the-art research, communications, and information processing equipment, which enhance every phase of operation. The firm's Web site, www.LPClaw.com, is one of the most innovative law firm Web sites in the region and contains a wealth of information, including research and legal links, as well as links to community activities and events. In 2000, Lyons, Pipes & Cook became the first U.S. law firm to purchase Keystone Professional, a fully integrated business application solution for professional service firms, which is destined to be an industry leader. All of these place the firm on the cutting edge of legal technology.

Lyons, Pipes & Cook is actively involved in the community. The firm values community service and encourages all attorneys and staff to take proactive roles. Additionally, the firm has members who volunteer their time to serve on Mobile Bar Association Committees, State of Alabama Disciplinary Commission, and the Alabama State Bar Board of Examiners, among others.

The mission of Lyons, Pipes & Cook is to provide excellent, results-oriented legal services to clients, serving them with loyalty and professionalism, while keeping their future best interests in mind; to maintain the integrity of the firm; and to ensure a quality work environment. Through focus and dedication to these principles, Lyons, Pipes & Cook will continue to be one of the South's leading law firms for another hundred years.

(above) Lyons, Pipes & Cook attracts top legal talent—attorneys who not only have the knowledge, experience, and sound judgment needed to be successful, but who combine these attributes with caring, compassion, and community involvement.

(left) The staff at Lyons, Pipes & Cook is supported by state-of-the-art research, communications, and information processing equipment to enhance every phase of operations.

PIERCE, LEDYARD, LATTA, WASDEN & BOWRON, P.C.

Pierce, Ledyard, Latta, Wasden & Bowron, P.C., is a full-service law firm that offers Mobile and the greater Gulf Coast a broad range of legal services including admiralty, appellate practice, commercial law, corporate and transactions practice, labor and employment, litigation, wills and estates, and governmental law. The firm is committed to a service-minded philosophy that gives top priority to client satisfaction no matter how large or small the matter.

The Firm's History

The firm was founded in 1991 by a group that included Don Pierce and Forrest Latta. Mr. Pierce drew upon his 32 years of litigation and managerial experience with Mobile's largest law firm, and Mr. Latta brought experience in business and insurance litigation. Over the next few years the firm quickly attracted some of the state's most accomplished practitioners. Real estate and transactions expert Goodman Ledyard joined within six months. The next year Bill Wasden left his position as general counsel to Alabama's governor to join the firm. In 1997 one of the state's most active litigators, Ed Bowron, moved his practice to the firm, and the following year Alabama's senior maritime practitioner, Abe Philips, established the firm's admiralty and maritime department.

Having celebrated a decade of service, the firm has grown rapidly to keep pace with the needs of its clients, and has more than quadrupled in size since its founding. Now with 25 lawyers, and a support staff in excess of 40, the firm is among the largest in South Alabama and the northern Gulf Coast of Florida and Mississippi.

The firm's attorneys have been committed to serving the community by offering volunteer legal services to the poor. They serve on public boards and charities, and are actively involved in their local churches. The firm also has been honored to represent many non-profit business and professional associations in forums ranging from state courts to the U.S. Supreme Court. Those include the Business Council of Alabama, Defense Research Institute, National Association of Insurance Commissioners, Alabama Defense Lawyers Association, National Association of Mutual Insurance Companies, Product Liability Advisory Council, and Insurance Environmental Litigation Association.

Affiliations

Pierce, Ledyard, Latta, Wasden & Bowron, P.C. is the only south Alabama member of the American Law Firm Association (ALFA). ALFA is the oldest and largest non-profit association of law firms operating worldwide. ALFA membership is limited to one firm in each geographical region. Membership is by invitation only and follows a rigorous application and peer review admissions process. All member firms operate independently, combining the unique advantages of a respected local law firm with the strengths and resources of an international law capability. There currently are more than 118 ALFA member firms across America and in Canada, Europe, Asia, Latin America, and Australia. Over 7,000 lawyers and solicitors in ALFA's member firms handle both litigation and transactional matters, with practices in every legal specialty.

The firm and its lawyers also hold memberships in many leading practice organizations, such as the International Association of Defense Counsel, Federation of Insurance and Corporate Counsel, Defense Research Institute, Maritime Law Association, Product

(above) From left: Edward G. Bowron, Goodman G. Ledyard, Forrest S. Latta, Donald F. Pierce, and H. William Wasden.

(right) Pictured from left: Linda Sims (seated), Berna Sellers; W. Perry Hall, Goodman G. Ledyard (seated), and Joy A. Jaye.
Photos by Jane Tucker Photography

Liability Advisory Council, Trial Attorneys of America, The Alabama Real Estate Attorneys Association and Southeastern Admiralty Institute. Several firm members have held state and national leadership positions in those organizations.

Practice Areas: Client Services and Litigation Representation

Pierce, Ledyard, Latta, Wasden & Bowron, P.C., has developed a reputation as a trusted counselor and legal advisor to local, national, and international businesses; privately-held companies; state and local government; and individual clients, offering a full range of legal services as both trial advocates and as legal advisors in non-litigation settings. The firm attempts to develop a partner relationship with its clients, the goal of which is to define the most efficient, practical approach rather than "one size fits all." The firm's constant goal is to exceed client expectations, distinguishing it in both client service and value.

The firm's practice encompasses a wide variety of legal service areas. The admiralty and maritime lawyers represent shipowners, operators, P&I Clubs, and other marine interests. The firm's appellate practitioners handle appeals from trials and frequently also appear as counsel for *amici curiae* non-parties. The firm's commercial lawyers have forged a growing practice in business reorganizations, creditors' rights, and bankruptcy, representing domestic lenders as well as the financial interests of insurance and commercial finance companies. As the central activity of the firm's commercial practice, the real estate transactions personnel offer a complete range of legal services related to the ownership, development, and management of real property, including acquisition and disposition of real property, financing, leasing and workouts, foreclosure, bankruptcy, and restructurings.

Underlying all practice areas is the firm's litigation capability. Litigation advocacy at all forum levels is one of the firm's primary strengths, with the firm's litigators practicing before federal and state trial and appellate courts and administrative agencies throughout Alabama and the greater Gulf Coast. The firm also handles arbitration, mediation and alternative dispute proceedings, and represents clients in investigations by state and federal agencies such as the Department of Justice, the Treasury Department, and the IRS.

Commitment to Clients and Community

The lawyers and staff of Pierce, Ledyard, Latta, Wasden & Bowron are committed to serving Alabama and the region through the pursuit of excellence in the practice of law. The firm's practice has continued to evolve to fulfill that commitment as its lawyers serve a rapidly changing world. In honoring that commitment, the firm also advances the interests of the legal profession, the judicial system, and the community. Having just celebrated its first decade of service, the firm salutes the City of Mobile on the historic occasion of its Tricentennial.

(above) Pictured from left: John Charles S. Pierce, C. William Daniels, Jr., W. Pemble DeLashmet, and Abe L. Phillips, Jr.

(left) Donald F. Pierce.

Photos by Jane Tucker Photography

ARMBRECHT JACKSON LLP

Armbrecht Jackson LLP is one of the oldest law firms in Alabama, tracing its roots to the late 19th century. Will Armbrecht, considered to be the firm's principal founder, was a noted jurist with a national reputation as an authority on municipal finance and served as U.S. Attorney under Republican presidents from 1904 to 1913. In the more than 100 years since its founding, Armbrecht Jackson has grown into a major regional firm with 39 lawyers licensed to practice in six states.

Armbrecht Jackson represents a wide variety of clients, including companies involved in banking, commercial lending, oil and gas, lumber and timber, stevedoring, international aviation, international shipping, shipbuilding and repair, and paper and chemical manufacturing, as well as railroads, insurance companies, and various medical and other professionals and their underwriters. In addition, the firm represents a number of trusts, individuals, and non-profit organizations.

Armbrecht Jackson's attorneys try cases in state and federal courts in the region, as well as before administrative agencies such as the Public Service Commission and the State Oil and Gas Board. The firm handles virtually every type of lawsuit, primarily on the defense side or as corporate plaintiffs. Recently, the firm has been involved for the defense in a number of high-profile lawsuits, such as the Amtrak train derailment disaster in Bayou Canot and multi-million dollar class action lawsuits against oil and gas companies, insurance companies, banks, and computer software companies, as well as medical malpractice suits against doctors and hospitals throughout the region.

In its corporate and business practice, the firm offers a full range of legal services to businesses and professional associations, and its areas of expertise include banking and finance; taxation, ERISA, and estate planning; real estate; oil, gas, natural resources, and utilities regulation; health care; labor relations and employment; intellectual properties; international trade; and securities law. Yet the firm's departmental structure is sufficiently flexible to allow an attorney specializing in one area of practice to work with any other lawyer in the firm, according to the individual needs of the client. The client's needs come first, and each client is able to tap into the expertise of any of the firm's team of 39 attorneys, 16 of which have been listed in "The Best Lawyers in America©" in various areas of practice.

Community service and civic pride are top priorities at Armbrecht Jackson. The firm is a major supporter of the Mobile Bar Association's Pro Bono program—offering legal services to area residents who cannot afford to hire an attorney.

Armbrecht Jackson's century-old legacy is as solid as its reputation: Quality service for every client.

No representation is made that the quality of the legal services to be performed is greater than the quality of legal services performed by other lawyers.

(right) Shown are lawyers Scott Brown, Connie Armbrecht, and Mary Carol Ladd.

GOTTLIEB, BARNETT & BRIDGES, LLC

Gottlieb, Barnett & Bridges is a Mobile-based consulting engineering firm with an international reputation for engineering services used in the design of waterfront facilities, material-handling equipment, and other marine and industrial related applications. The firm was founded in 1954 as Ewin, Campbell & Gottlieb, and in the 1990s opened a second office in Elizabeth, New Jersey, that specializes in facility and container yard planning and construction management.

Since 1956, Gottlieb, Barnett & Bridges (GBB) has worked closely with Sea-Land Service, Inc., handling a broad range of consulting and design engineering work for Sea-Land's global containerized shipping facilities—beginning with an initial assignment to design and manage the building of the world's first container-handling cranes. Ten of these cranes were built in Mobile and installed on the world's first fully-containerized vessels. Since then, GBB has designed most of the shipboard cranes used by Sea-Land and has written specifications for all of its shore-based cranes at U.S. ports on the Atlantic, Pacific, and Gulf Coasts, as well a ports in the Caribbean, Europe, Mid East, Far East, and Australia. GBB continues to work closely with Maersk Sealand, CSX World Terminals, and CSX Lines to plan, design, modify, and relocate cranes, as well as to design facilities at home and abroad.

GBB has extensive experience consulting with port authorities around the world—from New Orleans and New York to Dubai and San Juan—conducting feasibility studies, providing expert recommendations, and following up with detailed design services for virtually every aspect of port development.

GBB offers engineering services to shipyard-related industries and has worked with clients such as Friede Goldman Halter, Bender Shipbuilding, Atlantic Dry Dock Corp., Atlantic Marine, Inc., and Alabama Shipyard, Inc. These projects include the design of shipbuilding ways, piers and bulkheads, and erection yards.

In addition to maritime-related industries, GBB handles new plant design and modifications to existing heavy-industry facilities, such as Kerr-McGee, Hess Oil Corporation, Texaco, and Degussa Corporation.

With a top-notch staff of world-class civil, structural, mechanical, and electrical engineers, Gottlieb, Barnett & Bridges is proud of its reputation as the firm of choice for handling major projects requiring innovative solutions to complex and challenging problems.

(above) Alabama State Port Authority, McDuffie Import Facility. GBB provided conceptual planning, detailed engineering design, and equipment procurement services for this coal and iron ore import facility.

(left) Salalah Port Services Company, Port Salalah, Salalah, Oman. GBB provided conceptual planning, engineering review, and equipment procurement services for this state-of-the-art container transhipment facility.

CLARK, GEER, LATHAM & ASSOCIATES, INC.

Clark, Geer, Latham & Associates is a multi-disciplined engineering, architectural, and planning services firm founded in 1974. With expertise in all phases of project management—from conception to completion of construction-Clark, Geer, Latham (CGL) serves major industrial, commercial, private, and governmental clients throughout the southeast.

CGL's greatest strengths are found in its high level of technical capability, dedication to customer service, and commitment to the highest professional standards. As a result, the firm has established a number of long-term client relationships representing a broad spectrum of the market—including various industries, food distribution, commercial, educational, recreational, waterfront development, and religious concerns.

Widely respected for its comprehensive approach to engineering, architecture, and planning, CGL offers a full complement of services. Engineering services include civil, structural, mechanical, and electrical design. In addition, the firm offers environmental and construction permitting, preparation of bid documents, and construction management services. CGL's architectural services include master planning, and architectural programming, design, and modeling. The firm's planning services encompass site analysis, zoning studies, flood plain analysis, and overall master planning.

Working with clients throughout the country, CGL has built an impressive portfolio of projects that demonstrate the firm's unique capabilities. For example, CGL was responsible for all aspects of the design and construction management of a world-class wood chip handling facility in Theodore, Alabama. In addition, CGL has been involved with a number of large food distribution facilities across the southeastern United States. Several of these facilities encompass nearly 10 acres under roof and include minus 20-degree freezer space as well as conventional warehousing. The design and construction management of the Mobile area's newest marine liquid bulk terminal, which services deep-draft vessels, is another project in which CGL's capabilities were instrumental. CGL is also proud of its professional contribution to the development and construction of several of the newest facilities in the Mobile County Public School system.

The firm is led by J. M. Clark—one of CGL's founders who brings more than 40 years' experience to the job—and Thomas E. Latham, a registered Professional engineer in more than 30 states with dual degrees in mechanical and civil engineering. Together they lead a team of dedicated professionals in providing exceptional service to valued clients.

(above) Sysco Food Services of Central Florida, Palmetto, Florida.

(right) Mobile Bay Woodchip Center, Theodore, Alabama.

STUDIO G!

For Steve Goraum, owner of Studio G!, "taking a picture" is much more than just pushing a button. "When I take a photograph," says Goraum, "I'm telling a story. By taking an ordinary idea—combined with thought, planning, and clean, crisp execution—I can turn that idea into something unique and individual for my client."

Goraum developed a passion for photography as a teenager, and soon the native Mobilian sought formal training. A bachelor's degree from the prestigious Brooks Institute of Photography in Santa Barbara gave Goraum a solid technical and creative foundation for his future work.

After graduation in 1983, several years at a photography department within an Oklahoma City ad agency further prepared him for life as a professional photographer. "That experience taught me that the work isn't about being an *artiste*. It's about understanding a client's needs and delivering an excellent product." In 1988, when Goraum decided to open his own studio, he returned to his hometown.

Today, the walls of Studio G! are lined with striking, glossy color prints illustrating Goraum's meticulous approach to his craft for clients like Exxon, Minolta/QMS, Masland, Milliken, and Time/Life. One of his most challenging assignments was to photograph an $8,000-magnetic-resonance stereo speaker to convey a sense of sound and motion. Sixty-one exposures on a single sheet of film taken over a period of 1.5 hours provided the perfect stroboscopic image. One of Goraum's most enjoyable assignments was a two-week stint in Paris, working with French models, photographing a series of posters promoting French food and wines.

For a national "product shot" assignment, Goraum was able to indulge another passion, scuba-diving. Submerged in an enormous aquarium, he withstood 52-degree water to capture the exact moment a fish struck the client's lure.

In addition to product photography, industrial photography constitutes a large part of Goraum's work load—a challenge he enjoys "I find it satisfying to take a mundane work environment, and by using light and shadow and the basic tools of the trade, turn the shot into something really special," he says. "It's like being a magician."

Goraum also works his photographic magic in Studio G!'s fully equipped, 6,800-square-foot studio, where he can shoot products as large as luxury automobiles in a perfectly controlled environment. Keeping one step ahead of technology is another Studio G! specialty—from high-quality digital photography to web-delivery of the finished product.

"I'm a lucky man," says Goraum. "I've been pursuing photography since I was 14 years old, and enjoy every minute of it. It's nice to be able to make a career out of something you love." The picture-perfect life.

22690

CHAPTER THIRTEEN

Real Estate, Development & Construction

Photo by Steve Goraum/Studio G!

THOMPSON ENGINEERING

When Henry Seawell and Thompson Engineering are confronted with a compelling problem, they work out a plan to solve it. Whether designing a massive floating building that connects directly to a land-based hotel, or assembling a world-class firm that offers a comprehensive range of engineering services, the method is the same—strategic thinking and a systematic approach. Founded as a small testing lab in 1953, Thompson Engineering today is a dynamic, wholly employee-owned company with more than 200 people on staff. This unusual organizational structure has allowed for carefully planned corporate growth and the expansion of services in a broad range of engineering-related disciplines, points out Seawell, company president and CEO. In fact, says Seawell, Thompson may be the only company in the U.S. that offers such a complete array of services—from conceptual planning, engineering design and consulting, geotechnical engineering and environmental planning, to permitting, construction management processes, and quality-assurance testing.

Having tripled its workforce and quadrupled revenues in a recent six-year period, Thompson has become one of the largest engineering companies in the southeast—doing business in 26 states, and Central America. But Seawell is committed to the Mobile area—the strength of its economy and the well-being of its workforce. All of Thompson's financial business is conducted locally—with corporate profits remaining in the city. In addition, almost all of the company's directors, stockholders, and employees are from the Mobile/Baldwin County area.

High-Profile Projects

One glance at their project portfolio, and it's easy to see how essential the planning process is to everything Thompson Engineering undertakes. When the company became involved in the City/County Government Plaza project, their work included soil and foundation analysis and a redesign of the subterranean structures that reduced vibrations and protected neighboring historic buildings from damage. Thompson's planning saved the county more than $1 million. And the project incurred no budget overruns and no legal claims—an impressive accomplishment for a job of this magnitude and sensitivity.

In two other noted Mobile undertakings—the construction of Hank Aaron Stadium and the British Steel DRI Mill—Thompson's full service in-house staff collaborated with governmental and industrial managers to design site-foundation systems that trimmed more than $2,000,000 from construction budgets. The company's environmental studies, soil analyses, process systems techniques, and quality assurance helped create viable pollution-free downstream discharges. At the stadium site, a productive, highly visible wetland area that effectively filters pollutants from storm water remains an attractive feature at the private/public entertainment park.

In addition to high-profile regional jobs, Thompson serves many nationally recognized clients—including Ruby Tuesday, Rite Aid, and The Southern Companies. On many of these projects, Thompson handles all of the engineering, architectural, and quality assurance services. Another notable service contact includes the

(above) Engineering design and foundation recommendations for the 120-year-old Alabama State Capitol in Montgomery.

(right) A key player in both the initial and second-generation industrial development of the Middle Bay Port, as well as, the development of the area around the Theodore Industrial Canal.

design and construction management of Caesar's World Indiana—the largest riverboat casino in North America.

And for the "floating building" problem mentioned earlier—Thompson tapped its marine-engineering capability and expertise in the offshore drilling industry to design the world's largest sea-anchored, semi-submersible barge structure for the Beau Rivage in Biloxi.

Achieving Goals

A serious commitment to a carefully conceived strategic plan drives every step that Thompson takes. A training program for all employees, from senior management to staffers on the "front lines," ensures that all Thompson personnel are continually working to accomplish the company's goals—a key concern of and primary benefit for the company's employee-owners.

Seawell takes pride in the fact that Thompson is proactive in its business practices—and becomes neither "overly expectant" during a good economy nor tentative in a weak one. By steadily pursuing its strategic goals, the company remains strong regardless of external influences. "In essence," says Seawell, "we flatten the ups and downs."

TCO, Incorporated

One of the keys to Thompson's success is its affiliation with TCO, an employee-owned engineering holding company with eight subsidiaries—Thompson Engineering, Pope Engineering and Testing, Richburg & Rickett, Harper & Garratt Engineering, Watermark Design Group, Thompson Industrial Services, and Thompson Transportation and Infrastructure. These subsidiaries, of which each employee is a TCO stockholder, enable Thompson to bring a broader range of value-added services to each project—from architectural and master planning services to material testing, surveying, and construction management.

Although earlier perceptions persisted regarding Thompson and its holding company's aggressive business growth plan, the Mobile/Baldwin County community now understands that the TCO affiliates each are independently operated companies with a common goal of quality responsive service.

The innovative TCO corporate approach is a model local firms can follow that will enable them to remain in the Mobile area through internal capitalization—producing entrepreneurial owner-employees and preventing impersonal absorption into out-of-town business concerns. TCO's chief executive views maximum small business employment and the maintenance of net revenues within the local community and banking system as essential to the future growth and prosperity of the community.

Just The Beginning

The past few years have been a time of amazing growth for Thompson Engineering—meriting it a spot on the Mobile Area Chamber of Commerce's "Future 30" list. The company has also exceeded every strategic goal it has set for itself—an accomplishment that Seawell is particularly proud of. "We're a new-generation corporate model driven by client demand for seamless service. At Thompson, an overriding commitment to quality characterizes everything we do. And this," Seawell says animatedly, "is just the beginning."

(above) Thompson Engineering has played a significant role in the redevelopment of Historic Downtown Mobile and the Mobile River Waterfront.

(left) Assuring the preservation of historic structures, such as the Greek Orthodox Church in Malbis.

VANCE McCOWN CONSTRUCTION COMPANY, INC.

To call Vance McCown Construction (VMC) a general contracting company is really an over-simplification. "We're design/build contractors," says Vance McCown, VMC founder, "who act as the link that unites the owner/developer, the design consultants, and the contractor."

Specializing in commercial, institutional, and industrial construction, VMC has earned a reputation as a full-service construction partner. By participating in every aspect of the construction process—from initial design to final inspection—VMC works hard to anticipate potential problems, with the goal of completing each project on time and within budget.

Since its incorporation in 1983, VMC has established solid working relationships with an impressive roster of clients such as Rex TV, Kimberly-Clark, Inchcape Shipping, the Federal Bureau of Investigation, AmSouth Bank, and Providence Hospital.

McCown is quick to credit one person in particular for contributing to his success. In fact, you might say Vance McCown knows the construction business from the ground up, having learned from his father, Tom McCown—a realtor/contractor/developer experienced in building single-family dwellings as well as condominiums. Vance's father also taught him the importance of open communication with the client, the engineers, and everyone involved in a project.

(above) Federal Bureau of Investigation Project, Mobile, Alabama.

(right) Downtowner Corporate Center, Mobile, Alabama.

Total Involvement

Vance McCown Construction specializes in "total involvement" in every project, communicating openly and establishing a foundation of trust.

One example of VMC's total involvement with a client is Providence Hospital. VMC helped hospital administrators calculate site improvement expenses and select the best site for the new Rehabilitation and Wellness Center, then designed a structure that would blend in with the rest of the campus. So pleased was the administration with this project, that they turned to VMC again when it was time to construct an additional Providence Medical Office building, as well as a central laundry plant for Providence, Mobile Infirmary, and Spring Hill Memorial hospitals.

The VMC Team

VMC prides itself on the professional development of its staff. Courses like computer estimating training and product and quality control classes enable VMC associates to enhance their skills and provide exceptional customer service. Many employees who began working for VMC in the building trade have gone on to become project supervisors and managers. "The policy of promoting from within is a win-win situation," says McCown. Not only do the employees and the company benefit, but clients also have the advantage of working with project managers with extensive, practical, hands-on experience.

Butler Manufacturing

"Customization"—avoiding the "cookie cutter" look by bringing a fresh perspective to every project—is another specialty at VMC. For this reason, VMC does not employ a staff architect, preferring to contract with independent architects who possess the unique qualities and experience that are best suited to each individual job.

As a dealer for Butler Manufacturing, the leader in pre-engineered structures and building systems, VMC's renowned ability to customize projects is highly valued and respected. Such handsome buildings as the University of South Alabama's Mitchell Center and Southeast College of Technology belie the "pre-fab" image of their pre-engineered structural steel frames.

In addition, the design of the Mitchell Center's framework helped minimize loss of floor area and maximize seating area, while simplifying the framing of the concourse and seat decks. "Through our partnership with Butler Manufacturing, we're able to offer our clients handsome, attractive, sturdy, well-designed buildings," says McCown, "plus, a 20-year-warranty on the roof."

Long-Term Relationships

"Repeat business," says McCown, "is somewhat unusual in the construction industry, with many single-project clients." VMC, however, has developed an excellent working relationship with a number of clients over the years—some for as many as 18 years. Among the impressive "regulars" on VMC's client list: Rex TV and Appliance (18 years), Gleason & Associates (10 years), Metcalfe & Company (10 years), Robert Meador Warehousing (10 years), and Providence Hospital (8 years).

A quick glance at VMC's portfolio of completed projects reveals a striking array of styles and designs—from the classic simplicity of Eaton Square in Spring Hill and Gus's Azalea City Manor Restaurant to the handsome functionality of the World Omni Financial Center and the Ciba-Geigy Distribution Center.

Yet no matter how diverse the design, VMC remains committed to one goal: providing quality design and construction services that not only meet, but exceed, client expectations on every project.

(above) Rex TV & Appliance, a satisfied customer providing repeat business for VMC since its incorporation in 1983.

(below) Structural steel frame furnished for the University of South Alabama Sports Arena.

J.S. WALTON & CO., INC.

One visit to the office of J. S. Walton & Co., Inc., a leading heavy, highway, and industrial contractor in the Mobile area, and it's easy to see this is a company that takes great pride in its history and tradition. "We're in our third generation," says company president Norman J. Walton Jr., gesturing at a vintage black-and-white photo hanging on the wall. Norman, along with his brother William R. Walton, company vice-president, oversees the business established by the man in the photo—their grandfather, John S. Walton Sr.

Founded in 1919 in Brandenberug, Kentucky, one of the company's first jobs was building sidewalks in the small town of Princeton, Kentucky. After a move to Gardner, Florida, in 1927, the company built four bridges before relocating to Mobile. In 1945, Norman J. Walton Sr. and John S. Walton Jr. joined their father's firm, and continued to perform extensive construction work in the heavy, highway, and industrial areas. As the holder of "Alabama Contractor's License #31," J. S. Walton & Co., Inc., is one of longest-operating construction companies in the state.

(above) J. S. Walton & Co., Inc. has been instrumental in the development of the transportation network for Mobile and Baldwin Counties, recently completing The Foley Beach Express.

(right) The diversity in construction that J. S. Walton & Co., Inc. provides to its clients is shown by The Foley Beach Express.

The Road to the Future

The Walton's respect for their company's heritage is coupled with a progressive attitude about the business's future. As a specialist in heavy, highway, and industrial construction, drainage projects, and plant-site development, J. S. Walton & Co. has played a key role in a number of projects contributing to Mobile and Baldwin Counties' explosive growth —from the region's transportation infrastructure to downtown redevelopment.

J. S. Walton & Co. was instrumental in completing one of the area's most ambitious road-construction projects, the Foley Beach Express. Designed to alleviate the high volume of traffic to Gulf Shores, and to serve as an evacuation route, the Express project consists of three separate phases: a 7.5-mile roadway from Alabama Highway 59 South to Baldwin County Highway 20, a 6.4-mile roadway from Highway 20 to the Toll Plaza, and the approaches for the toll bridge across the intercoastal waterway to Canal Road. J. S. Walton & Co. built the first phase as a project for the City of Foley and participated in the second phase with a privately owned company. During the 15-month construction project, J. S. Walton & Co. moved more than 1,500,000 cubic yards of excavated material and was awarded the prestigious 2001 Build Alabama award for new highway construction by the Alabama Branch of the Associated General Contractors of America.

The company's road construction projects have had a dramatic effect on the quality of life in the area. The widening of University Boulevard greatly improved access to the University of South Alabama, the expansion of Highway 98 in Fairhope helped facilitate an extremely high traffic flow, and the rehabilitation of Water Street was an important element in energizing downtown re-development.

A major player in the region's industrial development, J. S. Walton & Co. has provided extensive plant-site developments in Mobile and surrounding areas. J. S. Walton & Co. also handled site development for Naval Station Mobile at the Navy Homeport and a runway addition at Bates Field.

Quality People, Corporate Success

J. S. Walton & Co. takes great pride in its safety record—having participated in a number of high-risk jobs without incident. "This is really a tribute to our employees," says Norman and William Walton, "and the active role they take in the company's safety program. The quality of our people is what makes our company so successful." Some J. S. Walton & Co. employees have been with the company for more than 40 years.

Involvement in the community is top priority, and J. S. Walton & Co. actively supports the Mobile Area Chamber of Commerce, South Alabama Regional Planning Commission, Mobile Area Boy Scouts of America, and the Delchamps Senior Bowl.

J. S. Walton & Co. is an active participant in a number of professional organizations including the Alabama Branch, Associated General Contractors of America, the Alabama Road Builder's Association, Inc., and the Mobile County Road Builder's Association.

J.S. Walton & Co., Inc., a name synonymous with quality, stability, and safety throughout the Mobile area, has been a part of Mobile's past growth, and is an active part of the present, with a dedicated eye cast toward the future, remaining ever sensitive to the special construction needs of its many clients along the Gulf Coast.

(above) J. S. Walton & Co., Inc. is active in the growth of Fairhope with such projects as US 98.

(left) The widening of University Boulevard in front of the University of South Alabama in Mobile reduced much of the traffic gridlock that previously existed.

HOSEA O. WEAVER & SONS, INC.

State-of-the-art Hot Mix Asphalt Plant located in Mobile.

Hosea Weaver—born "four miles behind the Castleberry post office"—got his start in construction close to home in Conecuh County in 1938. In 1952, he moved to Mobile County and began his own company, H. O. Weaver Construction. By day he dug fishponds for clients. By night he performed maintenance on his bulldozer to keep it running.

In 1955, Weaver Construction was awarded its first county contract, and two years later, its first state contract. Hosea changed the name of the business to Weaver & Morris Construction Co., Inc., when he took on a partner, Joe Morris. Morris died in 1969. Weaver's sons, Paul and Calvin, started their own company, Hosea O. Weaver & Sons, Inc., in 1973 with the help of their father, and in 1985 they bought their father's business, retaining the Weaver and Sons name.

Today, half a century since its founding, Weaver & Sons is a respected, full-service highway and industrial sitework contractor, with more than 175 employees, specializing in hot-mix asphalt manufacturing and laydown, site excavation and grading, and the installation of stormwater and sanitary sewers.

Asphalt Division

Weaver operates three hot-mix asphalt plants: two in Mobile County and one in Clark County. As Mobile's only locally owned and operated asphalt company, Weaver & Sons possesses a unique sense of responsibility to the community, as exemplified by its newest facility—a state-of-the-art plant on Cut-Off Road. In keeping with the company's "good neighbor" policy, Weaver & Sons attractively landscaped the site with Leland cypress, live oaks, slash pines, and sweet gums. A handsome eight-foot privacy fence helps screen the plant site from the surrounding community. And the company's use of rail service for off-loading greatly reduces the amount of truck traffic, and the resultant wear and tear on the road.

In designing the site's detention pond, Weaver & Sons exceeded the environmental regulations. Run-off water meanders through a maze of concrete "fingers," decreasing the siltation of Three-Mile Creek. The planting of grass and wetland species such as lilies and canes further filters the water.

The plant utilizes the industry's newest technology, such as computer-controlled calibration instruments, resulting in more precise mixes that resist rutting and drain better than traditional asphalt. And an innovative system of condensers captures and directs escaped steam back into the mixing tank, virtually eliminating odors.

Paul Weaver, company president, points with pride to the industry's environmental record—recycling 80 percent of removed material back into the manufacture of new asphalt.

Construction Division

The bulk of the company's construction projects consists of road and highway work for the state, as well as private site work—such as for large shopping centers and industrial sites. A key figure in west Mobile's expansion, Weaver & Sons paved most of Schillinger Road from Howell's Ferry to Theodore-Dawes, as well as University Boulevard from Ziegler to Moffet. Weaver has also participated in high-profile projects in Baldwin County, performing site work for Rock Creek and Historic Malbis, as well as a drain-and-pave project on Highway 59.

When asked to cite a particularly challenging project, Paul Weaver doesn't hesitate. "The rehab and widening of I-10 in downtown Mobile," he says. The $30-million job involved constructing additional lanes inside and outside the existing ones, removing the old concrete roadway, and replacing it with new asphalt. In undertaking this job, Weaver became the area's first contractor to crush, size, and recycle the removed concrete back into the hot-mix asphalt used for resurfacing. Operating under a strict time limit with a "penalty/bonus" clause, Weaver completed the I-10 project ahead of schedule, earning the maximum bonus and garnering the Quality Award from the Alabama Asphalt Pavement Association.

Weaver & Sons has also played an important role in the region's industrial development. The company worked closely with the engineering team for the Degussa plant in Theodore Industrial Park, devising an effective drainage system for the site. Weaver also performed the site work for the IPSCO Steel Mill.

A Tradition of Excellence

With a legacy of quality service, Weaver & Sons works very hard to ensure customer satisfaction with a company-wide "Quality Control, Quality Assurance" program. The company is also committed to industry and community improvement through affiliations with the Mobile Area Chamber of Commerce, National Asphalt & Pavement Association, Alabama Business Council, Associated General Contractors of America/Alabama Section, Alabama Asphalt Pavement Association, Alabama Roadbuilders Association, and Mobile County Roadbuilders Association.

"Making asphalt," observes Paul Weaver, "is a lot like making a cake. By blending together an exact combination of the finest ingredients, you get the highest quality product—Weaver & Sons recipe for success."

(above) From left, Calvin Weaver, Hosea Weaver, and Paul Weaver.

(left) Theodore Dawes Road under construction.

CUMMINGS & WHITE-SPUNNER, INC.

Marl Cummings, president of Cummings & White-Spunner—a leading real estate developer in Mobile—can sum up the reasons for the company's success in a single word: experience. "This company has seen it all in 50 years. We know this area like we know the back of our hand," says Cummings. "And the fact that we're still here after all the ups and downs in the economy is no accident."

Founded in 1954, Cummings & White-Spunner is a major shopping center developer in the area, offering a variety of services to its clients, including: property management, leasing, investment properties, residential lots, land development, commercial brokerage, and shopping center development and redevelopment.

After concentrating on residential building during the 1950s and 1960s, the company began specializing in commercial and retail development in the 1970s, with an emphasis on strip shopping centers. From 1985 to 1994, Cummings & White-Spunner was the foremost developer of Delchamps Shopping Centers.

Growth in a Changing Market

"Our traditional core business is changing," says Cummings. "National shifts in the retail arena are affecting us here on the Gulf Coast. But because of our experience in the retail area, we're successfully changing with it."

"Re-purposing" existing properties is an essential part of commercial development today. Cummings & White-Spunner has helped a number of clients successfully relocate into existing properties that have been customized to meet their specific retail needs, eliminating the inconvenience and expense of new construction.

In 1996, Food World vacated its store in Regency Square and moved to a new location within the same shopping center, re-opening as an upscale Bruno's Supercenter. Cummings & White-Spunner reconfigured the former Food World property into an attractive retail outlet for the HomePlace, a popular housewares store, quintupling the return to investors.

Cummings & White-Spunner worked with Wiener's, a national family clothing store, to help them successfully open two Mobile stores in re-configured vacancies in the Dauphin Square Shopping Center and Cottage Village Shopping Center. Cummings & White-Spunner has also participated in the redevelopment of vacant Scotty's stores, handling one such project on Dauphin Street and another at Airport Boulevard and Schillinger Road.

Says Cummings, "Tenants may change, but your investment can still bring a return if you know how to meet the challenges and seize the opportunities. And we do."

(above) Merrill Lynch Pierce Fenner and Smith, 601 North Section Street, Fairhope, Alabama. *Photo by Thigpen Photography*

(below) Regions Financial Center, Hillcrest Road, Mobile, Alabama. *Photo by Thigpen Photography*

Growing Markets in Mobile and Baldwin Counties

Cummings & White-Spunner is playing an important role in the development of the market's major growth areas—Baldwin County and west Mobile. The company has several developments on the Eastern Shore, including Blakely Square Shopping Center in Spanish Fort, and the Merrill-Lynch complex in Fairhope. With a joint venture partner, Cummings & White-Spunner is developing three parcels of land in the vicinity of the Riviera Outlet Centre, one for a major Lowe's Home Improvement Center.

For west Mobile, Marl Cummings foresees even greater expansion as utilities and sewer service become more available. The company has long been a force in the area's development, having handled such projects as Ambassador Plaza at Airport Boulevard and Schillinger Road, and Regions Financial Center on Hillcrest Road. Cummings & White-Spunner has a long association with Regions Bank, dating back to its days as Merchants National, and worked closely with the bank to help relocate several key departments, including Investments and Residential Mortgage

Loans to its attractive new location. Cummings & White-Spunner is actively exploring options for redevelopment in another regional growth market, downtown Mobile.

A Strong Reputation

Cummings & White-Spunner is a member of the International Council of Shopping Centers, the global trade association of the shopping center industry, with 39,000 members in more than 75 countries. The company is active in the Mobile Area Chamber of Commerce, Mobile Area Association of Realtors, and the Mobile Commercial Real Estate Exchange Club whose membership consists of qualifying commercial realtors with a certain high level of education and experience in the field.

Cummings & White-Spunner is owned by Marl Cummings and Rudolph Turner, and is licensed in Florida as well as Alabama, with developments in Panama City and Panama City Beach.

The key to the company's success after half a century of service is quite simple, in the opinion of Marl Cummings. "We've found our niche," he says. "We stick to what we know. We do it, and we do it well. And that translates into more than two million square feet of retail and mixed use space that we've developed in the Mobile metropolitan area."

With its strong market share, Cummings & White-Spunner has been able to capitalize on the changes that have taken place over the years in the local market. "When someone new comes to town, they look around and decide to call the company that is represented in every part of the city. Our reputation is so strong, people come to us. Literally, our reputation precedes us—and it's a good one."

(above) Lowe's Home Improvement Warehouse, Airport Boulevard and Schillinger Road, Mobile, Alabama. *Photo by Thigpen Photography*

(left) Hillwood Shopping Center, Cottage Hill Road and University Boulevard, Mobile, Alabama. *Photo by Thigpen Photography*

SAAD REALTY GROUP, L.L.C.

Working in concert with Saad Development Corporation, Saad Realty Group, L.L.C., has become a premier commercial and industrial real estate brokerage firm in Mobile and Baldwin counties. With the focused objective of meeting and exceeding the commercial and industrial real estate brokerage needs and expectations of its clients and customers, Saad Realty Group offers a complete package of brokerage services ranging from sales and leasing, property management, buyer/tenant representation, and capital and corporate services. These services have been successfully accomplished with all types of commercial properties including office buildings, retail centers, medical facilities, industrial properties, and unimproved land.

An innovative solution Saad Realty Group offers to help meet and exceed the goals of its clients and customers is a unique service called Fee Development. Fee Development Services involves providing all the necessary services for the development of a project from "Concept To Completion." The services offered range from feasibility and cost analysis, site selection and development, selection of engineering and architectural teams, selection and supervision of construction personnel, and the administration of the entire permitting process to the eventual location and placement of end-users for the completed project. One example of a Fee Development project by Saad Realty Group is Heron Lakes, an upscale neighborhood consisting of 125 residential lots for Skyline Country Club and Golf Course in West Mobile.

In order to provide the highest quality of service, the professional agents of Saad Realty Group each specialize in diverse fields of expertise to accommodate the myriad of commercial, investment, and industrial real estate needs required by each client and customer. These agents' unique, professional specialties and their skillful utilization of timely resources and technology all reflect the premier status of Saad Realty Group; they stand ready to meet any need that may arise, whether it would be office space, retail centers, large tracts of unimproved land, investment, and/or industrial properties.

With the continued growth and expansion of Mobile and Baldwin Counties along with the continuing efforts of its professional agents and staff striving to provide the highest quality comprehensive real estate services, Saad Realty Group will continue to be a premier commercial and industrial real estate brokerage firm. The strategic alliance of Saad Development Corporation and Saad Realty Group has allowed the two companies to catapult themselves to the forefront of the Mobile and Baldwin counties commercial and industrial real estate market. By combining their experience, talents, and resources the two companies empower their clients and customers to meet lofty goals. By offering their expertise, Saad Development Corporation and Saad Realty Group assure their clients' success.

(above) Infirmary 65 Building Mobile, Alabama. Home Offices of Saad Realty Group, L.L.C., and Saad Development Corporation.

(right) Hilton Square Office Plaza Mobile, Alabama. A six-story +/- 121,112-square-foot office complex managed by Saad Realty Group and sold by Saad Realty Group as an investment property.

SAAD DEVELOPMENT CORPORATION

Adhering to the philosophy "Building a Better Tomorrow," Saad Development Corporation has been doing just that across the Southeast. By offering the most comprehensive range of development services, Saad Development has brought an unheard of level of commitment to its clients and customers. By lending its more than 20 years of combined experience in Commercial/Industrial and Investment Services, Property Management, as well as Corporate and Capital Services, Saad Development has helped its clients and customers not only achieve but exceed their needs and goals for the future.

Working closely with its real estate brokerage affiliate, Saad Realty Group, L.L.C., Saad Development is able to focus on development project details such as site acquisition and development, feasibility studies, as well as market and cost analysis. This unique positioning of the two companies working in tandem towards a common goal has enabled Saad Development to set and reach new standards once inconceivable in the Southeast's commercial and industrial real estate industry. While Saad Realty Group initially establishes the relationship process by representing the client and/or customer in identifying and locating property, the trust and confidence that grows out of the relationship many times leads the client to retain Saad Development to develop the property.

A crucial element in Saad Development's success over the years is its ability to anticipate, comprehend, and exceed the commercial real estate market's needs. As an increasing number of local, regional, and national companies prefer to lease rather than own their facilities; Saad Development has met this need by cultivating strong, long-lasting build-to-suit relationships. Over the years, Saad Development has developed properties from "Concept To Completion" for such nationally known clients as Federal Express, Hollywood Theaters, and Nationwide Mutual Insurance as well as Blockbuster Video and Bellsouth Mobility, now known as Cingular Wireless. While cultivating and building its relationship with

Federal Express, Saad Development has developed such "Concept to Completion" projects for Federal Express in Alabama, Georgia, Kansas, Louisiana, Tennessee, and Texas.

With a strong infrastructure and favorable business climate in place in Mobile and Baldwin counties, as well as the Southeast, the potential for growth, both new development and re-development, is tremendous. In further refining and enhancing the services offered to meet this new growth head on, Saad Development Corporation's outlook for the future is bright. Continuing with its professional innovations and cutting-edge technology and skills, as well as time tested commercial real estate development solutions for its customers and clients, Saad Development Corporation is successfully facilitating the goal to "Build A Better Tomorrow."

(above) Federal Express Corporation, Nashville, Tennessee. Warehouse/ Distribution Center, one of several built-to-suit by Saad Development Corporation and managed by Saad Realty Group, L.L.C.

(left) BellSouth Mobility now Cingular Wireless, Mobile, Alabama. Local Office and Retail Center built-to-suit by Saad Development Corporation and managed by Saad Realty Group.

VOLKERT & ASSOCIATES, INC.

Few businesses have had as profound an effect on the central Gulf Coast area as Volkert & Associates. From the I-10 Twin Bridges across Mobile Bay to the Perdido Pass Bridge in Baldwin County, Volkert has been instrumental in the planning, designing, and engineering of some of the region's most visible landmarks.

(above) Interstate 165 North Section carries traffic from Interstate 65 into downtown Mobile and represents Volkert's engineering design capabilities.

Rated in the top one percent of all engineering/architectural firms in the U.S. by *Engineering News-Record*, Volkert has evolved from its 1925 founding in New Orleans into one of the nation's leading consulting and design firms, with 500 employees in 12 offices and seven states. Headquartered in Mobile, the company comprises three divisions: Volkert & Associates, Inc., Volkert Construction Services, Inc., and Volkert Environmental Group, Inc.

At the heart of the business is Volkert & Associates, a full-service engineering and architectural design firm specializing in transportation, aviation, architectural, utilities, and port/waterfront design, as well as right-of-way acquisition, surveying, planning, and landscape architecture. Volkert's high-profile projects include the Cochrane/Africatown USA Bridge, the Mobile Regional Airport Terminal Complex, I-10 Bayway, McDuffie Terminal at the Port of Mobile, several schools in Baldwin County, and I-165, North Section. Nationally, Volkert has been recognized for its work in designing the Visitors' Center Complex at Arlington National Cemetery, airport and highway commissions throughout the southeast, and projects for the Ports of Miami and Tampa. The firm's diverse design projects include bridges, highways, stadiums, and utilities, as well as buildings and complexes for educational, industrial, healthcare, and military uses.

Through its Construction Services Division, Volkert offers construction engineering and inspection services to clients like state departments of transportation and local water and sewer systems, supervising projects to ensure they are completed according to specifications. Volkert also provides complete program management, serving as the owner's representative—selecting design engineers and architects, handling contractor bidding, negotiating contracts, managing construction engineering, and inspection—while maintaining project schedules and the client's budget. The firm provides program management for major clients such as the Mobile County Public School System and Alabama State Docks.

(below) The design of the South Alabama Regional Planning Commission's 11,000-square-foot office building in Mobile's Church Street East Historic District showcases Volkert's architectural expertise.

Since the early 1970s, Volkert Environmental Group has compiled an impressive record in a broad range of projects such as environmental impact studies for major thoroughfares, commercial property assessments, wetlands mitigation, hazardous waste studies, ecological and coastal zone studies, storage tank management, and groundwater resource evaluation and management. Employing leading-edge technology, the company develops innovative solutions to problems in sensitive environmental areas.

Recognized for excellence by the National Society of Professional Engineers, the American Consulting Engineers Council, the U.S. Department of the Navy, the U.S. Department of Defense, and the State of Alabama Engineering Hall of Fame, Volkert & Associates brings creativity and cost-effectiveness to each design and engineering project it undertakes. As the company celebrates more than 75 years in business, Volkert remains committed to helping build a comfortable and pleasant environment, and to improving the quality of life in our communities.

SOUTHERN EARTH SCIENCES

Founded by Dr. James E. Laier in 1976, Southern Earth Sciences was originally established with the goal of providing the construction industry with innovative solutions to unusual foundation problems. In the quarter century since its founding, Southern Earth Sciences' range of services has grown to encompass virtually every aspect of geotechnical engineering, construction materials testing, and environmental consulting. With five offices in three states, Southern Earth Sciences has successfully completed more than 3,000 significant projects.

Southern Earth Sciences employs a staff of 68 engineers, geologists, field and laboratory technicians, engineering assistants, and support personnel. Because of its multi-disciplinary staff, Southern Earth Sciences has developed an integrated project-management approach to problem solving that makes it unique in this region.

The firm's primary focus is on offering the construction industry comprehensive consulting and materials testing in three primary areas: environmental services, geotechnical and geological services, and construction services.

Responding to an increased emphasis on environmental quality and protection, Southern Earth Sciences evaluates compliance for both governmental and private-sector clients. Services include site assessments and evaluations, landfill and solid waste management, underground storage tank contracting, and asbestos abatement. Southern Earth Sciences has extensive experience in resolving landfill and hazardous waste problems, offering site selection and auditing, groundwater contamination testing, and closure services for landfills and energy-to-steam facilities.

The Geotechnical and Geological department specializes in identifying potential problems in project plans and construction specifications, helping to maximize use of available property and avoiding the need for costly remedial work. Geotechnical and geological services include engineering analysis and design, field drilling, cone penetrometer testing, investigation services, laboratory testing, and instrumentation. Southern Earth Sciences conducts foundations studies of all dimensions, from pavement analysis to landslide and slope stability.

In both the AASHTO-certified concrete and soil laboratory and the field, Southern Earth Sciences offers a complete range of inspection and testing services for construction materials. An experienced staff of ACI-certified, registered field technicians allows Southern Earth Sciences to monitor quality at new construction sites small projects to full-time quality control testing and inspection on major projects. Services include soil testing, bridge inspection, dipstick technology for flatness testing of concrete slabs, and pile integrity testing.

Southern Earth Sciences is an active member of numerous professional organizations, including the American Council of Independent Laboratories, American Society of Civil Engineers, American Society for Testing Materials, and National Water Well Association.

With a reputation for reacting quickly and effectively to its clients' needs, Southern Earth Sciences is committed to providing quality service that gets the job done.

Southern Earth Sciences has the only electronic cone penetrometer currently operating in Alabama.

WHITE - SPUNNER CONSTRUCTION

White-Spunner Construction is a leading Mobile-based commercial construction company founded in 1978. Though the company's work is concentrated in the southeast, White-Spunner Construction has completed projects in 22 states, as far north as Detroit and Connecticut, and as far west as San Antonio and Kansas City—a geographic service area unique in the Mobile market.

White-Spunner Construction has worked with a variety of Fortune 500 companies including Home Depot, Publix, Winn-Dixie, Coca-Cola, General Mills, and K-Mart, and has formed lasting relationships with a number of these clients.

A principal reason for White-Spunner Construction's strong repeat business, according to Vice President Roy Largue, is the company's ability to offer design/build services from an owner's perspective. White-Spunner works with all members of the construction team—client, site contractor, and civil engineer—to create the most comprehensive, cost-effective design possible.

(above) Whitney Bank.

(below) Hank Aaron Stadium.

A prime example is the Hank Aaron Stadium project, which was $4 million over budget as originally designed. In cooperation with BayBear's management, city officials, and others, White-Spunner designed a plan to bring the stadium in on time and within budget. A reduction in the number of seats not only reduced construction costs, but also enhanced the stadium's friendly, intimate atmosphere. A switch from aluminum to pre-stressed concrete further reduced costs. Working seven-day weeks—at times during sub-freezing weather and snow—White-Spunner Construction completed the stadium in time for opening day, just seven months later. "It was an incredible project," says Largue. "And it's turned out to be one of the best things to happen to Mobile. Working with the mayor, the city council, and BayBear's management was a good experience." White-Spunner is also acting as construction manager for the city on the Mobile Art Museum.

The company's portfolio contains such commercial, industrial, and multi-family projects as the Myrtle Beach Factory Outlet in Myrtle Beach, South Carolina; Boynton Lakes Plaza in Lantana, Florida; the Riviera Center Factory Outlet; Whitney Bank Headquarters; and McGregor Square. The company also handled construction on the Coca-Cola Bottling Company in Robertsdale; and in Mobile: QMS Research & Development, Regency Gates Apartments, and Fairway Apartments at Spring Hill College.

One of the strengths of White-Spunner Construction is its ability to adapt quickly in a changing market. "We're adept at satisfying a number of commercial construction needs—from outlet malls and industrial complexes to multi-family and assisted-living facilities," says Largue. "We're aggressive, we're efficient, and we do the job right."

COASTAL LAND TRUST

The Mobile-Tensaw River Delta is a network of rivers, streams, bayous, and creeks that meander through 400 square miles of swamps, marshes, and river bottomlands. It is the second-largest river delta in America—behind the Mississippi River Delta—and is the nation's largest inland delta. So impressive is this sprawling aquatic ecosystem, the U.S. Congress has declared it a National Natural Landmark.

Containing more than a quarter-of-a-million acres of wetland habitats, the delta is home to a rich diversity of plant life including the green-fly orchid, scarlet hibiscus, and golden canna, as well as live oaks, southern magnolias, and bald cypress. Animal life is equally plentiful with more than 100 species of birds, 40 mammals, 100 reptiles and amphibians, and 120 fish species.

Yet for years, the delta has been under attack by industrial pollution, dredging, irresponsible development, and various forms of abuse and neglect. In 1970, more than 50,000 acres of the delta were closed to commercial fishing due to mercury contamination. And a number of species—such as the panther and Florida black bear—have either disappeared or are close to extinction.

Recent years, however, have seen an increased awareness of the vital role the delta plays in the seafood, forestry, and recreation industries, as well as natural flood control and water purification. One of the driving forces in the conservation and preservation of the delta is the Coastal Land Trust—a local, private, non-profit 501(c)3 group founded in 1986. The work of the Coastal Land Trust has augmented the major acquisitions resulting from major efforts of the Administration of Governor Don Siegelman with special effforts by Conservation Commissioner Riley Boykin Smith.

With an initial loan of $4 million from the Nature Conservancy, made possible by the R. K. Mellon Foundation, the Coastal Land Trust was able to buy more than 18,000 acres of privately owned delta property to be managed and protected as a public trust by Alabama's Department of Conservation and the U.S. Army Corps of Engineers.

Says Skipper Tonsmeire, volunteer president of the Coastal Land Trust, "Things in the delta are better today than they were in the mid-1980s when the Coastal Land Trust was formed. Today there are 80,000 acres of publicly held land in the delta." To date, the Coastal Land Trust has been responsible for the conservation of more than 40,000 acres of critical wildlife habitat for multiple uses, whether fishing, hunting, birdwatching, camping, or taking field trips. In addition, the Coastal Land Trust has helped to create an awareness of the crisis the delta faces. Says Tonsmeire: "We're all lucky to live here in this part of the country with all of the advantages of the Gulf Coast. But when you consider that this is the second fastest growing county in the state, we need to be extra vigilant to ensure that we maintain the natural resources that make our place so great."

The Coastal Land Trust also maintains a lodge located on 750 acres north of Spanish Fort near Hurricane. This lodge has been used by the Sierra Club, the Nature Conservancy, the Boys & Girls Club, the Mobile Chamber of Commerce, and Alabama School of Mathematics and Science.

The directors of the Coastal Land Trust are Art Dyas of Fairhope, Win Hallett of Mobile, David Morine of Virginia, Fred Stimpson of Mobile, and Skipper Tonsmeire of Fairhope. David Morine was the former Director of Land Acquisitions for the Nature Conservancy and was instrumental in the establishment of the Coastal Land Trust, the Bon Secour Natural Wildlife Refuge, and the Weeks Bay Estuarine Research Reserve. Former directors include the late G. Sage Lyons of Mobile and Henry Bryars of Fairhope and others.

None of what has been accomplished would have been possible without the support of Congressman Jack Edwards, a tradition that continued under Congressman Sonny Callahan.

Tidings from Mobile Bay.
Photo by Steve Goraum

J.F. PATE AND ASSOCIATES

J. F. Pate and Associates Contractors is a highly respected general contractor with roots in the community dating back to 1927, when Mr. J. F. Pate formed a family-owned-and-operated construction company. In 1984, the company merged with V. L. Taylor, Contractor, Inc., to become J. F. Pate and Associates.

"We're a third generation company," says John E. Pate who, along with V. L. Taylor, owns the company. "We have supervisors who've been with the company for more than 40 years. That's a wealth of experience we bring to every job." Pate and Associates is widely regarded for its dependability and trustworthiness with a great deal of repeat business.

Pate and Associates operates on the principal of "direct officer involvement" in the work process. Each officer maintains daily contact with the job superintendent and the owner's representative. This hands-on approach gives the company complete control of each project from start to finish, ensuring the quality workmanship for which J. F. Pate and Associates is so well known.

The company is licensed to do business in Alabama and Mississippi, and employs 50 people full-time. At any one time, Pate may employ as many as 150 additional workers as projects warrant.

Pate and Associates specializes in commercial construction with an emphasis on churches, schools, and hospitals. The company's portfolio of projects is an impressive one, representing work for a variety of area clients. A few of the company's school projects are: UMS-Wright, St. Paul's, Fairhope High School, Central Baldwin Middle School, and Mertz Elementary School, as well as renovations and additions for the University of Mobile, University of South Alabama, and Spring Hill College. Pate & Associates has built a number of medical facilities for Mobile Infirmary, Thomas Hospital, and U.S.A. Medical Center. The company has also built worship facilities for Dauphin Way Baptist Church, Christ United Methodist, Our Savior Catholic, Springhill Baptist, and Ahavas Chesed Synagogue. Other high-profile clients include the Mobile Museum of Art, the Country Club of Mobile, the Grand Hotel, and Integrity Music.

J. F. Pate and Associates is a member of a number of professional organizations, including the Construction Industry Association, Mobile Area Chamber of Commerce, National Federation of Independent Businessmen, Associated General Contractors of America, and Business Council of Alabama.

(above) UMS-Wright Athletic Facility. *Photo by Aaron Tesney*

(right) Dauphin Way Baptist Church. *Photo by Aaron Tesney*

THE PELICAN GROUP, INC.

The Pelican Group, wholly owned by Alton R. Brown, III, SCSM/CLS, is a Mobile-based real estate company whose primary services are the leasing, management, development, and renovation of neighborhood and community shopping centers ranging in size from 100,000 to 250,000 square feet.

Brown, who has been active in real estate since 1977, was associated with Herman Maisel and Company, Inc., serving as principal developer and as the firm's vice president. When the company was sold, Brown and a partner formed a new company to take over the development and expansion activities of the firm. In 1993, Brown acquired all outstanding interests in the company. In 1997, the company was renamed The Pelican Group, Inc.

Because of his extensive background in real estate, Brown brings a wealth of knowledge and specialized skills to the business, including site identification and acquisition, construction permitting, development planning, tenant lease negotiation, construction administration and supervision, property management, and lease administration.

The Pelican Group's management portfolio includes neighborhood and community shopping centers from Maine to Florida, with the majority of its business concentrated in the mid-Atlantic states and northeast Florida. The company is involved in the development of small, heavily anchored neighborhood and community shopping centers in Maryland, Pennsylvania, and West Virginia, as well as the development of free-standing properties for selected retail tenants, demonstrating the company's specialization in the development of rural sites in and around major metropolitan areas such as Washington D.C., Baltimore, Maryland, and Jacksonville, Florida.

Active in retail real estate on an industry level, Brown is a member of several state and local organizations, as well as the International Council of Shopping Centers—the global trade association of the shopping center industry. Brown has earned the association's designation as a Senior Shopping Center Manager and Certified Leasing Specialist—one of only a few thousand in the nation. Having served in a number of state and divisional offices, Brown currently serves as national chairman of the environmental sub-committee that oversees such environmental issues as wetlands regulation and permitting, Brownfields and hazardous wastes, growth management, and air quality. In May of 2000, Brown received the ICSC's Trustee's Distinguished Service Award, one of approximately 45 given out in the 40-year history of ICSC.

Brown has developed more than 2.3 million square feet of retail real estate, including such shopping centers as Westwood Plaza Shopping Center and Ecor Rouge Shopping Center in the Mobile/Baldwin area. On the east coast, retail developments include Fox Run Shopping Center in Prince Frederick, Maryland, and Laurel Glen Shopping Center in Lexington Park, Maryland.

Citing employment figures, Brown points out the role retail real estate development plays in today's market. "Our industry employs about 10 percent of the nation's non-agricultural work force and contributes billions of dollars in tax revenues," he says. "I want the public to see that retail real estate development is a strong, positive economic engine. It's an industry of which I'm proud to be a part."

(above) The Pelican Group, Inc., staff from left: Alton R. Brown, III, SCSM/CLS, Monica S. Butler, Cheryl H. Smith, and Miranda R. Hensley.

(left) Fox Run Shopping Center, Prince Frederick, Maryland.

J.C. DUKE & ASSOCIATES, INC.

J. C. Duke & Associates is a full-service general contractor serving both the Gulf Coast's industrial and commercial markets. From its founding in 1988, the company has successfully met the competitive demands of the marketplace with innovative, cost-effective building methods and an emphasis on the client-contractor team approach—resulting in quality projects built on time and within budget.

Led by a senior management team with more than 100 years' combined experience in industrial and commercial construction, J. C. Duke & Associates is proficient in a wide range of industrial and commercial contracting services. Services range from routine industrial cleaning and painting by small crews to multi-million dollar commercial and industrial projects requiring complete construction teams. J. C. Duke has earned a reputation for meeting near-impossible challenges—such as completely replacing an outdated industrial fire water system without disrupting the plant's operation or production. The company also offers quick-response repair services for commercial and residential emergencies. Teams are organized through the emergency restoration division for dispatch to any location in the region within a matter of hours.

A few projects recently completed by J. C. Duke & Associates include the Aviation Center Mobile, all of the Phenolchemie plant buildings at Theodore Industrial Park, the IPSCO administration building, Escambia Middle School, Westlawn and Elsie Collier Elementary Schools, and the 42-acre Sportplex facility in Gulf Shores.

Because of its commitment to safety, quality control, and efficiency, company policy calls for "in-house" performance of key activities like site work, concrete work, and masonry work. The full-time safety department promotes a high standard of performance, resulting in consistently low EMR ratings and more efficient job practices. Many of the company's trained work force are "HazWoper" certified, and have earned additional safety certifications necessary for work in typical plant environments. The company's total approach to safety is based on a simple but effective philosophy: "safety demands better planning, and better planning results in better performance."

J. C. Duke is dedicated to the successful completion of projects through effective planning, conscientious management, timely performance, and hard work. The company's experienced planners, managers, supervisors, and workers have compiled an impressive record of outstanding projects completed on time and within budget. The J. C. Duke team of professionals looks forward to serving the people and industries of Mobile, continuing the tradition of quality, which has been its trademark since the company's founding.

(above) J. C. Duke's key personnel in front of its office at 1716 Industrial Park Drive, Mobile, Alabama.

(right) A front elevation of the administration building at the Phenolchemie plant site; one of the many buildings J. C. Duke constructed for the company.

COASTAL BUILDERS, INC.

Coastal Builders, Inc., is a full-service general contractor offering design and construction service in five Gulf Coast states. The company's in-house capabilities include concrete, masonry, carpentry, steel and pipe fabrication including field installation, millwright, and pre-engineered buildings. This combination makes Coastal Builders (CBI) a leading contractor in the commercial, industrial, institutional, and multi-family residential markets.

CBI, originally founded as Case Construction by John P. Case in 1971, was incorporated as Coastal Builders, Inc., in 1978. Mr. Case's corporate philosophy of cultivating teamwork and empowering staff members to specialize in specific fields of interest has shaped and guided the company's growth for 30 years. The result is a general contracting firm that offers comprehensive, in-depth service in a variety of disciplines.

With one of the best masonry teams in the country, CBI has successfully completed restoration and building projects for Jacintoport, IPSCO Steel, Leinkauf School, and many others. CBI also specializes in the forming, pouring, and finishing of concrete ranging from small monolithic pours to multi-level high-rise placements. In addition to in-house form, frame, and finish carpentry expertise, CBI craftsmen at the company's new state-of-the-art millwork fabrication facility in Mobile, produce specialty wood millwork products to include wood door and window units, trim, moldings, etc. CBI's dedicated pipe-and-steel-fabrication facility meets the needs of industrial clients and is U, R, and S code stamp qualified.

As the Mobile representative for CECO Pre-Engineered Steel Buildings for over 30 years, CBI is backed by CECO's 60-plus years' experience in fabricating buildings nationwide.

The firm has completed several high-profile community projects including the renovation of Ladd-Peebles Stadium. All work was accomplished, including managing complex safety issues, without incident, while maintaining the operability of the facility. CBI also performed the restoration of Leinkauf School, one of the city's oldest, after a devastating fire. The job was "constructed-in-place," so that the partial outer walls still standing would not have to be removed. Using master craftsman techniques, CBI restored the masonry to its original design and color.

CBI has also earned a reputation for its quality work in building high-rise condominiums, which includes construction of a total of 12 projects over the past six years with the largest being the Admiral's Quarters with a project cost of $45 million. Some of these condominium projects include Tidewater, Admiral's Quarters, Marlin Key, Plantation Palms, The Pass, and The Dunes, all located along the central Gulf Coast.

The building of new institutional structures and renovation of existing facilities is another area of strength for CBI, with numerous church projects including St. Lawrence Catholic Church, Wade Baptist Church, and Trinity Presbyterian Church, with other projects presently under construction.

While offering a diverse field of capabilities, CBI strives for excellence and renews its commitment to all of its clients through integrity, honesty, and dependability while striving to become a more cost-effective asset to its current and future projects.

CBI's Web site, located at www.coastalbuildersinc.com, gives a more in depth view into the company's craft abilities through project pictures, reference lists, and company information to aid potential clients in selection of a full-service provider for their projects in the construction industry.

(above) Leinkauf School, Mobile, Alabama.

(far left) Admiral's Quarters, Orange Beach, Alabama

(left) Ladd/Peebles Stadium, Mobile, Alabama.

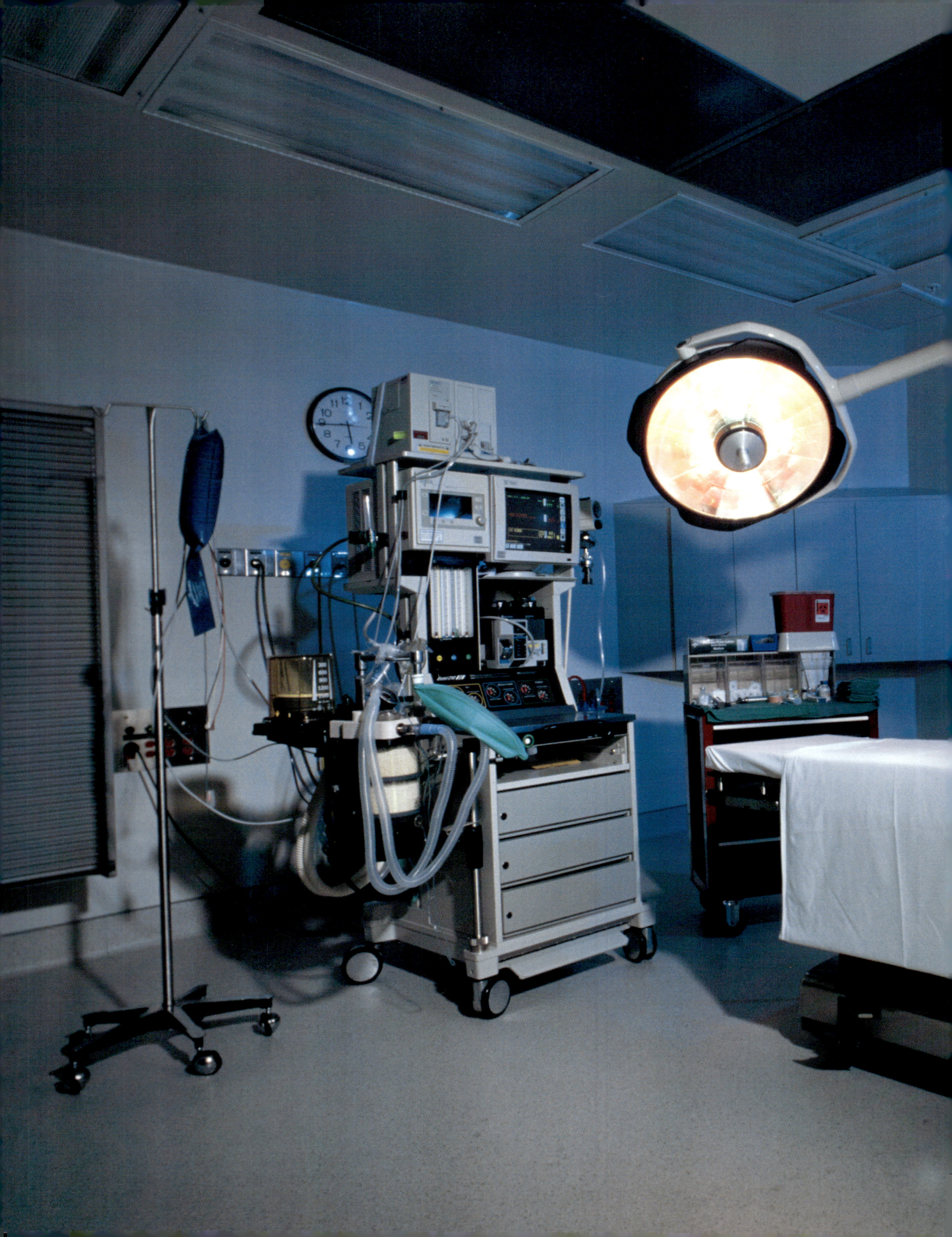

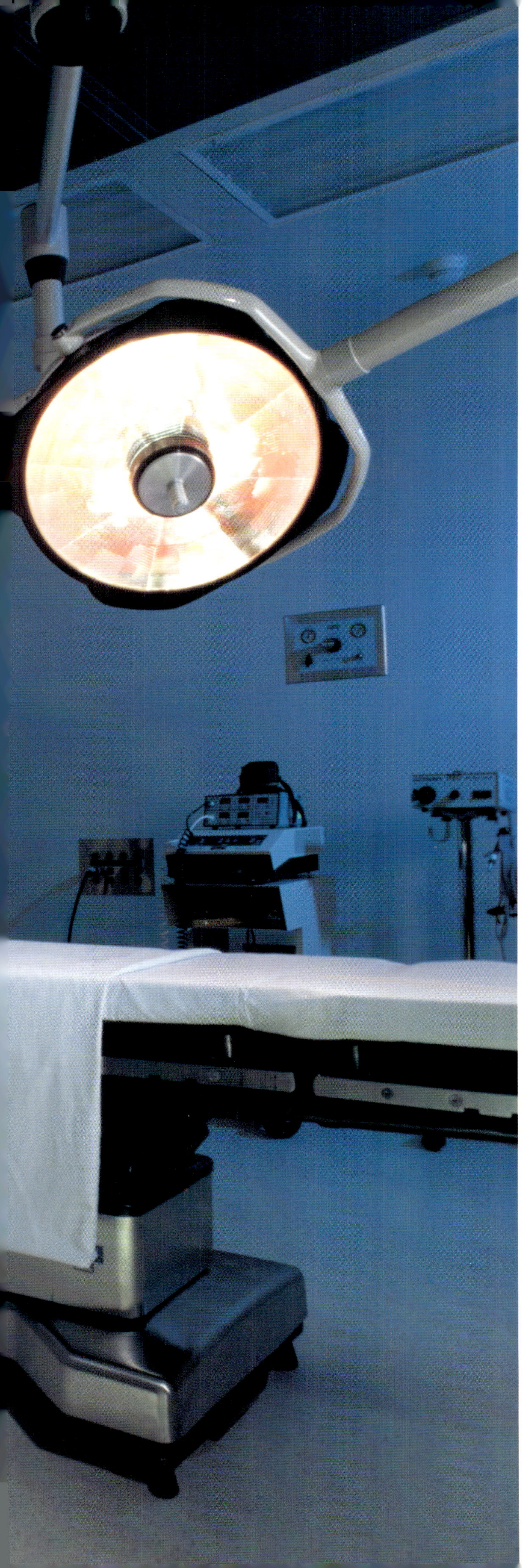

CHAPTER FOURTEEN

14

Health Care

Photo by Steve Goraum/Studio G!

UNIVERSITY OF SOUTH ALABAMA HOSPITALS

With a tradition of service whose roots date back more than 170 years, University of South Alabama Hospitals exemplify the term "medical excellence." Comprising four facilities on three separate campuses, USA Hospitals, in conjunction with the USA College of Medicine, form the region's most comprehensive health-care system.

Founded in 1830, the City Hospital of Mobile—later known as Port Hospital, then Mobile General Hospital—provided medical care for the citizens of Mobile during crises ranging from the Civil War to yellow fever epidemics. As a key element in the establishment of the USA College of Medicine, ownership of Mobile General Hospital was transferred to the University of South Alabama in 1970. Renamed the University of South Alabama Medical Center, the hospital became the primary teaching facility for the new medical school.

University of South Alabama Medical Center

The University of South Alabama Medical Center (USAMC) is a 346-bed acute care facility and major referral center for southern Alabama, southern Mississippi, and sections of northwest Florida—the area's sole source of a number of critical medical services. The region's only Level One Trauma Center is located at USAMC, providing the highest level of emergency care available. In conjunction with the Trauma Center, SouthFlite USA—the University's medical transport helicopter—brings advanced life support and rapid transport to patients within a 100-mile radius of Mobile.

Recognized as one of the nation's leaders in its field, the USA Regional Burn and Wound Center provides critical care for patients in a four-state area, using an interdisciplinary approach that treats the physical, social, and emotional needs of patients. In addition, the USA Regional Transplant Center conducts the area's only organ transplant program, treating patients for renal failure and end-stage complications from hypertension and diabetes.

As a research hospital and active member of several national protocols, USAMC is able to provide the most current treatments and therapies in a number of specialties. The USA Regional Stroke Center participated in the development of a new drug that, administered early, can actually reverse the damage caused by stroke. The USA Comprehensive Sickle Cell Center, one of only 10 such National Institutes of Health-funded centers in the country, is dedicated to caring for those with the disease, and conducting research that may ultimately lead to a cure.

(above) Dr. Betty Pace, associate professor of cell biology and neuroscience, leads the way in sickle cell research at USA's College of Medicine.

(right) Dr. Richard Zweifler, director of USA's Regional Stroke Center, examines a CT brain scan. USA's nationally recognized stroke center is actively involved in both research and treatment of strokes.

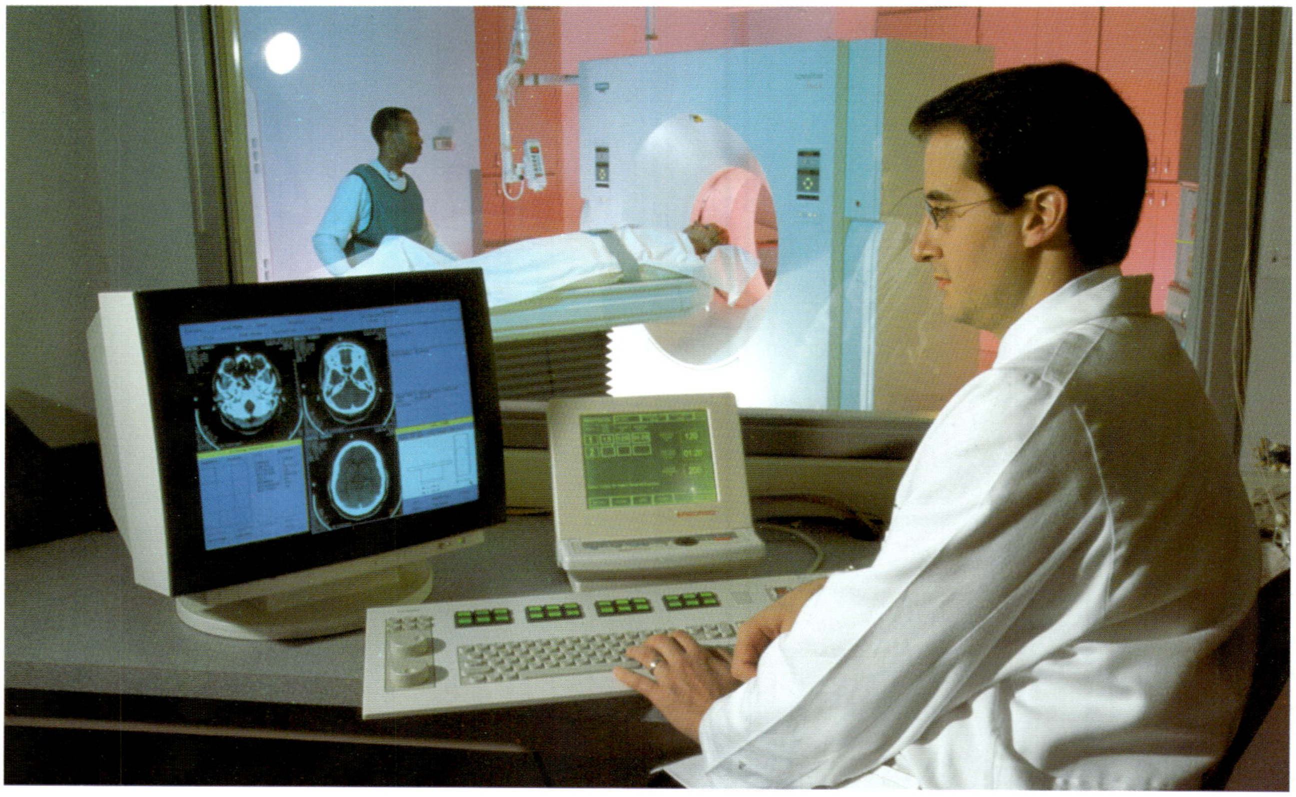

USA Knollwood Hospital & USA Knollwood Long Term Care Hospital

A 100-bed acute care facility in west Mobile, USA Knollwood Hospital offers medical and surgical services, as well as a 24-hour emergency center. In addition to a Regional Stroke Center, a number of unique health-care options are available at USA Knollwood, including the Women's Health Center, USA Digestive Diseases Center, USA Epilepsy Center, and the USA Sleep Disorders Center. USA Knollwood is also home to the region's most comprehensive outpatient surgery center. As the city continues its westward expansion, USA Knollwood will grow in importance as a provider, in conjunction with the other USA Hospitals, of premium-quality care for the entire region.

The University has embarked on an ambitious plan to create the first academic cancer research institute in the upper Gulf Coast region. Through the USA Cancer Institute, USA College of Medicine faculty will research new cancer drugs and treatment techniques and provide patients with greater local access to state-of-the-art cancer treatment. The Institute will be based at USA Knollwood Hospital, but will involve the entire USA Health System. It will provide a single location for coordinated comprehensive cancer care—prevention, diagnosis, treatment, and research.

Also located on the Knollwood campus is USA Knollwood Long Term Care Hospital, a regional referral center, and one of only a few such facilities in the country. Designed for patients who need functional restoration, rehabilitation, and medical management for an average of three to six weeks, USA Knollwood Long Term Care Hospital provides subacute and rehabilitative services to patients with spinal cord injuries, orthopedic conditions, pulmonary disease, neuromuscular disease, stroke, severe burns, and multiple traumas. A multidisciplinary approach combines physical, occupational, and speech therapy, along with therapeutic recreation and rehabilitative nursing to help each patient attain functional independence.

USA Children's & Women's Hospital

As one of only five such free-standing facilities in the country, USA Children's & Women's Hospital is dedicated solely to the care of women and children. With a strong emphasis on family-centered care, the hospital provides expectant mothers with comfortable, home-like settings for delivery, along with the most sophisticated medical treatment available. In addition, the Neonatal Intensive Care Nursery provides life-saving services for all babies born within a 100-mile radius.

With a sensitivity to the special physical and emotional needs of children, USA Children's & Women's Hospital delivers care in an environment designed to reduce the anxiety of hospitalization. Through the Child Life Program, certified child life specialists work with young patients to help them understand their hospital experience. The Class Act Program enables school-aged youngsters to continue their education with certified Mobile County Public School teachers, reducing absences and the associated anxiety. The Star Brite Network provides young patients directed Internet access, allowing them to communicate with children in hospitals across the country.

Reaching Out

University of South Alabama Hospitals are continually improving methods of community outreach. Telemedicine, a sophisticated telecommunications network, allows long-distance doctor-patient interaction and diagnosis. Thus, a doctor in Mobile can treat a patient 33 miles away in Bayou La Batre. With Teleradiology technology, physicians at outlying clinics and hospitals throughout South Alabama are able to transmit high-resolution x-rays for diagnosis by specialists at USA Medical Center.

As the region's leading educational and referral centers, University of South Alabama Hospitals are firmly committed to the mission of medical service and education for the benefit of all citizens.

(above) SouthFlite brings advanced life support to patients at accident scenes and those who are critically ill in hospitals and require transport for advanced care. Using their speed and direct flight capabilities, the helicopter and crew can reach cities and towns 100 miles from Mobile in just over 40 minutes.

(left) A quiet moment with a newborn at USA Children's and Women's Hospital, where approximately 4,000 babies are born each year.

CARDIOLOGY ASSOCIATES

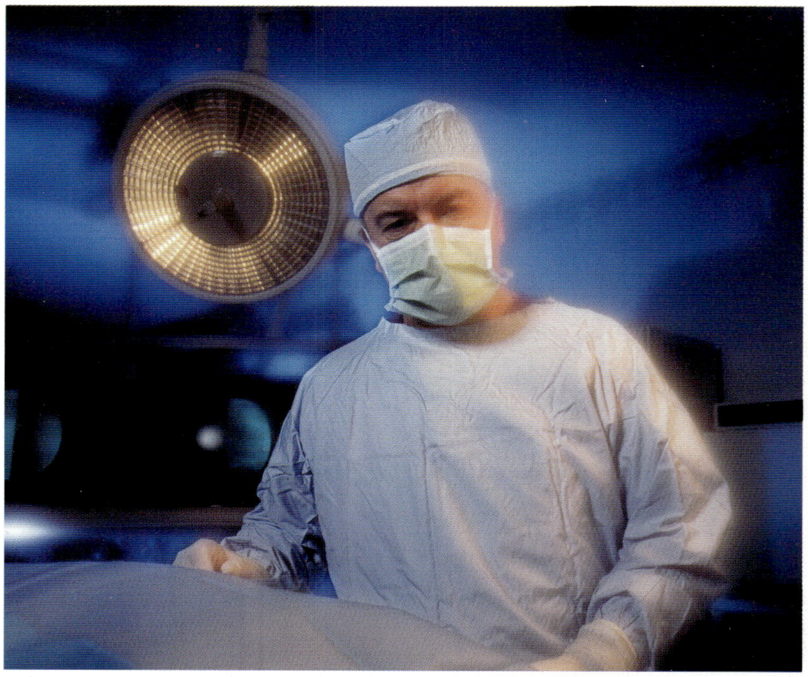

(above) Cardiologist Gerry M. Phillips, M.D., F.A.C.C., begins an angioplasty procedure in the cardiac catheterization lab.

(below) The Cardiology Associates Team. Pictured, first row from left: Fabio Leonelli, M.D., Wail Hashimi, M.D., Kenneth Burnham, M.D., Brian Dearing, M.D., Erik Eways, M.D., Eliyya Abbud, M.D. Second row, from left: Stephanie Grosz, M.D., Frank Bunch, M.D., Richard Chernick, M.D., William Hayes, M.D., Gerry Phillips, M.D., Vance Chunn, Administrator, Kenneth Francez, Jr., M.D., David Mayer, M.D., Andrew Morrow, Jr., M.D., Lynn Arnold Batten, M.D. Not pictured: Charles Parrott, M.D., Anne Hackman, M.D., William Denney, M.D., and Mary Honkanen, M.D.

To the physicians of Cardiology Associates, the human heart is more than just an organ—it is an abiding mystery, symbolizing the wellspring of life. Their dedication to unraveling this mystery is the core of their mission—to provide the most comprehensive, highest quality cardiovascular care to adults and children on the Gulf Coast.

Founded by Gerry M. Phillips, M.D., in 1985, Cardiology Associates offers the region's most progressive treatment modalities for adults and children with heart problems. Under the leadership of Dr. Phillips and his partners, the group has established a team approach to the practice of medicine—offering a wide array of services including: invasive and interventional cardiology, adult and pediatric cardiac catheterization, balloon angioplasty and stents, pacemakers, electrophysiologic studies, radio-frequency catheter ablations, implantable defibrillators, and peripheral vascular interventions.

In addition, Cardiology Associates' clinical and non-invasive cardiology services include: nuclear cardiology, echocardiography, stress testing, holter monitoring, EKGs, peripheral vascular studies, and transtelephonic pacemaker monitoring.

Under the supervision of the Director of Clinical Research, Cardiology Associates participates in National Clinical Research Studies—an on-going regimen of device trials and pharmaceutical studies. This participation allows the physicians access to leading-edge technology and drugs that would not be available otherwise.

The physicians of Cardiology Associates provide the most comprehensive cardiovascular care in the community and offer a number of services that are unique to their practice alone. These include:

- The area's only physician-directed clinic fully dedicated to the diagnosis and treatment of cholesterol and lipid disorders.
- A comprehensive heart failure clinic led by the area's only physician fellowship trained in heart failure. His clinical model is being adopted at area hospitals for the treatment of heart failure patients.
- The only team of pediatric cardiologists in the area and the only ones along the tri-state Gulf Coast who perform pediatric heart catheterization.
- Multiple physicians fellowship trained in the diagnosis and treatment of peripheral vascular disease.
- A full complement of specially trained physicians, called Electrophysiologists, dedicated to the detection and treatment of heart rhythm disorders.

Cardiology Associates offers full-time comprehensive cardiac care at five locations in Mobile and Baldwin Counties, as well as outreach clinics in rural areas and other communities such as Jackson, Atmore, Chatom, Troy, and Montgomery.

As knowledge of the workings of the cardiovascular system continues to grow, the physicians of Cardiology Associates renew their commitment to the exploration of effective new modes of cardiac care, as well as their commitment to the ultimate quest—unraveling the mystery of the heart.

INFIRMARY HEALTH SYSTEM

With a century-old tradition of service to the community, Infirmary Health System—the region's largest health-care provider—is committed to bringing the highest quality medical care to the citizens of southwest Alabama.

Established in 1897, in response to the request of a group of concerned citizens led by world-renowned author Augusta Evans Wilson, the Mobile Infirmary Association laid the groundwork for the opening, in 1910, of the Mobile Infirmary. Since moving to its current location in 1952, the medical center has grown to become a state-of-the-art, 704-bed acute care facility—the largest non-governmental, not-for-profit hospital in the state.

In addition to the hospital, Infirmary Health System encompasses an impressive network of health-care resources. The J. L. Bedsole/Rotary Rehabilitation Hospital is the only comprehensive acute rehabilitation facility in Mobile. Infirmary Home Health Agency offers highly skilled care to patients in the comfort of their own homes. Infirmary Hospice Care provides medical care and support services for terminally ill patients and their families. Infirmary Home Medical Services maintains a full line of homecare equipment and supplies. In addition, Infirmary-65 offers convenient access to an extensive array of diagnostic tests, including open MRI and bone densitometry.

Infirmary Health System also reaches out to surrounding areas by means of Infirmary-Eastern Shore that serves the medical needs of the rapidly growing Baldwin County area, as well as Thomasville Infirmary, Washington County Infirmary and Nursing Home, Grove Hill Memorial Hospital, and over 20 Infirmary medical clinics.

A key component of Infirmary Health System's total medical care is education. A program of seminars, classes, lectures, and support groups regularly addresses such wide-ranging issues as diabetes, spinal cord injuries, and sleep disorders.

Utilizing donated funds—such as memorials, honorariums, and special gifts—the Infirmary Foundation continues the institution's tradition of providing quality health care. More than $2.5 million has been distributed by the Foundation to help purchase medical equipment, underwrite special community projects, and provide scholarships. Thousands of lives have been enhanced through the Foundation's contributions to Mobile AIDS Support Services, Ronald McDonald House, Child Advocacy Center, United Cerebral Palsy, Strickland Youth Center, and the Infirmary's School Nurse Program.

Having established a benchmark for excellence, Infirmary Health System remains strong in its commitment to providing quality, cost-effective, convenient health care.

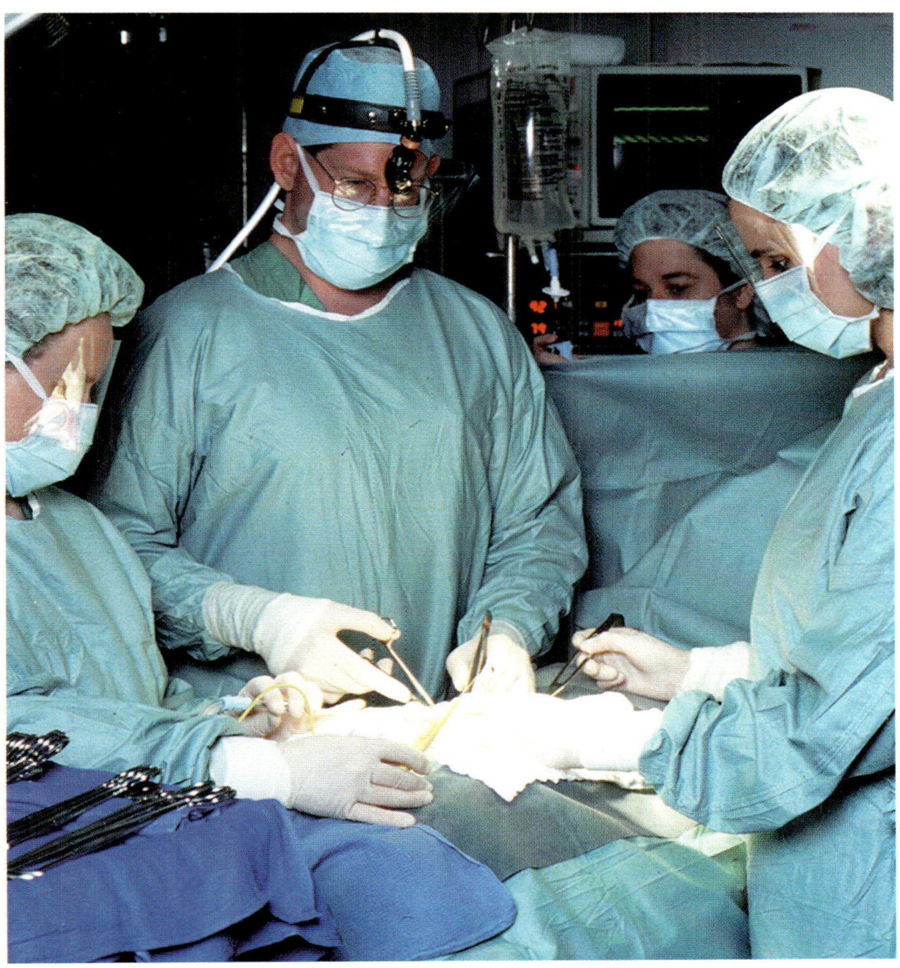

(above) Mobile Infirmary Medical Center is a state-of-the-art, 704-bed acute care facility—the largest non-governmental, not-for-profit hospital in the state.

(left) With more than 30 operating rooms in service, the Infirmary is one of the leading hospitals in the state in the number of procedures performed each year.

PROVIDENCE HOSPITAL

One look at Providence Hospital's sleek, curvilinear profile, and it's obvious that this is no ordinary medical center. The innovative cloverleaf-shaped towers house a patient-friendly "pod configuration" in which each room is private, and less than 10 feet from a nurse's station. The building's interior design is representative of Providence Hospital's mission to serve the community, helping those in need with a spiritually based, values-driven healing ministry.

Providence Hospital, founded in 1854 by the Daughters of Charity as a 60-bed infirmary, has grown into a major 349-bed full-service regional hospital. Providence Hospital is a member of Ascension Health, a unique health organization that unites the Daughters of Charity and the Sisters of St. Joseph Health Systems in a 15-state network. Providence Hospital's mission is clear: "Rooted in the loving ministry of Jesus as healer; we commit ourselves to serving all persons, with special attention to those who are poor and vulnerable. Our Catholic health ministry is dedicated to spiritually centered, holistic care which sustains and improves the health of individuals and communities. We are advocates for a compassionate and just society through our actions and our words."

Though a distinct emphasis is placed on spirituality there is no proselytizing. The makeup of the hospital staff reflects a great diversity of religious beliefs, and less than 20 percent of the hospital's patients, at any given time, are Catholic.

As a part of its mission, Providence is committed to providing the newest technology and services, such as Miraluma imaging, the first FDA-approved nuclear medicine test for detection of breast cancer. The hospital was also the first in the region to offer the Biosense Carto Mapping System for the treatment of arrhythmia. And, in conjunction with Vanderbilt University Medical Center, Providence is participating in a groundbreaking study on stem cell transplantation.

In response to specific community needs, Providence instituted the Early Heart Attack Care and Early Brain Attack Care programs to educate the public about the early warning signs of heart attacks and strokes. The Chest Pain Center, a dedicated unit within the Emergency Department, assesses and intervenes in the early stages of an impending heart attack, helping to reduce the possibility of serious damage.

Complementing the hospital's services is the Providence Medical Office Plaza, which is a four-building complex that houses the Cancer Center and Diabetes Center along with more than 150 physician offices representing every major medical specialty and subspecialty. Adjacent to the hospital is the newest building on campus, a 100,000-square-foot state-of-the-art facility in which the Outpatient Center, Ambulatory Surgery, the Providence Heart Center, and other services are located. A 155-acre area surrounds the hospital campus and is the site of the hospital's Rehabilitation and Wellness Center and the Providence Park Office Plaza.

With a dedication to serving the community according to its statement of values—service of the poor, reverence, integrity, wisdom, creativity, and dedication—Providence Hospital leads the way in providing high-quality health care to the people of the central Gulf Coast.

(above) Built on its current site in 1987, Providence Hospital is a 349-bed full-service regional hospital and the centerpiece to the surrounding 155-acre medical campus.

(right) Providence Hospital is a member of the largest Catholic health system—Ascension Health, a unique health organization that unites the Daughters of Charity and the Sisters of St. Joseph Health Systems in a 15-state network.

SPRINGHILL MEDICAL CENTER

With an emphasis on providing high-quality clinical care in a family-focused environment, Springhill Medical Center has established a reputation for offering its patients the "best of both worlds." As a 250-bed hospital—each room private and attractively decorated—Springhill Medical Center is "small" enough to offer attentive, personalized care. As a complete medical-surgical facility with full diagnostic capabilities and 24-hour emergency room, Springhill Medical Center is "large" enough to offer the comprehensive health care you'd expect from a regional leader.

Founded in 1975 as a small 50-bed facility, Springhill Medical Center has grown into a campus-style medical center consisting of the main hospital (Springhill Memorial), two medical office buildings, The Cancer Center, the Gerald L. Wallace Auditorium and Annex, the HeartCare Center, the Athletic Club, the Center for Well-Being, and the Rehabilitation Institute.

Keeping pace with its physical growth, Springhill Memorial offers an impressive choice of clinical options, such as full surgical services, including open-heart procedures, and comprehensive women's and children's care with full labor and delivery suites and a pediatric special care unit. In-patient and out-patient radiation and chemotherapy are offered at The Cancer Center, designed for the comfort and convenience of patients with its own easily accessible entry. Full diagnostic capabilities include lab, X-ray, MRI, CT Scan, and heart catheterization. And board-certified emergency medicine physicians are on duty 24 hours a day, 7 days a week in Springhill Medical Center's Emergency Room.

As a leader in new and innovative treatment modalities, Springhill Medical Center was the first hospital in the area to offer lithotripter therapy, the non-surgical treatment of kidney stones. The region's first Sleep Center and Chest Pain Clinic were also established at Springhill Medical Center, providing much-needed services to southwest Alabama. One of the hospital's newest offerings is the Wound Care Program. Utilizing a multi-disciplinary team of medical professionals, and innovative technology like Hyperbaric Oxygen Therapy, Springhill Medical Center is able to more effectively treat stubborn and problem wounds such as diabetic ulcers, and resolve infections and increase healing in certain toxic poisoning cases and trauma wounds.

It is, perhaps, in the area of educational outreach that Springhill Medical Center has most distinguished itself. Through an extensive lecture series, on-going childbirth classes, comprehensive diabetes education, and up-to-date parenting classes, Springhill Medical Center helps equip thousands of Mobile-area residents with the information needed to lead healthy lives. In addition, the importance of emotional growth and healing is recognized in the hospital's full slate of organized support groups.

With more than 25 years of service to the community, Springhill Medical Center looks to the future while remaining committed to its mission: "... to efficiently provide health care that is unmatched in quality, convenience, and benefit of use in a courteous and family-oriented manner."

BLUE CROSS AND BLUE SHIELD OF ALABAMA

Blue Cross and Blue Shield of Alabama's Mobile district headquarters at 4750 Airport Boulevard.

Blue Cross and Blue Shield, America's oldest and largest health-care insurer, consists of 47 independent, locally owned member companies nationwide under the coordination of the Blue Cross and Blue Shield Association. Collectively, Blue Cross and Blue Shield Plans provide health-care coverage for 77.4 million people in the 50 states, the District of Columbia, and Puerto Rico—25 percent of the U.S. population.

Blue Cross and Blue Shield of Alabama (BCBSA) is the largest provider of health-care benefits in the state, providing coverage for more than 3 million people at 26,000 companies and government agencies. The company pays more than $5.6 billion in benefits each year—95¢ of every dollar it receives—to such members as State of Alabama employees and public school teachers, as well as the employees of BellSouth Services, the city of Mobile, Alabama Power, Ruby Tuesday, Regions Bank, SouthTrust Bank, and Colonial Bank. The Mobile division of BCBSA serves 5,703 employer clients in 13 south Alabama counties from its main office and two satellite offices in Foley and Andalusia.

As the first prepaid health-care plan in America, Blue Cross traces its roots to 1929 when an official at Baylor University introduced a plan that guaranteed Dallas schoolteachers 21 days of hospital care for $6 a year. Other employee groups in Dallas soon joined the plan, and the idea quickly attracted nationwide attention. By 1939 the Blue Cross symbol was officially adopted by a commission of the American Hospital Association as the emblem for plans that met certain guidelines. In 1960 the commission was replaced by the Blue Cross Association. The Blue Shield concept grew out of the lumber and mining camps of the Pacific Northwest at the turn of the century. Employers who wanted to provide medical care for their workers paid monthly fees to medical service bureaus or groups of physicians. The Blue Shield symbol was informally adopted in 1948 by a group of nine plans that eventually became the National Association of Blue Shield Plans. By special acts of the state legislature, Blue Cross of Alabama was created in 1936 and Blue Shield of Alabama was created in 1948.

In an era of increasingly expensive health care, BCBSA constantly strives to reduce costs, improve quality, and provide the best value to its customers. Perhaps the best indicator of Blue Cross's commitment to its "customer first" policy is the fact that the company regularly retains more than 98 percent of its customers from year to year. A big part of this customer satisfaction, says Michael Phillips, district manager of BCBSA, is the freedom their members have in choosing which doctor to see and when. "People want control in the decision-making process," says Phillips, "and that's what we at Blue Cross and Blue Shield of Alabama strive to provide."

CARDIO-THORACIC & VASCULAR SURGICAL ASSOCIATES, P.C. (CTVSA)

For thirty years, the name CTVSA has been synonymous with excellence in the fields of cardiac, thoracic, and vascular surgery. Led by a distinguished team of eight surgeons, and supported by an outstanding staff of nurses and surgical assistants, Cardio-Thoracic & Vascular Surgical Associates has performed more than 15,000 open-heart procedures, 6,000 major vascular procedures, and 2,000 lung and chest-wall operations.

The group's physicians practice at all Mobile hospitals, as well as Thomas Hospital in Fairhope and South Baldwin Hospital in Foley. With a long-standing reputation for clinical and technical excellence, CTVSA receives patient referrals from throughout the Gulf Coast area.

Since its founding in 1971, the physicians of CTVSA have been dedicated to providing the finest care in their specialties, as set forth in the practice's mission statement: "To provide our patients with the highest standards of care in cardiac, thoracic, and vascular surgery. To provide our patients and their families with compassionate care. To educate and inform our patients and their families regarding prevention and treatment of cardiovascular disease. To maintain current standards of excellence through continuous medical education of our surgeons and associated health-care professionals. To foster excellent comprehensive health care."

Each of the surgeons of CTVSA is board-certified in his specialty. Drs. Frank McPhillips and Greg McGee hold special certificates in vascular surgery from the American Board of Surgery. Drs. John Stone, William Johnson, Mark Gonçalves, Trey Pluscht, Terry Stelly, and John Boyer are certified by the American Board of Thoracic Surgery. Dr. Johnson also holds a special certificate of vascular surgery from the American Board of Surgery.

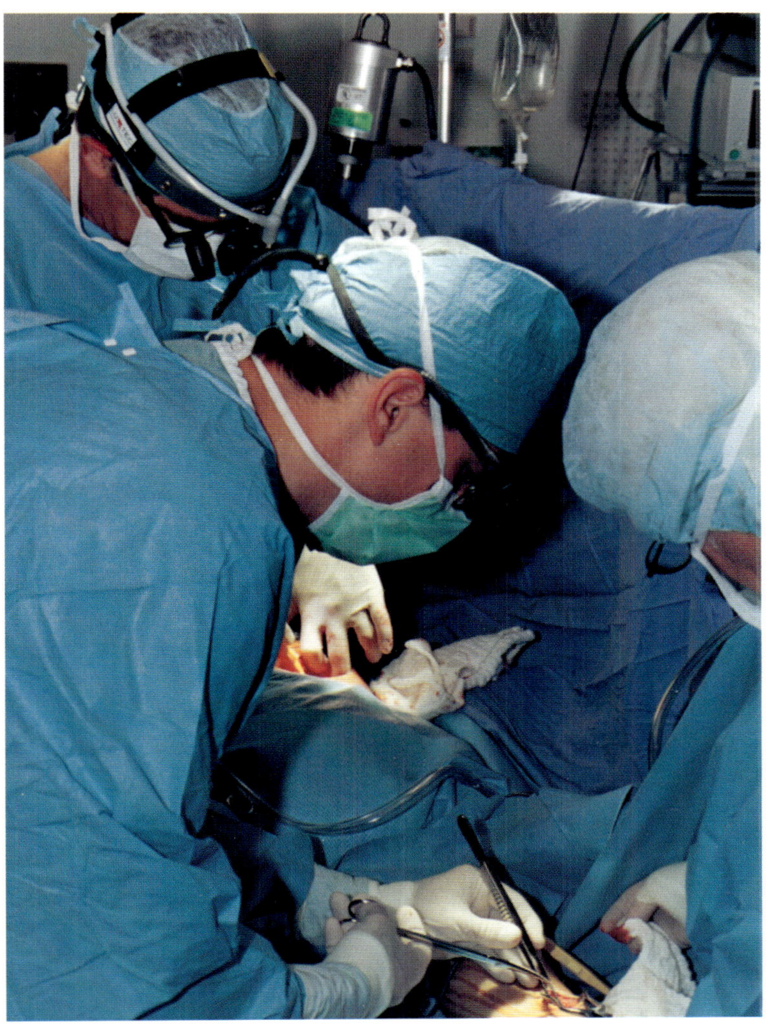

The surgeons of CTVSA believe that continuing education is an essential part of maintaining the highest standards of care for their patients. Through continuous training and re-training at national and international seminars, CTVSA brings the most innovative, sophisticated surgical procedures to the Gulf Coast.

In the field of cardiac surgery, CTVSA physicians routinely perform complex valve repair and replacement procedures, as well as surgery for a wide range of aortic aneurysms. CTVSA surgeons are renowned for their expertise in the new area of "beating heart" operations—which allow coronary artery bypasses to be constructed without the use of the heart-lung machine—and transmyocardial laser revascularization, another recently-introduced treatment option.

Drs. McGee and McPhillips are respected leaders in the field of vascular surgery—pioneering the use of revolutionary techniques in minimally invasive treatment of aneurysms and arterial blockages.

The physicians of CTVSA are members of many prestigious medical societies, both locally and nationally, including the Society of Thoracic Surgeons, Southern Thoracic Surgical Associates, the Southern Association for Vascular Surgery, the John W. Kirklin Surgical Society, and the Denton A. Cooley Cardiovascular Surgical Society.

CTVSA is committed to providing the highest standard of medical care—from careful pre-operative evaluation and meticulous surgical technique to attentive post-operative care—with integrity, compassion, and a dedication to excellence.

(above) Bottom row, from left: Peter Pluscht, III, M.D.; Mark A. Gonçalves, M.D.; William E. Johnson, III, M.D.; and Frank L. McPhillips, M.D. Top row, from left: John W. Boyer, M.D.; Terry C. Stelly, M.D.; Gregory S. McGee, M.D.; and John E. Stone, Jr., M.D.

(left) Dr. Johnson and surgical team.

ANESTHESIA SERVICES, P.C.

Founded in 1953, Anesthesia Services is the oldest anesthesia group in Mobile, and one of the largest in the state—with 25 board-certified anesthesiologists and 40 anesthetists. Anesthesia Services is an open-staff group practicing at Mobile Infirmary, Providence Hospital, Mobile Surgery Center, SurgiCare, and Dauphin West.

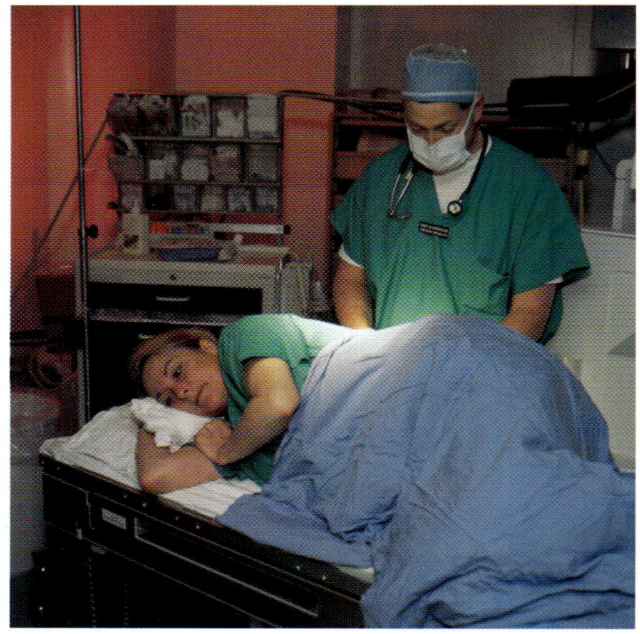

Anesthesiology is the practice of medicine devoted to the relief of pain and the care of the surgical patient before, during and after surgery. In the past two decades, the anesthesiologist's role in total health care has expanded greatly. In addition to administering anesthesia to surgical patients, the anesthesiologist functions as a perioperative physician who evaluates patients before surgery, consults with the surgical team, provides pain control and support of life functions during surgery, supervises care after surgery, and medically discharges patients from the recovery unit.

A sub-specialty of increasing importance for Anesthesia Services is that of pain management and control. A variety of nerve blocks helps manage the intractable or chronic pain caused by conditions such as cancer, arthritis, and back and hip injuries.

"There is a growing national awareness that people don't have to suffer," says Dr. Michael H. Lasecki, a member of Anesthesia Service's practice. "And as the baby boom generation continues to age, they will be subject to more pain syndromes and chronic pain." The future prospect is far from bleak, however, according to Lasecki. "We are at the beginning of a new era of tremendous advances in modalities for treating pain."

Anesthesia Services partners with the University of Alabama-Birmingham Medical School, in providing the clinical rotation for students in the Nurse Anesthesia Graduate Program. Eight students per year qualify for the rigorous training, which requires students to have earned a Bachelor's degree with a 3.0 average and to have completed at least one year's work as a critical care nurse. The benefit to the community of the nurse anesthetist program is enormous, says Dr. Lasecki, Medical Director of the school in Mobile. "We're helping ensure that this region is well served in the field of anesthesiology today as well as in the years to come." Anesthesia Services was also the first in Alabama to utilize the services of physician assistants who specialize in anesthesia, a valuable manpower resource for Mobile.

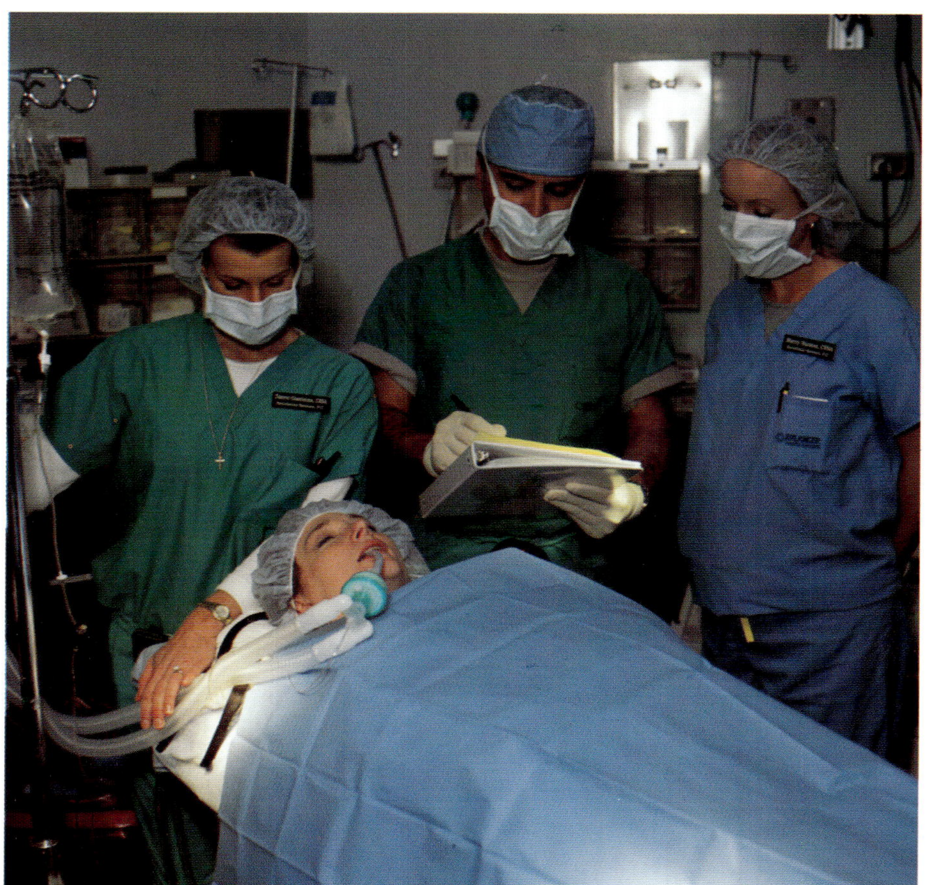

Anesthesia Services is a member of the Mobile Area Chamber of Commerce, Better Business Bureau, Business Council of Mobile, and an active supporter of Camp Rap-a-Hope, a summer camp sponsored by the Medical Society and Medical Alliance of Mobile County for children living with cancer.

PRIMEHEALTH

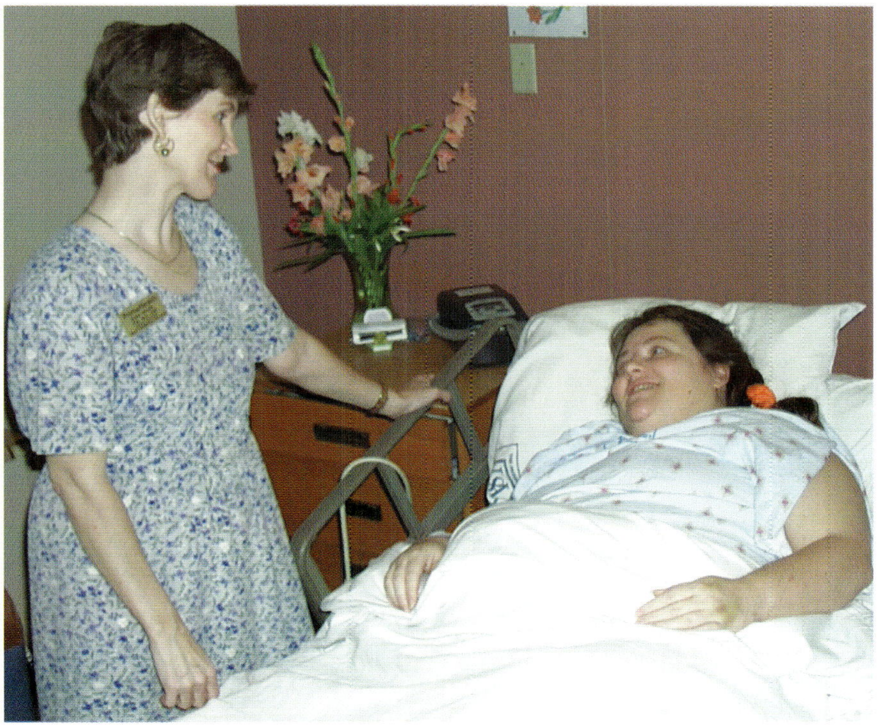

PrimeHealth makes people the most important part of healthcare. "We Make You Important" is more than a slogan at PrimeHealth, says Kathryn Parks, executive director. "It is our compelling focus . . . how we behave day after day."

Parks says making people the most important part of healthcare is the focus of every PrimeHealth employee. It results in quality service to PrimeHealth members and employers who offer PrimeHealth. It helps make healthcare more personal and comfortable. It takes into account people's feelings, concerns, the value of their time, and their opportunities to contribute to their own health.

PrimeHealth strives to make both members and employers important. PrimeHealth employees help develop department objectives to deliver superior service and ways to implement them; methods to measure their effectiveness. They share the results with fellow employees, customers, and prospects. Employees are recognized for their efforts to make members important and encouraged to be creative and operate with initiative.

Some of the benefits PrimeHealth employees have created for members are:

• Healthcare guidelines that help infants, children, adults, and older adults get the full benefit of today's medicine.

• Healthcare reminders that help members protect their health by reminding them to get important exams such as pap smears and mammograms.

• Recommendations of health seminars that can help members restore their health or protect it.

• Visits to hospitalized PrimeHealth members that help them feel comfortable with their healthcare coverage and their treatment.

Some of the benefits PrimeHealth employees have created for businesses are:

• More health benefit plans at varying costs to make it possible for more businesses to offer healthcare insurance to employees.

• Increased employee loyalty as employees become aware of the quality service provided by PrimeHealth.

•- Healthier employees who can contribute more to helping the business compete.

• Participation of employees in helping to control healthcare costs by building healthy habits.

PrimeHealth employees make all of the benefits they provide even better with their attitudes and initiative, says Parks. She cites the actions of PrimeHealth customer service representatives and clinical services nurses as examples.

"On their own initiative, our service representatives recognize opportunities to suggest our services to members," Parks says. "When they are speaking to new mothers, they often recommend that they utilize our infant healthcare guidelines to protect their baby's health. When our clinical nurses visit hospitalized members, they recommend health seminars and other services that will help these patients when they are discharged. PrimeHealth employees are always on the lookout for ways to make our members important."

PrimeHealth services more than 20,000 members through a provider network of 1,300 physicians and 250 provider groups.

(above) Visits to hospitalized members are part of PrimeHealth's focus on making members the most important part of healthcare. This PrimeHealth nurse is making sure the patient is comfortable with her healthcare coverage and her treatment.

(left) Helping employees get all the benefits of their healthcare coverage is another way PrimeHealth makes people the most important part of health care. This PrimeHealth marketing representative is explaining free health services available from PrimeHealth.

Let's talk at

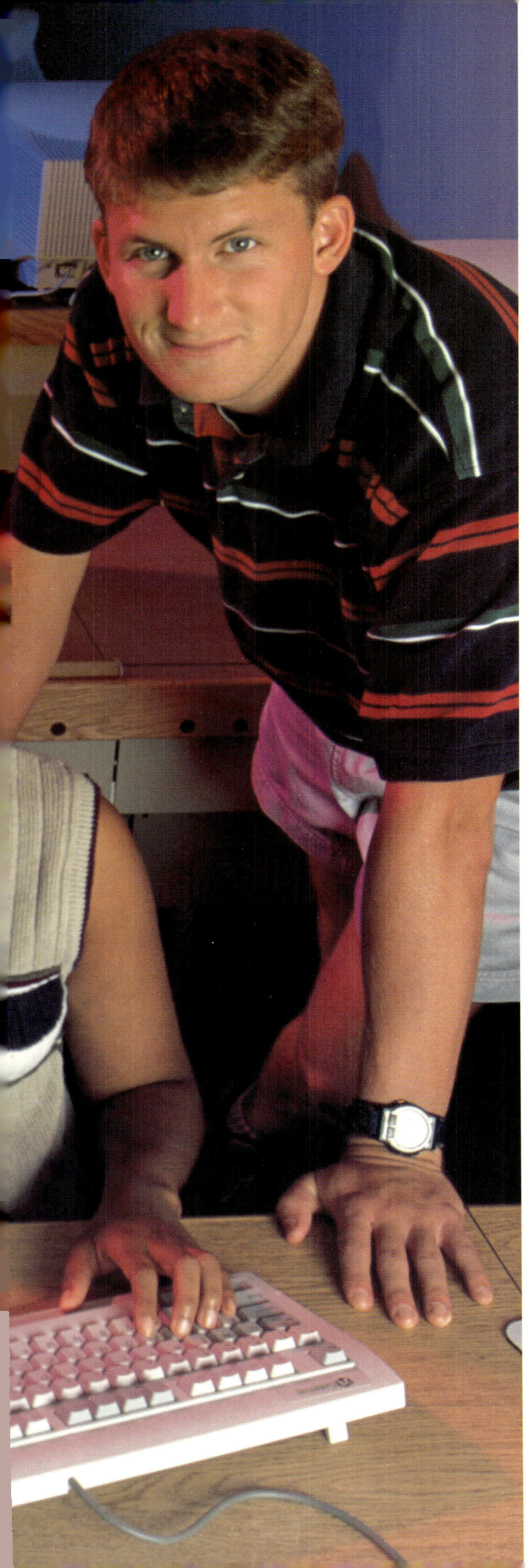

CHAPTER FIFTEEN

15

Education

Photo by Courtland W. Richards/University of South Alabama Photographer

UNIVERSITY OF SOUTH ALABAMA

With a mission to teach, conduct research, provide public service, and deliver quality health care, the University of South Alabama—in its brief 40-year history—has had an astonishing impact on the quality of life on the central Gulf Coast. Having graduated more than 47,000 students, the University has earned a reputation as a leading center of high-quality, accessible, undergraduate, graduate, and professional education. And as an institution with a $1 billion annual impact on the region and state, the University of South Alabama (USA) has established itself as a key factor in the area's economic development.

Since it was chartered by the Alabama Legislature in 1963, the University has experienced exponential growth and witnessed a number of major milestones. In 1964, the first classes began at the University's west Mobile campus with an enrollment of 276 students. In 1973, 25 students entered USA's newly chartered College of Medicine. During the next decade, the University's first Ph.D. program was instituted, and the Baldwin County campus was established. Today, USA's enrollment of approximately 12,000 makes it the state's fourth largest university.

USA forged an exciting new direction in 1998, naming V. Gordon Moulton as the successor to the University's first president, Dr. Frederick P. Whiddon. A member of the USA family for more than 35 years—as teacher, department head, dean of Computer and Information Sciences, and vice-president—President Moulton brings to the position a vision for the future grounded in the University's four-fold mission.

A Mission to Teach

As is true of every great university, teaching is at the heart of USA's mission, with a commitment to educating the whole person. USA fulfills this commitment by fostering the individual's ability to think critically and analytically, to communicate effectively, to acquire information and apply it to problem solving, and to understand the globally diverse context in which knowledge is applied.

With more than 80 undergraduate and 25 graduate programs available, USA students receive a solid liberal arts education and acquire marketable skills for success in the workplace in a variety of academic disciplines: the Colleges of Allied Health Professions, Arts and Sciences, Mitchell College of Business, Education, Engineering, Medicine, Nursing, and the Schools of Computer and Information Sciences, and Continuing Education and Special Programs.

(above) The bronze jaguar sculpted by USA alumnus Sam Nettles stands in the Mitchell Center Plaza as a symbol of campus pride. The sculpture was donated by Abe Mitchell, and Mayer and Arlene Mitchell, all of Mobile. The Mitchells are longtime benefactors and friends of the University.

(right) As Mobile's finest multipurpose facility, named in honor of the Mitchell family's philanthropic support of education and the University of South Alabama, the Mitchell Center has become a focal point of student activities and community life. Brothers Abe and Mayer Mitchell founded Mobile's highly successful Mitchell Company, whose residential and commercial real estate development activities span the entire southeastern United States.

The student/teacher ratio of 17:1 and average class size of 20 are indicative of USA's ability to offer the top-quality education of a major university in combination with the personalized attention of a smaller college. Adding to the University's rich academic culture is the diversity of the student population—representing 40 states and 95 foreign countries.

While USA's dedication to a traditional academic ethic remains strong, the University continues to develop new ways of meeting the diverse needs of students in a changing world.

"How do we, as an institution, deal with an evolving student population and its needs?" asks President Moulton. The traditional student profile of an 18-year-old enrolled in a four-year program continues to change, he points out, as more older and non-traditional students return to school. In fact, the average age of a USA student is 26. "Many of our students work full-time and have children, along with community commitments," he says.

For this reason, the University is investing in new and alternative methods of teaching, such as "distance" learning via the Internet—allowing students anywhere in the world the opportunity to earn a USA degree, while customizing the educational experience to fit their busy lifestyles. USA also offers an extensive schedule of evening and weekend courses at both its main campus and Baldwin County campus in Fairhope, to further accommodate students with full-time jobs and other special scheduling needs.

The University's academic reputation continues to grow with the addition of innovative offerings such as the nationally recognized e-commerce degree program that focuses on the use of technology in business and the Accelerated College Enrollment Program that allows high school seniors in Mobile County to take college classes at USA while finishing high school.

(above) The Mitchell Center is now home to Mobile's historic Waterman Globe. The 1,360-pound rotating globe was restored by the USA College of Engineering after being in storage for nearly 25 years.

(left) USA's College of Allied Health Professions offers students hands-on experience with the latest in health-care technology.

A Mission to Conduct Research

As one of the state's leading universities in competitively funded research, the University of South Alabama takes part in research projects and scholarly activity in all academic areas. "Tens of millions of research dollars are awarded annually to our faculty members—for salaries, laboratories, and equipment," points out Moulton. "The total economic impact is in excess of $75 million."

(above) Mobile Mayor Mike Dow, a USA alumnus, delivers the 2000 fall commencement address at the Mitchell Center. USA President Gordon Moulton is seated to Dow's right. Historically, more than 47,000 graduates have started their professional lives with a degree of distinction from USA.

(right) Students in the USA School of Computer and Information Sciences prepare for new opportunities in technology.

With contract and grant research dollars at an all-time high, the work done at the University positively affects every area of community life—from the environment and health care to business and the arts. Recent research projects have included studies as diverse as the biology and ecology of Mobile Bay and its estuary system, a patented folic acid-related food additive that could reduce birth defects, and new processes for producing natural gas and for recycling tires into gasoline. Through USA's new Cancer Institute, the first academic cancer research institute on the upper Gulf Coast, USA College of Medicine faculty research new cancer drugs and treatment techniques and provide patients with greater local access to state-of-the-art cancer treatment.

By affording students the opportunity to gain hands-on research experience, the University is helping shape the academic and business leaders of the next generation.

A Mission to Provide Public Service

An essential element of the University's role in society is public service. USA reaches out to and serves the community in a number of important ways. The 10,000-seat Mitchell Center, in addition to being the home of Jags basketball, is a popular location for activities such as concerts, sports events, and numerous high school graduations.

The Laidlaw Performing Arts Center is a state-of-the-art venue for chamber music concerts, theatrical productions, literary readings, and other arts events. In addition, USA's partnership with the city in transforming the 75-year-old Saenger Theater into a downtown performing arts center has brought new vitality to the city.

One of the University's most far-reaching efforts is the Continuing Education program, which is open to all members of the community. Class offerings are diverse—ranging from interior design and creative writing to bird watching and karate—and are available at a nominal charge.

Perhaps the most profound community impact is felt in the University's role as one of the area's largest employers. Providing jobs for more than 5,800 Mobile-area residents, USA helps anchor the economy with a $1 billion economic impact on the region and state.

A Mission to Deliver Quality Health Care

In keeping with its mission to improve the quality of health care in the region, USA is dedicated to the education of physicians, health scientists, allied health professionals, and nurses.

The University's hospitals and clinics provide invaluable learning experiences for the next generation of health-care professionals, while medical research at USA continues to push back the frontiers of knowledge, leading to longer, more productive lives for everyone.

Each year, USA's clinics and three hospitals—USA Medical Center, Children's & Women's Hospital, and Knollwood—see more than 250,000 patients, bring more than 4,000 babies into the world, and administer quality care to all citizens. In addition, USA's SouthFlite helicopter provides life-saving transportation and treatment for those in critical need—the only service of its type in the area.

"An aging population means an ever-larger portion of the Gross National Product will be devoted to health care," observes Moulton. "It is essential that we prepare for this reality by providing an extremely high level of education for tomorrow's physicians, nurses, and health-care professionals," says Moulton.

The University's "Human Capital"

As the University of South Alabama embarks on an exciting new journey of growth and development, it enters a period of both introspection and outreach. Meeting face to face with students in a series of regularly scheduled "President's Table" sessions, President Moulton discusses a variety of vital issues to determine the most effective way the University can fulfill its top priority—serving the needs of its students.

At the same time, the University is reaching out to the community at large. "Part of this University's responsibility is to help create an environment in which learning is valued," says Moulton.

"Too often, education is viewed as a net drain, rather than a vital boost to the economy." A key element of Mobile's economic development, Moulton points out—beyond access to water, attractive land prices, and tax incentives—is providing a well-educated, thoroughly trained work force.

"The ultimate value of this University," concludes Moulton, "is the powerful, positive effect that our 'human capital' has on the betterment of the entire community. In this way, the University of South Alabama truly fulfills its mission." Learn more about USA on the Internet at www.southalabama.edu.

(left) The USA baseball team celebrates its victory in the Sun Belt Conference Tournament and takes its place as the 2000 tournament champions. The Jaguars have sent numerous players to the major leagues and have played in 19 NCAA tournaments. *Photo courtesy of Mobile Register*

(below) USA banking graduate Jonathan Hathcote of Theodore, Alabama, sports the look of success.

SPRING HILL COLLEGE

(above) According to a national Student Satisfaction Survey, Spring Hill students are more satisfied with their college on the whole than the national average. Challenging academic programs, small classes, and personal attention from caring faculty set Spring Hill apart from the crowd.

(below) The Avenue of the Oaks is one of the many landmarks on the beautiful 500-acre campus.

As the oldest college in the state of Alabama, and the third oldest Jesuit college in the United States, Spring Hill is recognized as one of the top private, liberal arts institutions in the nation. Built upon a strong academic tradition, the school has remained committed to its mission: to educate students to become responsible leaders in service to others. Guided by the Jesuit philosophy of *cura personalis*—care for the individual—the Spring Hill faculty educates the whole person. Preparing students for more than just a career, they prepare students for life.

Founded in 1830 by Michael Portier, first Bishop of Mobile, Spring Hill was originally a combination grammar school/high school/college for male students only. Since granting its first four degrees in 1837, Spring Hill has experienced dramatic growth. In 1847, the Jesuits assumed administration of the school under the leadership of Father Francis Gautrelet, S.J. Non-college level classes were discontinued in 1935, with coeds accepted full-time in 1952. Integrated racially in 1954, Spring Hill was cited by Dr. Martin Luther King, Jr., as one of the South's first schools to desegregate, and received notice in his "Letter From a Birmingham Jail."

In the years since, Spring Hill has maintained its status as one of the region's outstanding schools. Consistently ranked in *U.S. News &World Report*'s "Top 15 Institutions in the South," Spring Hill also ranks high in the listings for "Best Value." At the heart of the Spring Hill experience is a rigorous 60-hour core curriculum designed to develop the student's intellectual capacity for critical thinking, coherent writing, and articulate speaking. Through the combination of the core curriculum and specialized instruction in a major, students build their skills in analysis, synthesis, and judgment, and cultivate their quest for understanding and the desire for truth.

The curriculum is brought to life by an outstanding faculty—more than 90 percent of whom hold doctorates or the highest degrees in their field. The student-faculty ratio of 13 to 1 helps create a caring, personalized community throughout the College's eight academic divisions. A diverse population of more than 1,400 students from more than 36 states and 17 countries enhances the learning experience.

Beyond Academics

With more than 70 percent of students living in college residence halls and apartments, the campus is the center of a lively extra-curricular scene. More than 50 clubs and organizations offer students the opportunity to participate in a variety of activities—student government, fraternities and sororities, service clubs, campus ministry, academic and honorary societies, as well as arts organizations. The handsome Arlene Mitchell Theater provides hands-on theatrical experience in a state-of-the-art performing arts facility.

A primary component of Spring Hill student life is service to the community. The Metropolitan Service Award and Jesuit Service Award allow eligible students to complete their college education while working with others in the community—

children, the elderly, and those with special needs. Students are placed in well-structured programs—at schools, healthcare facilities, and community centers—that allow them to work in a meaningful way appropriate to their abilities, interests, and schedules. Devoting on average three hours per week of personal, one-on-one volunteer time, students gain an understanding of the needs of others and enjoy the experience of becoming friends with those they serve.

Nurturing The Body and Spirit

As part of its commitment to educating the "whole person," Spring Hill offers its students a variety of sports opportunities. The College is a member of the National Association of Intercollegiate Athletics and the Gulf Coast Athletic Conference. The Arthur R. Outlaw Recreation Center is home to the Spring Hill College Badger basketball teams, as well as an indoor pool, racquetball courts, and weight room. More than 20 teams provide students the opportunity to play lacrosse, rugby, soccer, flag football, and more at competition and club levels. Spring Hill is one of the very few colleges in the country with an 18-hole golf course on campus. Students may play year round, with no greens fees.

Founded in the tradition of Catholicism, Spring Hill places a great emphasis on each student's spiritual development. Campus Ministry fosters a culture of faith by promoting religious life in the college com-munity. The ministry staff offers numerous programs including retreats, reflection groups, and personal counseling. Students also participate in an annual mission trip to Mexico, Habitat for Humanity projects, and other spiritual-growth activities.

(above) With more than 50 clubs and organizations, there are many opportunities to meet new friends and get involved in campus life.

(left) Spring Hill is one of 28 Jesuit colleges and universities in the U.S. The College is heir to a successful system of Jesuit liberal arts education, a system that draws its traditions and ideals from four centuries of Ignatian spirituality, academic excellence, and educational wisdom.

Prepared For Life

With an academic heritage of more than 170 years, Spring Hill College is heir to a distinguished system of Jesuit liberal arts schooling, one which draws its traditions and ideals from four centuries of scholarly experience and educational wisdom.

In keeping with this heritage, Spring Hill has developed a compelling focus which embodies its distinctiveness: "The people of Spring Hill College, in community, work together to nurture learning for body, mind, and spirit. We take the time and make the effort to teach and act with justice, with care, and in the service of others."

ST. PAUL'S EPISCOPAL SCHOOL

With a mission to "prepare the whole person for a changing and challenging future," St. Paul's Episcopal School exemplifies the finest academic tradition of the classic well-rounded education.

Founded in 1947 with a single 20-student class, St. Paul's today—with more than 1,500 students in grades Pre-K through 12—is the largest Episcopal school in the continental U.S. This astounding growth, however, has not diminished the school's commitment to providing an excellent college preparatory education—intellectually, spiritually, physically, and socially.

St. Paul's rigorous academic curriculum is taught by a dedicated faculty—more than half of whom hold advanced degrees—and regularly results in a college-acceptance rate of 100 percent among graduating seniors. A hallmark of the school's educational program is its respected Fine Arts Program, highlighted by a score of music courses offered in the specially designed Music Building—with practice studios, a music library, and chorus and strings rooms.

The school is also in the technological vanguard, offering Mobile's first laptop computer program, as well as wireless Internet access. In addition, students have access to more than 200 computers in classrooms and labs throughout the 35-acre campus.

St. Paul's educational philosophy and mission statement are grounded in Christian principles, with students taking part in a variety of religious activities including regular chapel services, religion classes, and ethics programs.

With an emphasis on health and wellness, St. Paul's is an ideal environment for students' physical development, with 70 percent participation in athletics at most grade levels. A recent winner of the All-Sports State Title for garnering six state championships in a single year, St. Paul's offers middle school and upper school students the opportunity to play on more than 30 inter-scholastic boys' and girls' teams. Although it has earned more than 100 state championships since 1976, the school is especially proud of the Girls' Cross Country Team, which set a national record with 16 consecutive state championships.

St. Paul's encourages participation in student and community life through activities such as Presidential Classroom, Key Club, Quill and Scroll, Forensics Team, and scores of extracurricular and volunteer opportunities.

Throughout its 50 years, St. Paul's has excelled at providing excellent academics in a Christian environment, fulfilling its philosophy to "Educate the whole child in a caring way."

(above) Austen Johnson reads to his Little Brother, William Kneip, during a Big Brother/Little Brother activity at St. Paul's.

(below) Jennifer Justice works on her laptop computer as B.J. Chaney and Lizzie Slaton look on. St. Paul's students are able to access the wireless Internet service anywhere on the campus.

Photo by Dale Moore

HOST
MOBILE
SPRING HILL AVE
GOVERNMENT BLVD
DAUPHIN ST
MOBILE
RIVER
VingCard

CHAPTER SIXTEEN

16

Marketplace & Attractions

Photo by Steve Goraum/Studio G!

Mobile Renaissance

MOBILE GREYHOUND PARK

On August 6, 1973, an overflow crowd of more than 6,000 began arriving for opening night at Mobile Greyhound Park two hours before the first race. Traffic was backed up for nearly half-a-mile. When the first night's "handle" of more than $180,000 was totaled, it was clear—Mobile Greyhound Park was an instant success.

The excitement continued to build, and as more and more fans were drawn to the park, an additional race was added to each program and the season was extended. Exciting new wagering combinations were added, like the Twin Trifecta, resulting in a single jackpot of more than $73,000.

The crowds at Mobile Greyhound Park haven't been the only victors, however. The biggest winners of all have been the people of Mobile County. For every dollar wagered at the park, a portion goes directly to improving the quality of life for all Mobile-area citizens.

Since its opening, Mobile Greyhound Park has contributed more than $115 million in taxes to the schools, municipalities, and agencies of Mobile County.

The University of South Alabama—a primary beneficiary of dog track funding—has received more than $40 million over the years, helping establish one of the southeast's leading medical schools. Dog track funding has been vital to other educational institutions as well, such as S. D. Bishop State Junior College, the Alabama School of Math & Science, and the Mobile County Public School system—the recipient of more than $18 million in dog track funding.

Mobile Greyhound Park has had a profoundly positive impact on virtually every phase of life in the county—with contributions of more than $18 million to the city of Mobile, and funding for municipalities like Prichard, Chickasaw, Saraland, and Bayou La Batre, which have received more than $7 million dollars for high-priority public works projects. In addition, the County Law Enforcement and Firefighters Pension Fund was created with more than $6 million in dogtrack funding.

To attract new visitors, Mobile Greyhound Park began simulcasting thoroughbred racing from racetracks across the country, including Aqueduct, Belmont, Saratoga, and Churchill Downs. The park also simulcasts greyhound races from other parks.

The park is open year-round, offering nine performances a week and 12 to 14 races each performance. With a capacity of 7,000, the park also features an attractive clubhouse, offering the relaxation of fine dining with the excitement of world-class greyhound racing.

For the past quarter of a century, Mobile Greyhound Park has provided thousands of hours of fun, excitement, and entertainment. The park has been a crucial part of the area's growth, and as the region continues to develop it will remain an important source of funding. Thanks to Mobile Greyhound Park, the citizens of Mobile County are the true winners.

(above) Excited fans cheer their favorite greyhounds "down the stretch."

(right) Mobile Greyhound Park animal handlers, resplendent in their tuxedos, pose with San Tan Sachet the 2000 winner of the Port City Puppy Classic.

The battleship ended its journey more than 4,000 feet from the existing shoreline. The park was created from material dredged from the bottom of the bay to create the two-mile channel needed for the ship's return.

A Day's Adventure

The USS *Alabama*, with nearly two-thirds of its 680-foot-length accessible to visitors, offers an up-close, first-hand look at life on board a battleship. Everything from the captain's cabin and navigating bridge to the crew's berthing spaces and mess hall is open for inspection. And while the ship is the center of attention at the park, a number of exciting attractions have been added over the years that have turned the park into a daylong adventure.

A tour through the submarine USS *Drum* gives visitors a taste of what it was like to wage war from deep beneath the sea. A crew of 7 officers and 65 enlisted men served aboard the *Drum*, which earned 12 Battle Stars during WWII. The sub has recently been moved onto land to help visitors appreciate the size of the sub, 311 feet long with a 27-foot beam. The *Drum* ranks eighth in enemy tonnage sunk during WWII. On the third Saturday of every month, a submariner conducts a personal tour of the *Drum*, offering unique insight into the workings of the sub.

The nearby Aircraft Pavilion, a 36,000-square-foot air-conditioned facility, houses most of the Park's 23 vintage warplanes dating back to WWII, including a B-52 Stratofortress, an A-12 Blackbird spy plane, and a P-51 Mustang dedicated to the Tuskegee Airmen. A variety of military equipment and artifacts from Korea, Vietnam, and Desert Shield/Desert Storm commemorate more recent veterans. A 15-passenger flight-simulator ride lets visitors experience the thrill of being a test pilot. The pavilion is dedicated to the 28 Alabama recipients of the Medal of Honor and contains a Wall of Honor inscribed with the name of every Alabamian who gave their life in the 20th century. A second black granite wall holds the names of the 1,213 Alabama citizens who perished in Vietnam.

A short distance away stands a bronze life-size sculpture of a veteran reading names etched on a black granite wall modeled after the Vietnam Memorial in Washington. Funded by local veterans, the monument is dedicated to Mobile and Baldwin County citizens who gave their lives in Vietnam.

Recent additions to the park include a Korean War memorial, whose design incorporates elements of the country's landscape and a 400-foot fishing pier where national and international fishing tournaments are held. A seawall is currently being built, which will allow visitors to walk all the way around the battleship.

To Secure Our Peace

USS *Alabama* Battleship Memorial Park is a key part of the region's tourism and travel industry. Since 1965, the park has generated more than $125 million in direct economic benefit to the Mobile area and more than $275 million to the state. The park, an independent agency of the state operated by the USS *Alabama* Battleship Commission, is completely self-sufficient and receives no taxpayer money for daily operations.

The battleship is a major visitor attraction, says Tunnell, but above all it is a wonderful way for Mobile to show the nation the effort it took to secure our peace. "Alabama has 9,582 war casualties from WWI through today," he says. "The park is dedicated to their memory and to all Alabama veterans of the armed services. They're the reason we're here today."

(above) The air-conditioned Aircraft Pavilion houses many historic aircraft and honors the 28 Alabama recipients of the Medal of Honor. It serves quite admirably as a site for corporate social functions, weddings, retirements, and other ceremonies. *Photo courtesy of the USS Alabama Battleship Commission*

(left) Battleship Memorial Park honors Alabama veterans of all United States conflicts as evidenced by this stirring memorial to the 1,213 Alabama veterans who made the ultimate sacrifice in Vietnam. *Photo courtesy of the USS Alabama Battleship Commission*

MOBILE GREYHOUND PARK

On August 6, 1973, an overflow crowd of more than 6,000 began arriving for opening night at Mobile Greyhound Park two hours before the first race. Traffic was backed up for nearly half-a-mile. When the first night's "handle" of more than $180,000 was totaled, it was clear—Mobile Greyhound Park was an instant success.

The excitement continued to build, and as more and more fans were drawn to the park, an additional race was added to each program and the season was extended. Exciting new wagering combinations were added, like the Twin Trifecta, resulting in a single jackpot of more than $73,000.

The crowds at Mobile Greyhound Park haven't been the only victors, however. The biggest winners of all have been the people of Mobile County. For every dollar wagered at the park, a portion goes directly to improving the quality of life for all Mobile-area citizens.

Since its opening, Mobile Greyhound Park has contributed more than $115 million in taxes to the schools, municipalities, and agencies of Mobile County.

The University of South Alabama—a primary beneficiary of dog track funding—has received more than $40 million over the years, helping establish one of the southeast's leading medical schools. Dog track funding has been vital to other educational institutions as well, such as S. D. Bishop State Junior College, the Alabama School of Math & Science, and the Mobile County Public School system—the recipient of more than $18 million in dog track funding.

Mobile Greyhound Park has had a profoundly positive impact on virtually every phase of life in the county—with contributions of more than $18 million to the city of Mobile, and funding for municipalities like Prichard, Chickasaw, Saraland, and Bayou La Batre, which have received more than $7 million dollars for high-priority public works projects. In addition, the County Law Enforcement and Firefighters Pension Fund was created with more than $6 million in dogtrack funding.

To attract new visitors, Mobile Greyhound Park began simulcasting thoroughbred racing from racetracks across the country, including Aqueduct, Belmont, Saratoga, and Churchill Downs. The park also simulcasts greyhound races from other parks.

The park is open year-round, offering nine performances a week and 12 to 14 races each performance. With a capacity of 7,000, the park also features an attractive clubhouse, offering the relaxation of fine dining with the excitement of world-class greyhound racing.

For the past quarter of a century, Mobile Greyhound Park has provided thousands of hours of fun, excitement, and entertainment. The park has been a crucial part of the area's growth, and as the region continues to develop it will remain an important source of funding. Thanks to Mobile Greyhound Park, the citizens of Mobile County are the true winners.

(above) Excited fans cheer their favorite greyhounds "down the stretch."

(right) Mobile Greyhound Park animal handlers, resplendent in their tuxedos, pose with San Tan Sachet the 2000 winner of the Port City Puppy Classic.

BELLINGRATH GARDENS & HOME

It was an uncommon sight for a quiet Sunday afternoon in 1932. Automobiles lined the roadway, bumper to bumper, for miles around Theodore, Alabama. Though it was the depths of the Great Depression, curious Mobilians had turned out in droves for their first opportunity to see the splendid garden Walter and Bessie Bellingrath had carved out of the wilderness.

Under doctor's orders to relax, Walter Bellingrath had bought some waterfront property in 1917 for a fishing camp. Later while touring Europe, he and his wife were so impressed with the country gardens and homes, they decided to create their own estate at the site of the camp on Fish River.

In the 70 years since that first public viewing, Bellingrath, which is listed on the National Register of Historic Places, has become one of the most popular destination gardens in the country. More than 200,000 visitors annually enjoy magnificent year-round blooms amid the serene beauty of Mirror Lake, the Great Lawn, the Oriental-American Garden, and the lavish Rose Garden and Conservatory.

(above) Fall cascade chrysanthemum display.

(left) Spring azalea display.

The Gardens' 60 magnificently landscaped acres, set within a 1,000-acre semi-tropical rain forest, creates a lovely setting for the handsome 15-room Bellingrath Home popular "America's Castles" series. Perched atop a bluff overlooking the river, the Bellingrath Home contains the family's collection of fine crystal, porcelain, silver, and furniture, displayed as it was in the days when Walter and Bessie made it their home.

While Bellingrath—known as "The Charm Spot of the South—has long been one of the region's premier gardens, it has recently experienced an extraordinary renaissance. In 1999, Dr. William Barrick joined the Gardens as executive director. Formerly the director of Georgia's famed Callaway Gardens, Barrick brings more than 30 years of horticultural experience and achievement to the position. Under Barrick's direction, Bellingrath has implemented a Master Plan to restore the garden to its original grandeur, including the renewal of the lush tree canopy and forest around Mirror Lake. The plan also calls for the development of an herb garden and an "event" garden for weddings and corporate functions, as well as the expansion of the rose garden. New facilities will include an education building, a gallery for the Boehm porcelain, and a tearoom and cafeteria.

"We see these improvements as a way to polish and refine a lovely jewel," says Barrick. "Uppermost in our minds was the question: 'What would the Bellingrath's do today?' Their vision created this work of art. It is encumbent upon us to interpret and expand upon that vision, to offer visitors a one-of-a-kind garden experience."

THREE GEORGES'

In 1917, three Greek immigrants named Georgio opened the doors to a new store and a future legend—a combination deli/soda fountain/candy shop named "Three Georges'." Following a fire that damaged the store, George Pappas bought out his partners and, in 1929, opened George's Candy Store, one of Mobile's sweetest traditions. In the 70 years that followed, the store passed from George, Sr., to George, Jr., then to George, Jr.'s widow, Euple. And though another family now owns the store, some things never change—like the dark, sweet Brazilian chocolate, made from a secret recipe that has made Three Georges' famous.

"We were engaged when we bought the business," says Scott Gonzalez of his personal and professional partnership with his wife. "I had given Siobhan a box of chocolates from George's while we were dating, so the store had already played a part in our courtship."

Though the convention center had not yet been constructed and most of the buildings to the west of the store were vacant when they assumed ownership, Scott and Siobhan decided to commit to staying downtown. "We were sort of a lone star' on Dauphin," Gonzalez says. "But downtown has boomed, and our plans have grown right along with it."

After taking over the business, the Gonzalezes reinstated the shop's original name—the first of many steps to return the store to its "roots." They preserved the authentic atmosphere of the shop, retaining the massive mahogany sideboards lined with candy-filled glass jars, black and white tile floors, and marble slabs for candy making. Also, to restore the original three services of the first store, the Gonzalezes added an old-fashioned soda fountain downstairs, and an upstairs balcony for lunch.

In 1997, the Gonzalezes acquired another Mobile tradition, H. M. Thames Pecan Company and its well-known Nuthouse stores. This marriage of sweet and salty businesses has been a happy one, resulting in a total of four stores in the Mobile area and a successful internet/mail-order business that ships worldwide.

The couple purchased yet another Mobile landmark—the Scottish Rite Temple, now known as The Temple. The building is available for wedding receptions, parties, concerts, Mardi Gras balls, graduations, reunions, and other special events. Plans also call for big band dinner dances and dinner theater productions by local artists to be held at The Temple in the near future. And the Gonzalezes aren't finished yet. New stores in west Mobile and Pensacola are on the drawing board.

With the intensive labor involved in rehabbing three Mobile landmarks, it would be easy to assume that the Gonzalezes are ready to slow down. Not so, says Scott. "We're finally reaching the point where we're not just restoring buildings, we're restoring businesses. And that's exciting."

(below right) Scott, Siobhan, and McClean Gonzalez

(below) Georges Candy Shop circa 1930s a popular landmark on the downtown landscape during one of Mobile's many parades.

ENTERPRISE INDEX

Degussa Corporation
PO Box 868
Theodore, Alabama 36590
Phone: 251-443-4000
Fax: 251-443-1609
E-mail: charles.story@degussa.com
www.degussa.com
Pages 212-213

DuPont Agricultural Products
PO Box 525
Axis, Alabama 36505
Phone: 251-679-5300
Fax: 251-679-5126
Page 234

EnergySouth, Inc.
2828 Dauphin Street
Mobile, Alabama 36606
Phone: 251-450-4774
Fax: 251-471-2588
www.energysouth.com
Pages 186-189

The Finch Companies, Inc.
1505 Telegraph Road
Mobile, Alabama 36611-2211
Phone: 251-457-6671
Fax: 251-452-7220
E-Mail: twfulton@mindspring.com
www.finchco.com
Pages 216-219

Gottlieb, Barnett & Bridges, LLC
3600 Springhill Business Park, Suite 200
Mobile, Alabama 36608-1212
Phone: 251-344-1913
Fax: 251-342-3229
E-mail: GBBMobile@gbbmobile.com
www.gbbmobile.com
Page 259

Heritage Planning Group, P.C.
1420 Government Street
Mobile, Alabama 36604
Phone: 251-476-8011
Toll-free: 800-494-8440
Fax: 251-476-8014
E-mail: gaynell@heritageplanning.com
www.heritageplanning.com
Page 249

Hosea O. Weaver & Sons, Inc.
PO Box 8039
Mobile, Alabama 36689
Phone: 251-342-3025
Fax: 251-342-0108
E-mail: weavsons@bellsouth.net
Pages 270-271

Industrial Valve
5310 Highway 45
Mobile, Alabama 36613-2416
Phone: 251-675-5282
Fax: 251-675-1377
E-mail: mobile@indvalve.com
www.indvalve.com
Page 236

Infirmary Health System
PO Box 2226
Mobile, Alabama 36652
Phone: 251-435-2400
Fax: 251-435-3920
www.mimc.com
Page 289

J. C. Duke & Associates, Inc.
1716 Industrial Park Drive
Mobile, Alabama 36693
Phone: 251-661-4888
Fax: 251-661-1181
E-mail: J.C.Duke@Zebra.net
Page 282

J. F. Pate and Associates
23 Midtown Park Drive West
Mobile, Alabama 36606
Phone: 251-476-2500
Fax: 251-476-2508
E-mail: lkearns@jfpate.com
Page 280

J. S. Walton & Co., Inc.
PO Box 863
Mobile, Alabama 36601
Phone: 251-344-0282
Fax: 251-344-3854
E-mail: jswalton@bellsouth.net
Pages 268-269

Kimberly-Clark Corporation
PO Box 2447
200 Bay Bridge Road
Mobile, Alabama 36652-2447
Phone: 251-330-3000
Fax: 251-452-6318
www.kimberly-clark.com
Pages 222-223

Lyons, Pipes & Cook
PO Box 2727
Mobile, Alabama 36652
2 North Royal Street
Mobile, Alabama 36602
Phone: 251-432-4481
Fax: 251-433-1820
www.lpclaw.com
Pages 254-255

Magnolia Mortgage Company, LLC
1550 South University Boulevard
Mobile, Alabama 36609
Phone: 251-660-5025
Toll-free: 800-952-5025
Fax: 251-661-2835
E-mail: timwilkes@magmtg.com
www.magnoliamortgagecompany.com
Page 250

Masland Carpets
716 Bill Myles Drive
Saraland, Alabama 36571
Phone: 800-633-0468
Fax: 251-675-7772
E-Mail: info@maslandcarpets.com
www.maslandcarpets.com
Page 233

Minolta-QMS
One Magnum Pass
Mobile, Alabama 36618
Phone: 251-633-4300
Fax: 251-633-7253
www.minolta-qms.com
Pages 204-207

Mitsubishi Polysilicon
7800 Mitsubishi Lane
Theodore, Alabama 36582
Phone: 251-443-6440
Fax: 251-443-6406
www.mpsac.com
Page 232

Mobile Airport Authority
1891 Ninth Street
Mobile, Alabama 36615
Phone: 251-438-7334
Fax: 251-694-7667
E-mail: maa@mobairport.com
www.mobairport.com
Pages 192-193

Mobile Area Chamber of Commerce
451 Government Street
PO Box 2187
Mobile, Alabama 36652-2187
Phone: 251-433-6951
Fax: 251-432-1143
E-mail: info@mobilechamber.com
www.mobilechamber.com
Pages 242-243

Mobile Area Water and Sewer System
207 North Catherine Street
Mobile, Alabama 36604
Phone: 251-694-3100
Fax: 251-694-3448
E-mail: crambo@mawss.com
www.mawss.com
Pages 198-199

Mobile Greyhound Park
7101 Old Pascagoula Road
PO Box 143
Theodore, Alabama 36582
Phone: 251-653-5000
Fax: 251-653-9185
E-mail: MGP7101@bellsouth.net
www.mobilegreyhoundpark.com
Page 310

Mobile Paperboard Corp.
701 Mobile Street
Mobile, Alabama 36617
Phone: 251-478-6391
Fax: 251-478-5125
E-mail: cconrad@tngus.com
www.newarkgroup.com
Page 231

Mobile Register
401 North Water Street
Mobile, Alabama 36602
Phone: 251-433-1551
www.al.com/mobile
Pages 190-191

The Pelican Group, Inc.
PO Box 160403
Mobile, Alabama 36616-1403
Phone: 251-342-8600
Fax: 251-342-8744
E-mail: abrown0128@aol.com
www.pelicangrp.com
Page 281

Phenolchemie, Inc.
7770 Rangeline Road
Theodore, Alabama 36582
Phone: 251-443-3000
Fax: 251-443-3001
www.phenolchemie.com
Page 230

Pierce, Ledyard, Latta, Wasden & Bowron, P.C.
41 North Beltline, Suite 400
Mobile, Alabama 36608
PO Box 16046
Mobile, Alabama 36616
Phone: 251-344-5151
Fax: 251-344-9696
E-mail: dfp@pllaw.com
www.pllaw.com
Pages 256-257

PrimeHealth
1400 University Boulevard South
Mobile, Alabama 36609-2999
Phone: 251-342-6360
Toll-free: 800-236-9421
Fax: 251-380-3236
E-mail: glaughlin@primehealth.org
www.primehealth.org
Page 295

Providence Hospital
6801 Airport Boulevard
PO Box 850429
Mobile, Alabama 36685
Phone: 251-633-1360
Fax: 251-633-1411
E-mail: mknight@providencehospital.org
www.providencehospital.org
Page 290

Regions Bank
PO Box 2527
Mobile, Alabama 36622
Phone: 251-690-1578
Fax: 251-690-1368
E-mail: ccleverdon@regionsbank.com
www.regions.com
Pages 244-245

Saad Development Corporation
3290 Dauphin Street, Suite 600
Mobile, Alabama 36606
Phone: 251-478-7223
Fax: 251-478-7267
E-mail: sdc@saad.com
www.saad.com
Page 275

Saad Realty Group, L.L.C.
3290 Dauphin Street, Suite 600
Mobile, Alabama 36606
Phone: 251-478-7223
Fax: 251-478-3508
E-mail: srg@saad.com
www.saad.com
Page 274

Southern Earth Sciences
762 Downtowner Loop West
Mobile, Alabama 36609
Phone: 251-344-7711
Fax: 251-341-9488
E-mail: jlaier@soearth.com
www.soearth.com
Page 277

SouthTrust Bank
PO Box 1508
Mobile, Alabama 36633
61 Saint Joseph Street
Mobile, Alabama 36602
Phone: 251-431-9200
Fax: 251-431-9254
www.southtrust.com
Page247

Spring Hill College
4000 Dauphin Street
Mobile, Alabama 36608
Phone: 251-380-2280
Fax: 251-460-2195
E-mail: admit@shc.edu
www.shc.edu
Pages 302-303

Springhill Medical Center
3719 Dauphin Street
Mobile, Alabama 36608
Phone: 251-344-9630
www.springhillmemorial.com
Page 291

ST Mobile Aerospace Engineering, Inc.
2100 Ninth Street, Brookley Complex
Mobile, Alabama 36615
Phone: 251-438-8888
Fax: 251-438-8892
www.stmae.com
Pages 224-225

St. Paul's Episcopal School
161 Dogwood Lane
Mobile, Alabama 36608
Phone: 251-342-6700
Fax: 251-342-1844
E-mail: brutledge@stpauls.pvt.k12.al.us
www.stpauls.pvt.k12.al.us
Page 304

Stallworth Land Company
Highway 45
Vinegar Bend, Alabama 36584
Phone: 251-777-8401
Page 237

Stallworth Timber Co., Inc.
PO Box 380
Beatrice, Alabama 36425
Phone: 251-789-2151
Fax: 251-789-2189
E-mail: dstall@stallworthtimber.com
www.stallworthtimber.com
Page 238

Steiner Shipyard, Inc.
PO Box 742
8700 Hemley Street
Bayou La Batre, Alabama 36509
Phone: 251-824-4143
Fax: 251-824-4884
E-mail: wanda@steinershipyard.com
www.steinershipyard.com
Page 235

Studio G!
4356 Midmost Drive
Mobile, Alabama 36609
Phone: 251-343-5954
Fax: 251-343-5815
E-mail: stevegoraum@aol.com
www.gophotography.com
Page 261

Thompson Engineering
3707 Cottage Hill Road
Mobile, Alabama 36609
PO Box 9637
Mobile, Alabama 36691
Phone: 251-666-2443
Fax: 251-666-6422
E-mail: mmanning@thompsonengineering.com
www.thompsonengineering.com
Pages 264-265

Three Georges'
558 South Broad Street
Mobile, Alabama 36603
Phone: 251-433-1689
Fax: 251-433-3364
E-mail: mail@3georges.com
www.threegeorges.com
Page 312

University of South Alabama
USA Public Relations
307 University Boulevard AD 250
Mobile, Alabama 36688-0002
Phone: 251-460-6211
Fax: 251-460-7827
E-mail: kayers@usamail.usouthal.edu
www.usouthal.edu
Pages 298-301

University of South Alabama Hospitals
USA Medical Center
2451 Fillingim Street
Mobile, Alabama 36617
Phone: 251-471-7262
Fax: 251-471-7288
E-mail: scox@usamail.usouthal.edu
www.usahospitals.org
Pages 286-287

USS Alabama Battleship Memorial Park
2703 Battleship Parkway
Mobile, Alabama 36601
Phone: 251-433-2703
Fax: 251-433-2777
E-mail: ussalbb60@aol.com
www.ussalabama.com
Pages 308-309

Vance McCown Construction Company, Inc.
3213 Midtown Park South
Mobile, Alabama 36606
Phone: 251-478-4202
Fax: 251-478-4374
E-mail: vancevmc@aol.com
Pages 266-267

Volkert & Associates, Inc.
3809 Moffett Road
Mobile, Alabama 36618
Phone: 251-342-1070
Fax: 251-342-7962
E-mail: volkert@volkert.com
www.volkert.com
Page 276

White-Spunner Construction
2654 Cameron Street
Mobile, Alabama 36670
Phone: 251-471-5189
Fax: 251-478-3962
E-mail: rlargue@whitespun.com
Page 278

Whitney National Bank
25 North Beltline Highway
PO Box 9789
Mobile, Alabama 36691
Phone: 251-665-1700
Fax: 251-665-1638
E-mail: mfaulk@whitneybank.com
www.whitneybank.com
Page 246

WKRG 5
555 Broadcast Drive
Mobile, Alabama 36606
Phone: 251-479-5555
Fax: 251-473-8130
E-mail: tv5@wkrg.com
www.wkrg.com
Pages 200-201

BIBLIOGRAPHY

Bailey, Richard. *They Too Call Alabama Home: African American Profiles 1800-1999.* Montgomery, AL: Pyramid Publishing, Inc., 1999 (Copyright by Pyramid Publishing, Inc.)

Boyle, Charles J. *History of the Spring Hill College Campus: A Pelicans Eye View.* Mobile, AL: Spring Hill College, 1999.

Davis-Horton, Paulette *The Davis Avenue Story: The Place, The People, The Memories.* Mobile, Ala.: Horton, Inc., 1991. (Copyright by Horton,Inc.)

Delaney, Caldwell. *Remember Mobile. Mobile: The Haunted Book Shop, 1969.* (Copyright by Caldwell Delaney)

Delaney, Caldwell. *The Story of Mobile.* Mobile, AL: HB Publications from The Haunted Book Shop, 1994. (Copyright by Caldwell Delaney)

Gaillard, Frye; Gaillard, Nancy; and Gaillard, Tracy. *Images of America: Mobile And The Eastern Shore* Dover, New Hampsire: Arcadia Publishing, 1997. (Copyright by Frye, Nancy and Tracey Gaillard)

Gould, Elizabeth Barrett. *From Fort to Port: An Architectural History of Mobile, Alabama.* Tuscaloosa and London: The University of Alabama Press, 1988 (Copyright by the University of Alabama Press)

Hearin, Emily Staples. *Let The Good Times Roll* Mobile, AL: E.S. Hearin & W.B. Taylor, 1991. (Copyright by

Higginbotham, Jay. *Mobile! City By The Bay.* The Mobile Junior Chamber of Commerce, 1999 (Copyright by the Mobile Junior Chamber of Commerce)

Lovett, William J. *Mardi Gras in Mobile: A chronicle of Black Participation.* Mobile, Ala.: Mobile Area Mardi Gras Association, 1980. (Copyright by Mobile Area Mardi Gras Association)

Mathews, C. E. and Brown, Anderson. *Highlights of 100 Years in Mobile.* Mobile, Alabama: Powers Company, Inc., 1965. (Copyright by The First National Bank of Mobile)

McLaurin, Melton and Thomason, Michael. *Mobile: The Life & Times of a Great Southern City.* Woodland Hills, Calif.: Windsor Publications, 1981. (Copyright by Windsor Publications)

Rogers, William Warren; Ward, Robert David; Atkins, Leah Rawls; Flint, Wayne. *Alabama: The History of a Deep South State.* Tuscaloosa, AL: The University of Alabama Press, 1994. (Copyright by The University of Alabama Press)

Spencer, Warren F. *Raphael Semmes, The Philosophical Mariner.* Tuscaloosa: University of Alabama Press, 1997. (Copyright by the University of Alabama Press)

PERIODICALS

Alabama Seaport Magazine. Mobile, AL: Alabama State Docks, 2001. *The Mobile Register.* 2001. (Copyright by The Mobile Register)

WEB SITES

About, The Human Internet—www.mobile.about.com
Alabama Department of Conservation and Natural Resources—www.dcnr.state.al.us
Alabama Gulf Coast Convention & Visitors Bureau—www.gulfshores.com
Alabama State Docks—www.asdd.com
Alabama Wildlife Magazine—www.alawild.org
Baldwin County Economic Development Alliance—www.baldwineda.com
BayFest—www.bayfest.com
Bayou La Batre—www.gulfinfo.com
Blakeley Historic State Park—www.siteone.com/tourist/blakeley
City of Fairhope—www.cofairhope.com
City of Mobile—www.cityofmobile.org
County of Mobile—www.mobilecounty.org
Dauphin Island Park and Beach Board—www.dauphinisland.org
Dauphin Island Sea Lab/Estuarium—www.estuarium.disl.org
Eastern Shore Chamber of Commerce—www.eschamber.com
First Night International—www.firstNightIntl.org
Gulf Coast Exploreum Museum of Science—www.exploreum.net
Gulf Info—www.gulfinfo.com
GMAC Bowl—www.mobilealbowl.com
The Harbinger—www.theharbinger.org
Historic Mobile Preservation Society—www.historicmobile.org
Joe Jefferson Players—www.jjp.net
Landmark Tours—www.landmarktours.com
Library of Congress—www.lcweb.loc.gov
Lighthouse Depot Online—www.lhdepot.com
Main Street Mobile—www.mainstreetmobile.org
Mobile Area Chamber of Commerce—www.mobilechamber.com
Mobile Ballet—www.mobileballet.org
Mobile BayBears—www.mobilebaybears.com
Mobile Convention and Visitors Center—www.mobile.org
Mobile County Public School System—www.mcpss.com
Mobile Harley Davidson—www.mobileharley.com
Mobile Museum of Art—www.MobileMuseumOfArt.com
Mobile Mysticks—www.mysticks.com
Mobile Opera—www.mobileopera.org
Mobile Public Library—www.mplonline.org
Mobile Register—www.al.com
Mobile Steamboat Company—www.mobilesteamboat.com
Mobile Symphony—www.mobilesymphony.org
National Park Service—www.cr.nps.gov
Robert Trent Jones Golf Trail—www.rtjgolf.com
Saenger Theatre—www.mobilesaenger.com
Senior Bowl—www.seniorbowl.com
Soul of America—www.soulofamerica.com
University of Mobile—www.umobile.edu
University of South Alabama—www.southalabama.edu
U. S. Coast Guard—www.uscg.mil

Barbara Spafford would like to extend a special thanks to Jodi Swiderek and the staff at the Mobile Area Chamber of Commerce, especially Ashley Collins, Leigh Perry Herndon, and Deborah York.

INDEX

F

G

H

I

J

K

L

M

N